A Daughter Of Many Mothers

With the plethora of memoirs by Holocaust survivors, it might be easy to overlook this one by Rena Quint with Barbara Sofer, but it would be a big mistake to do so. Her story is unique and very dramatic and her odyssey following her liberation from the camps in search of her identity is unforgettable.

Dr. Efraim Zuroff,
Historian and Chief Nazi-hunter
of the Simon Wiesenthal Center and director of its Israel Office.

Reversing her childhood decision to repress the horrors of her past, Rena Quint shares her remarkable story with us. In doing so, she honors those who saved her and ensures that we will never forget this dark chapter in human history.

Dr. Amnon Gimpel,
Psychiatrist and author of Brain Exercises to Cure ADHD.

When I first met Rena Quint I found it hard to believe this eloquent and ebullient woman was the same person who had survived the Holocaust as an orphaned little girl. She is an inspiration.

Dr. Gerald Schroeder,
Author of Genesis and the Big Bang and The Hidden Face of God.

Rena's story, so beautifully told, is a paean to motherhood under the worst possible conditions. Because she's American, it's easier to identify with her. Every Hadassah group that meets Rena is moved to tears.

Barbara Goldstein,
Deputy Director of Hadassah Offices in Israel
and motivational speaker.

Rena Quint has been telling her story to educational groups and visitors to Yad Vashem for decades. Because of her ability to connect and vividly articulate her story, she has touched the hearts and minds of countless persons. Following the thread of her experiences in the tapestry of people, places and events that comprise the history of the Shoah, is what makes the Holocaust palpable for her listeners.

Dr. Robert Rozett,
Director of the Libraries at Yad Vashem.

Rena Quint has devoted a large part of her life to telling her story, which she does with a passion and class that takes the listener (and reader) on an unforgettable journey. Reading about Rena Quint is essential, for she is "the real thing", not just a story teller.

Phil Chernofsky,
Editor, Torah Tidbits, OU Israel Center, Jerusalem.

Rena Quint knows how to tell her unique story and connect it to people from diverse cultural and religious backgrounds worldwide. I have witnessed her interaction with Christian visitors at Yad Vashem. No one remains unmoved by her experiences. I warmly recommend this testimony presented in her book to Christian communities around the world.

Dr. Susanna Kokkonen,
Director, Christian Friends of Yad Vashem.

Rena is the first Holocaust survivor I met in person. I was deeply shaken by her story and moved by the kindness she showed towards me and my generation of Germans. And I can't describe the joy I felt of seeing and hearing how her life has turned out. It's a real life happy ending after such an unimaginable suffering. I'm glad she is sharing her story. The crimes committed during the Holocaust must never be forgotten.

Anja Reumschüssel,
Journalist, Hamburg, Germany.

Not only did Rena retain her faith despite the tragedies in her life, but by sharing her remarkable story she strengthens ours. *A Daughter of Many Mothers* is a must read!

Naomi Leibler, Hon. President World Emunah.

More than 20 years have passed since the first time I heard Rena tell her story. The venue was a packed hotel lobby in Cracow and the occasion was the eve of our first visit to Auschwitz, the culmination of our Jewish Heritage seminar in Poland. The students were as captivated with the story as they were with the person. Her story is so genuine, so innocent, so tragic, yet so beautiful. And just like the cycle of Jewish history which such a trip portrays so eloquently, in the end the light conquers the darkness.

Rena finished that session with a statement which has become an educational and inspirational motto for many of the students who have been touched by her story. She told us "We have to be the Jews they never got the chance to be!"

I have come to know Rena as a friend and a teacher and have heard her relate her experience countless times. The story never changes. No embellishment, no commentary. It is apparently as pure and heartfelt today as it was when the events unfolded in real time. It is astounding to see how this child of the Holocaust, drifting from one tragedy to the next, without a stable family support system, has become such a warm, competent, loving wife, mother, grandmother and educator.

Rena has truly become a personification of the beautiful Jewish Mother she never had a chance to know.

Jonty Maresky, M.D.

A Daughter Of Many Mothers

Rena Quint

~ with ~

Barbara Sofer

Mazo Publishers

A Daughter Of Many Mothers
ISBN: 978-1-946124-25-8
Copyright © 2017 Rena Quint and Barbara Sofer

Rena Quint
18 Graetz Street ~ Jerusalem, 93111 Israel
Tel: 972-2-5633-012 – Fax: 972-2-5662-707
Email: quint@inter.net.il

Barbara Sofer
Tel: 972-2-5665-479 / Cell: 972-50-894-6206
Email: bsofer@gmail.com
Web: www.barbarasofer.com ~ Befriend on Facebook

The authors are grateful to Lynn Gimpel for introducing them.

Dikla Meshulam designed the front cover showing Rena Quint's Quilt of Mothers.

Published by
Mazo Publishers
Chaim Mazo, Publisher
P.O. Box 36084 ~ Jerusalem, 91360 Israel
P.O. Box 10474 ~ Jacksonville, FL 32247 USA
Website: www.mazopublishers.com
Email: mazopublishers@gmail.com

Printed in Israel

To My Parents

– the ones who gave birth to me –
and
– the ones who raised me –

———•◆•———

To my devoted and beloved husband, Emanuel Quint

Manny and I have been blessed with four wonderful children
– Menucha, Naomi, Jodi, and David –
– and their spouses –
– and grandchildren –
– and great-grandchildren –

From one survivor, to a clan – Thank You, God.

CONTENTS

I am ready to die. I find a spot near a tree and lie down. Men, women, and children, some like me, not yet dead, lie here too. A breeze stirs my hair. It brings the stench of the dead, a smell that I am used to. Dying under a tree will be nicer than in the stinking barracks.

All the fences are lined with bodies, piled higher than a man standing tall – not that men stand tall anymore.

I am nine years old. I have spent most of my childhood in a ghetto, a work camp, concentration camps and a death march. Bergen-Belsen is the worst of all. There is no water, not even in the filthy puddles of yesterday.

Suddenly the quiet is broken. I hear an unfamiliar sound and look up. People are running. Men and women who never walk faster than a shuffle are running. I want to see where they are going, but I can't stand up. I'm sick. People who never talk louder than a whisper are shouting.

Soldiers in khaki uniforms are walking nearby. I can tell these aren't German soldiers by the way the prisoners greet them with shouts of joy. How strange. Some of the soldiers are throwing up. Nazi soldiers never throw up.

"*Ihr seid frei* – you are free," are words on the loudspeaker. "We are the English Army. Be calm. Food and medical help are on the way."

"*Frei. Frei* – We are free," women shout around me, in Yiddish. What does "free" mean? I do not understand. I am too sick and tired to move – I want my mother.

INTRODUCTION

I am invited by Hadassah, the Women's Zionist Organization of America, to spend two days with a group of American women who are visiting Poland. We spend a day in Warsaw, and the next day in Piotrkow, the city where I was born. I travel with Barbara Sofer, the co-author of this book. When we clear customs, Barbara turns to me and quietly asks how I feel coming back to Poland.

"How do you feel" is never a simple question to answer, especially for me. I blanch, catch my breath and think for a moment. I am trying to assess my feelings.

There are two of me. One person is Rena Quint in the spring of 2015 – an international speaker, a great-grandmother, an American who does *The New York Times* crossword puzzle, an Israeli citizen who has an elegant home and a loving husband and family. I frequently attend philharmonic concerts and cook gourmet dinners for friends and dignitaries.

And then there is the other person, little Fredzia Lichtenstein, born in 1935 in Poland, a little girl whose entire family is murdered in Holocaust. She is a child who survives in a country of cold, ice, snow, and pain – a motherless girl, frightened all the time, with no coat or shoes, no home, no food, no family.

The sun doesn't shine in the Poland of my youthful memories. But stepping outside in the bright sunshine of Warsaw with Barbara, there is undeniably the scent of spring flowers, forsythia and lilacs.

When we get to our hotel, it takes ten minutes to cross the street, because thousands of young people are running in a marathon.

Just a week earlier, there was a similar marathon in Jerusalem, where I live now. The runners look much the same, mostly young and trim, good-natured and cosmopolitan, wearing shorts and bright-colored mesh vests that keep them from sweating.

Our opulent hotel used to be called the Victoria Hotel, a showcase hotel for visitors under the Communist regime. It is as fancy as an American Hilton. Could this modern land be the same Poland of my childhood? How jarring this is with my memories.

At the hotel, the bellhop with a top hat(!) escorts me to a stylish room and I innocently, maybe even foolishly, ask him if it is safe to drink the tap water.

And then I briefly think back to April 1945, when I am imprisoned in the Bergen-Belsen concentration camp, when the Germans turn off the water supply. No food and no water for three days. To survive, we drink from puddles, where every kind of scum and pollution is floating. We drink that filthy water, anything to quench our thirst, until we are liberated by the British.

Even after liberation, 14,000 men, women and children like me die.

How could I have survived the Holocaust? How could anyone have survived?

A few hours later, our group visits the old Jewish cemetery of Warsaw. The guide points out one of the execution pits that served as a mass grave for many of the Jews of Warsaw.

This is the part of Poland that Fredzia remembers, where nine Jews out of ten are murdered, ninety-nine children out of a hundred. A country formed of piles of dead bodies. Daily executions.

I remember this, but what does this have to do with Rena Quint of Graetz Street, Jerusalem, with her many friends, a smartphone and grandchildren at Princeton and Stanford?

And then we drive the 80 miles of good highway to Piotrkow. Here is the familiar small city of my childhood, devoid of its thriving Jewish community. There exists a small Jewish community in Warsaw, even several kosher restaurants, frequented mostly by tourists, but today not one Jew lives in Piotrkow.

The lyrics and melody of a popular Israeli song go through my mind. "And the wheat is growing again." The song describes a valley after someone dear has died and the surprise of finding the wheat growing as usual despite the personal cataclysm that has taken place. More or less, it's translated: "It's not the same valley, nor the same house. You're not there and can't return … but the wheat is growing again." That's how I feel.

My birth family – mother and father, brothers, aunts, uncles, cousins – and neighbors are all dead, murdered in the Holocaust. Still, in Piotrkow, it's spring. Nursery school children are following their teacher in a straight line to a city park to play.

Jacek Bednark, researcher and our solicitous guide, points out a two-story brick building. "Here is where your grandmother lived. Here stood your mother's shop," he tells me.

Not a stranger's shop, or a storybook shop, but where my mother stood and met customers and earned a living. My mother's shop! I imagine her smiling at customers. I look for her in the alleyway.

We stop at the Piotrkow synagogue, a stately building with the Star of David still visible on the outside lamps. But now the glorious synagogue is a municipal library.

Outside of the building that was once the Piotrkow synagogue, a stately building with the Star of David still visible on the outside lamps.

If you know enough to ask the librarian to open the curtains on the southern wall, you can see the remains of the synagogue's *Aron Hakodesh,* the special, holy closet where the Torah scrolls were kept. You can see the bullet holes on the concrete walls, too.

The librarian doesn't show any emotion. Her face is placid, annoyed by the request and that I've interrupted her paperwork to show us those old bullet holes. She sighs, and then gets up from her desk where she is checking out books, and perfunctorily opens the curtain for us.

This was the synagogue where my parents were married by the well-known Rabbi Yehuda Meir Shapiro.

Seventy-two years ago, I managed to miraculously

Opening the curtains on the southern wall of the library, you can see the remains of the Aron Hakodesh where the Torah scrolls were kept when the building was the Piotrkow synagogue. You can still see the bullet holes, too.

escape from this synagogue when Jews were rounded up. And yes, both Rena and Fredzia remember that day.

From the synagogue, we go to see the apartment where my mother was born, another where my parents lived, the shops they owned, and the house in which my two brothers and I were born.

The deputy mayor of Piotrkow meets our group and speaks nostalgically about the days when the city had so many wonderful Jews – Jewish poets and painters, bakers and bookbinders, Rabbis and runners. And little Jewish children playing in the public parks. Like me.

There are no Jews left in Piotrkow today. When I go back, I seek one ... a girl named Fredzia ... who was once me ... and who I tried to leave behind ... but who keeps following me, like a shadow.

A Daughter Of Many Mothers

Chapter 1

MANY MOTHERS DAY

I think I'm ten years old. I'm climbing the monkey bars at recess. Rita is climbing higher up. She's the prettiest girl in my class. Her long blond hair is swinging in the sunlight, making a golden arc, as she reaches upward with strong arms. She's smiling and confident. She laughs out loud. She doesn't seem to have a care in the world.

"Oh, so that's how you are supposed to do it," I say to myself. I'm athletic, too, and can climb the bars and hang upside down. I have soft blond hair, clean and shiny, too. But I'm missing Rita's jauntiness. There is something unquantifiable about her embrace of childhood that I know nothing about. That's what I want. If I can't have it, I must at least act as if I do.

I get it now. You are supposed to just be able to play without worrying about what comes next. Or at least to pretend. You are not supposed to show that you're trying hard to survive, that you've become an expert at not dying.

I can do this, I tell myself. No one is going to see that I'm never relaxed. If I know how I'm supposed to feel and act as if that's the way, I do feel it might help. I've already gotten in trouble for my hyper-alertness.

I'm much bigger than all my classmates who started first grade at age six. There was no school in the ghetto. I know I'm different from all the other children.

Rita grew up in a comfortable home in Brooklyn with a bike and dolls and roller-skates. While she was taking swimming lessons and playing grown-up by wearing her mother's high heels, I was hiding in a ghetto, working in a slave labor camp, and eating soup that stank like garbage because it was made from garbage.

If you smelled that soup, you'd say you wouldn't eat it even if your life depended on it. But believe me, if your life depended on it, you'd devour it, and like Oliver Twist, standing in line with your bowl, ask for more. If your soup had a muddy potato peel in it, then it was your lucky day.

While Rita was picking out patent leather shoes for birthday parties, I was wearing open clogs in the snow and wrapping my feet with rags. Now I have pretty shoes. Oxfords for school and patent leather for synagogue.

I know that to be accepted one day by the girls in my class, I have to hide my shame at what I went through. I can do this. I'm good at changing identities.

For years I had to pretend I was a boy and I did that, too. I watched boys to see how they behaved and acted like them. When your life depends on it, you can do just about anything.

I need to study how the American girls act to learn how I am supposed to behave in my newest identity: American schoolgirl. I wish I didn't have to act, but PS 92 taught me that I had a lot to change to succeed in this new country.

Once upon a time, I lived in a lovely home in Poland. There I had a loving mother and father and two beloved brothers. The beds had crisp white embroidered sheets and my mother tucked me in with a soft down-quilt. Our table was set with real china. There were flowers on the table. We bought ice cream cones from the kiosk across the street. I had my own sled. Now all of that is gone. That mother and father and my brothers are all dead. Only I survived.

Now, like Rita, I live in a lovely home in Brooklyn. But how different are our dreams and nightmares!

To kids growing up in America, their exact birth date is very important. They buy rings with birthstones and read horoscopes in the newspapers. When I came to America, my birthday got lost along the way. I am using the birthday of a girl named Fannie. She is dead so she doesn't need her birthday anymore.

Girls are tougher to get to like me than mothers. I will wait and watch and act just like them and find out what can get them to like me. I know I can. I need to be strong and patient. I know not to cry.

Crying can be dangerous. The girls in my class cry sometimes. One of them cries because girls ostracize her. Another cries when she gets a C on a test. At first, the girls ostracize me, too. They don't like me. I'm different. But I don't cry or complain to the teacher or my mother. One day they will like me, too.

At first I fail all my tests, but I don't cry. I am strong and patient. Now I don't fail tests anymore. I have moved up from C's, too. Soon I will have all B's and then A's.

I have another problem, but this one can't be solved by watching others girls and learning how they solve it.

In school, we're learning about Mother's Day. For Mother's Day all the girls glue doilies and colored hearts on construction paper to make cards for their mothers. "My Mom," the girls say. I roll the words around on my tongue. "My Mom," that's how Americans say it.

I learn that Mother's Day is celebrated on the second Sunday in May in America. It's huge. Even a bigger holiday than your Mom's birthday, the girls say. Who of my many mothers do I honor?

Leah Globe is my sixth mother. Maybe even the seventh or eighth, I'm not sure. I speak of her as my mother, but I can't yet force myself to call her Momma. She understands.

What did I call the others? Momma, I think. Mein Momma. Momma, Momma, Momma, how many times did I call out to you in the night until I learned calling out in the night or day might cost me my life?

The teacher says that in 1934, US President Franklin D. Roosevelt approved a stamp commemorating Mother's Day in the United States.

That was before World War II, the teacher tells us. My teacher says that 60 million people died in the war. No one mentions anyone in specific, like my mother, my father, my two brothers. I look down at my desk so that no one can see my face, which might give something away. For the others in the class, "World War II" doesn't have much meaning, except for those whose fathers served in the army or navy.[1]

In 1935, in Poland, my birth mother was pregnant with me, her third child. It says in the encyclopedia that Mother's Day was celebrated in my birth country of Poland, too, since 1923. I wonder if my father, Poppa, brought Momma flowers. Perhaps Jews didn't celebrate Polish national holidays, but perhaps they did. Like so many parts of my life, I have no idea of the correct answers.

Girls like Rita have no idea of the scale of my losses. How could they? And that's how I want it.

In American elementary schools, girls use the word "cooties." They don't really have cooties. Everyone is so clean. I lived for years with lice crawling all over my body. If you didn't kill them, your skin turned black and then you died.

Who will want to climb the monkey bars with a girl

---

1   There were 16 million American soldiers and sailors who were called up. Who can relate to such numbers?

who went years without a real bath?

Who will want to play dolls with a girl who was pulled out from among thousands of dead bodies to be brought back to life?

Who will want to swap stories with a girl whose mothers always died?

My teacher says that the idea for Mother's Day in the United States grew out of a desire to heal after the American Civil War, an attempt to reunite families divided by the war, and to reach out to moms who had lost children on both sides. We learn that a woman named Ann Jarvis organized Mother's Day Work Clubs to fight the typhoid outbreaks, related to the war, in 1868. She tells us her daughter, Anna, took over the effort to establish a yearly day to honor her motherhood, and the day was officially established on May 8, 1914.

War, typhus, Anna. What do the other children know about this? I, too, am a child of war. I, too, nearly died of typhus. One of my mothers was named Anna. She's dead, too.

Traditions developed around Mother's Day in America. Bouquets are ordered. Some moms get breakfast in bed, boxes of bonbons, elaborate greeting cards expressing devotion and appreciation.

I want to show appreciation to my mothers, too, but I don't know how. So I learn about this holiday, and along with the other kids, glue doilies and colored hearts on construction paper cards and give Leah Globe, my newest mom, a Mother's Day card. But it isn't the same for me. Even though I copy what the other girls do, I can't talk about "Mom" the way they do.

It isn't that I don't love Leah. I do. I love her more day by day and Jacob, my new father. They are amazing parents. Nor is my standoffishness related to me being in the process of being adopted. I'm glad I'm being adopted. It's harder to give an adopted child away.

The issue is that I've already had so many mothers. In the past, every time I got a new mother, I lost her. Most of my mothers are dead. At least I think so. It is hard to know if they were just shipped out to a different place or went up in smoke. Loss and more loss is part of my life.

So, which of my many mothers should I be honoring? The other children in class all know.

Each time I lose a mother, I do have to absorb the loss. There is no time to be sad and cry. I must remain alert if I'm going to survive. I cannot have red eyes and a swollen nose from crying if I want the next mother to love me. Without a mother I won't survive.

How long will I have Leah Globe? She hugs me and tells me "forever," but in some matters I may be wiser than my new mother. She still has her original mother-in-law, who says she is now my grandmother.

But for me, life isn't like that. My mother let go of my hand and I ran. I can still feel her fingers loosening on mine as she let me go. The day she let go of my hand, she and my brothers went to their deaths. They were murdered by gas, or execution in the forest, or starvation. I don't know if they succumbed to disease or were buried alive.

Just imagine what it means to remember such things while you are climbing the monkey bars with carefree classmates.

I might think of her loosening her grip on my hand and, without thinking, loosen my own grip. A flash of memory might make me fall. I never want to fall. It's safer to forget.

Chapter 2

AT HOME WITH
MOMMA AND POPPA

"Hang on, Fredzia. Bumps ahead." That's my brother David talking. Duvi, Dubi, Davi, Davidil. What don't I call him?

We are bringing Momma's cholent to the bakery oven where it will remain from Friday afternoon until Saturday morning when we reclaim it and eat it for a big family lunch. Cholent is a delicious mix of beans and onions and meat that cooks all night.

We live in the center of the city of Piotrkow in the center of Poland.

The sled swerves and I tighten my arms around the black metal pot wrapped in its brown blanket. I breathe in the aroma of fried onions and potatoes and brace for the sled hitting a frozen tree root. Never mind. I'm good navigating bumps.

My mother, Sarah, Surah in Yiddish, was born in the smaller, rural town of Przyrow, but moved to Piotrkow after her parents died. Three of my mother's sisters – Aunties Bina, Leah, and Chava – lived in Piotrkow. Her other six siblings lived in or around the nearby bigger city of Czestochowa. The Messers, my mother's family, were in the cattle feed business. Auntie Bina, for example, ran the wholesale trade.

My mother was a businesswoman, too. She opened a paint store when she first moved to Piotrkow in the same building where one of her sisters lived. My aunt Leah (Laja) Messer, three years my mother's junior, came to Piotrkow to assist my mother in her shop.

When I first began my search for my mother's history I had a stereotype in mind of a stay-at-home Mom. As it turned out, I was the stay-at-home Mom in the United States and the women in my mother's family were all immersed in commerce.

When my kids were growing up in Brooklyn, there was concern about homes being painted with lead paint. In Poland, back when my mother ran a paint shop, lead-based paint was already recognized as a danger and prohibited. This is a good example of how we hold patronizing views about the Jewish communities in Europe before the war.

I've been told that I look like my mother. As far as I know, there are no photos of my mother. I have searched archives and city records as I struggle to reconstruct my personal history. With research, piece by piece, the picture of my family and the city where I grew up become clearer – not as a puzzle with whole pieces, but more as a patchwork quilt.

On my father's side, the family manufactured and sold clothing. My paternal grandparents were Yankel and Cyrla Lichtenstein. My father had four siblings, brothers Aaron and Zelik, a sister Ruchla, and Uncle David Mordechai. According to city records, Poppa was a "tailor," which was a general title in Poland between the wars when the tailoring business was largely Jewish. From the magnificent play, "Fiddler on the Roof," we have an enduring image of a hapless tailor named Muttle, who saves up to buy a sewing machine. It's an unlikely portrait of my father. Piotrkow wasn't a shtetl, a small country town like Anatevka in "Fiddler on the Roof." In

Piotrkow, "tailor" might also mean clothing manufacturer.

We know, again from city records, that my father had at least one stall in the market, and a tailor shop at 8 Szewska Street. He worked there from the end of 1930 when he was 24. He was also in the manufacturing business with his own line of clothing. I have the old Polish documents that confirm this. As part of her dowry, Momma gave Poppa two sewing machines and an oak tailoring table. And as part of her trousseau, she also contributed furniture, bed linens and tablecloths. I know this from documents that record my mother's prenuptial agreement, which was read aloud at their engagement. Imagine – a "prenup" in the 1930s in Poland! Getting Jewish brides and grooms to sign prenuptial agreements is an issue of contemporary Jewry in Israel and the Diaspora, but my parents signed one more than 80 years ago.

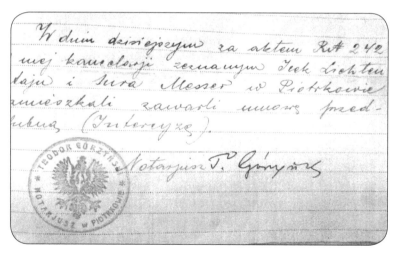

Rena's parents' prenuptial agreement was officially registered in the city records.

Repertorjum Nr. 2 4 2. Dnia ...

... roku tysiąc dziewięćset trzydziestego ...

Przedemną **Teodorem Górzyńskim** Notarjuszem przy Wydziale hipotecznym Sądu Grodzkiego miasta Piotrkowa, w kancelarji mojej w mieście Piotrkowie przy placu Trybunalskim w domu pod liczbą 7 znajdującym się w obecności ...

Rena's parents' prenuptial agreement was recorded in the Piotrkow city records. (An English translation is included in the appendix.)

• 29 •

According to city records, my parents were married in March 1930. My brother Joseph – Yossi – was born in 1931. Brother David appeared in 1933 and I was born on Wednesday, December 18, 1935.

My mother sold her shops around the time she got married, but she continued to work with my father. The business agreements were always in her name. Soon after my birth, we moved to a larger, better-appointed apartment on Czarnieckiego Square. My parents must have been doing well enough to be able to change homes, which was uncommon in Eastern Europe. The apartment was also listed in my mother's name.

These apartments weren't primitive structures like you see in the movie of "Fiddler on the Roof". Nearly all homes in Piotrkow had indoor plumbing, electricity, and radios. Many middle-class homes had beautiful paintings, often the work of local artists, who doubled as sign painters.

Every building had a janitor, what New Yorkers would call "the super." He was a Polish Christian with special assignments on the Sabbath, doing tasks that Jews couldn't do, such as lighting the fires.

Most families were middle-class, but there were also wealthy factory owners of tanneries and sawmills and poor families who needed support by the community.

The Jews of Piotrkow were proud of their city, even though it was not the more cosmopolitan Warsaw. Our city was well-known for its excellent Jewish school system, for both boys and girls. All Jewish children in Piotrkow could get a Jewish education, even if they came from poor families and couldn't pay the school fees.

There was the modern Jewish kindergarten of Maria and Roma Ginsburg, well-known in the area for innovative education. Dr. Maria Montessori's ideas of developing independence in young children were popular throughout Europe.[1] At the same time, the traditional Jewish cheder, with a more regimented school day and early reading was respected. Jewish children in Polish cities usually went to a combination of Jewish school and public school. A law in Poland required them to get a general education.

Movie theaters showed movies with Clark Gable, Marlene Dietrich and Charlie Chaplin. We also had separate mandolin and brass bands, and concerts by famous Yiddish and classical musicians.

Four-wheeled carriages and horses lined up at Trybunalski Place where my paternal grandparents lived, but there were also many cars. Three different Yiddish newspapers were published every week in Piotrkow. People joked that there was always plenty of newsprint to wrap the fish.

Tuesday and Friday were outdoor market days in Piotrkow. Horse-drawn wagons clip-clopped along the cobblestone streets, carrying fish and chickens and vegetables into town. On market days you might see a man carrying a gramophone with a huge horn-shaped speaker on a wheelbarrow playing songs of the famous cantor Yossele Rosenblatt. People stopped to listen and give him a coin. Other sellers offered used clothes and furniture, hawking what they called "altizachen." On the narrow streets near the Strawa Bridge the poorest women sold bruised apples and pears for fruit soup.

Fish was bought on Tuesdays, and kept in barrels filled with water in the basement until they were cooked on Thursday to get ready for Shabbat. Even the cats in Piotrkow seemed to know when it was Thursday, waiting on the window ledges for trimmings.

---

1   Anne Frank attended a Montessori school in Amsterdam.

We had a factory for seltzer water in the Jewish section of town, and samovars to keep coals burning and the water hot for tea.

Jews had lived in Piotrkow for more than 400 years. The first Jews came to Poland at the end of the 11th century, fleeing Western Europe because of the anti-Semitic attacks related to the First Crusade. Many more came after 1492, when Jews were expelled from Spain, Austria, Hungary and Germany. They were welcomed by wise rulers who counted on the refugees' prodigious commercial expertise to boost their economies. Polish Jews were accustomed to periods of relative quiet, punctuated by outbreaks of anti-Semitic violence. In Piotrkow itself, the synagogue was burned down in the 16th century, but in 1679, Jews were granted trading rights in the city and re-established the community. The expectation by local Jews was that after the anti-Semitic attacks, the pendulum would swing in the other direction, and life would return to "normal."

Millions of Polish Jews emigrated in the late nineteenth century, many to the United States, but on the eve of the Nazi occupation of Poland, 3.3 million Jews still lived in Poland, making it the largest Jewish community in the world. A play on words for the Hebrew word for Poland (po-leen) means "here we stayed." Nine hundred years is a long time to stay in one place.

The overall population of our city was 55,000, with about 12,000 of us Jews. That's 22 percent of the population. A number of Jews lived in the predominantly Christian parts of town, but the majority – like us – lived in a predominately Jewish neighborhood.

Yiddish was the language spoken at home in the Jewish quarter, but residents knew Polish to speak to non-Jews in everyday interactions, mostly in business and with the building janitors and household help. It wasn't unusual for non-Jews who had business with the Jewish community to know a smattering of Yiddish.

In terms of religious observance, Jews ranged from extreme piety to skeptical atheists. Because of the concentration of Jews, even the anti-religious knew when it was the Sabbath, and could usually be found engaging in lively arguments about ideology around their family's Sabbath table where tradition was observed.

Likewise, religious or not, the Jews were proud of the Jewish institutions: the magnificent Great Synagogue and the Jewish printing industry. Our Rabbi Moshe Chaim Lau was a celebrity in the Jewish world, considered the finest Jewish orator in Europe.

My parents were married in the Great Synagogue. Officiating at their wedding was the renowned Rabbi Yehuda Meir Shapiro, a cousin of Rabbi Moshe Chaim Lau, and the Rabbi who preceded him in the Piotrkow pulpit. Rabbi Shapiro developed the study program called Daf Yomi, still used by Jews all over the world, (including my family) in which a page of Talmud is learned every day in a seven-year cycle.

Because my parents were married by such an esteemed Rabbi, it's fair to assume that they were traditional or religious and that at least one of them came from a well-regarded family. My older cousin, Irving Cymberknopf, wrote in his memoirs that his own parents were religious, particularly his mother, my mother's sister Bina. Nonetheless, I have no way of knowing for sure if my parents strictly followed the family traditions, modified them, or rebelled against tradition.

My mother's dowry specified light oak furniture and the kitchen table was painted white.

The marriage license of Rena's parents was registered in the Piotrkow city records and signed by Rabbi Shapiro.

How odd it feels that I should know that we had a white kitchen table but know so little about my family that sat around it. What did we talk about at dinner?

In winter, Piotrkow was transformed into a white wonderland. Children skated almost before they walked. Parents tied skates onto shoes and with little chairs, children pushed themselves across the thick ice. The best skaters in Piotrkow were Renja and Romek Zacks, a sister and brother who waltzed like a prince and princess and pirouetted on the ice.

Little children in Poland also learned how to steer and balance on sleds, the way children in warm countries know how to ride bikes.

Carrying the cholent on a sled is my first clear memory. Perhaps I received that sled with handles like Bambi ears as a combined birthday present and Hanukkah present when I turned three. The Hebrew date of my birth is 22 Kislev, 5696, a few days before Hanukkah.

I like to think that on my third birthday, my many aunties and uncles and cousins came over and lit Hanukkah candles and sang songs. The Hanukkah story was certainly retold, how a small band of brave men and women opposed an empire that denied them their rights. Hanukkah delicacies of potato pancakes and hot jelly donuts were fried in goose fat. Children sat on the floor and played with dreidels – spinning tops with the Hebrew letters nun, gimel, hey and shin – the first letters for "a great miracle happened there."

Little did we know how much we would soon need a miracle.

The cholent pot I carried in my childhood had to be cool enough for me to hold inside the blanket, but still warm enough to feel good in my lap. I remember a stream that I thought was a river beyond our bakery. I have a visceral memory of hurrying, and of the contents of the pot smelling like ambrosia.

In the Piotrkow Yizkor Book (where memories of older survivors were collected), there's a story of Reb Itzhak Leib Rusak, a Hassidic baker, who would go to the ritual bath to immerse before the Sabbath. In the meantime, an assistant would accept all the different big pots of cholent that would arrive. According to the author, "the pots would be placed in the oven according to the status of their owners: the pots of the wealthy in the middle (so that they would not burn) right in front of the pots of the poor whose contents at times remained half raw."[2]

At candle-lighting, the baker shut the oven's heavy door, only to be opened with a shout of "Gut Shabbos" on Saturday. The bakery ovens in Piotrkow stayed hot all of Shabbat. After synagogue services, families lined up to get their pots, which the same assistant distributed. Each pot had a differentiating symbol or mark like a license plate.

As Shabbat approached, on the streets of the Jewish quarter, a man shouted, "Yidden, in shul arain – Jews, go to synagogue." The steam-powered flour mill blew its whistle three times. All the shops were padlocked and covered with heavy iron shutters. The horse-driven taxis, droskies, that made so much noise were all gone. Suddenly the city was silent. It was time for candle-lighting. Momma probably lit the simple brass candlesticks that most Jewish women in Poland received before getting married.

Here's how I imagine it:

I'm standing with my mother in the apartment on Czarnieckiego Place. We are dressed for Shabbat with matching aprons. Momma gives me a coin and places her own coin in the blue box for the "Keren Hayesod." It's important to give charity, tzedakah, she says. Boys and girls from Zionist clubs will come by later in the week to empty the boxes and send the money to Palestine, to buy land to grow oranges and olives.

Then she puts her hands over her eyes, swaying slightly as she says her prayers for Shabbat, and for the wellbeing of her family.

She chants the blessings over the candles: "*Baruch Ata*

---

2   *A Tale of One City*, 215.

Hashem Elokeinu Melech Ha'olam asher kidshanu b'mitzvatov vitzivanu l'hadlik ner shel Shabbat – Blessed art Thou, G-d, King of the Universe, who has sanctified us by the commandment to light Sabbath candles."

Sometimes she gets tears in her eyes and I get tears in my eyes just watching her, wondering what she is thinking and demanding of God.

I know this ceremony well. For over 58 years I have performed it every Friday night in my home.

When I put my hands over my eyes, I try to summon up my mother, whose face eludes me. My mother's scent and embrace must be locked somewhere in my memory bank. And then I bring to mind the mothers I have known and my children, my grandchildren, my great-grandchildren. And when I open my eyes, I'm back in the present, in Jerusalem. There is the scent of sweet Polish kugel in the oven. Guests are knocking at the door.

Chapter 3

TRYING TO REMEMBER OR TO FORGET

Should I remember? Forgetting is safer than remembering. How young am I when I make this draconian decision to forget?

It's a conscious wish from at least the time I was a child in America and I decided to bury my past, but I must have developed this defense mechanism/strategy to survive earlier on. Forget one mother just for a while so you can attach yourself to another.

I had to move forward to survive. I had to sacrifice excruciating memory, cutting away pieces of my heart.

Still, the past has a funny way of rising to the surface, chasing the present. Like a seed that reaches upward instead of sending its roots downwards, it seeks sunlight.

I am a great-grandmother and I still seek my mother's face in my own. I have hired researchers to find her image, alas with no success.

My beloved mother Sarah was less than 40 years old when she perished. I examine photos of myself at 40. I look into my children's faces and my grandchildren's seeking variations of the theme. Are the smile lines around my mouth inherited from my mother? The shape of my eyes? My laugh? I hear my great-grandchildren laughing. What a beautiful and familiar sound! But I wonder if that's my mother's laugh.

A portrait of my granddaughter Shani, painted by Leah Globe, hangs in our parlor. I'm always asked if that's me. "She looks so much like you." And, if I look like my mother, is this how my mother looked?

I don't even know where and when my parents were murdered. I don't know where they are buried. I mark their death on the 10th of the Hebrew winter month of Tevet, a fast day that marks the Babylonian conquerors surrounding Jerusalem in the year 588 BCE. That's the date that Holocaust survivors like me, who don't know when their parents died, chant memorial prayers for their lost loved ones. "*Yitkadal, vayitkadash shemai rabba...* Magnified and sanctified may the Great Name be in the world created by the Divine will...." The Jewish prayer for the dead celebrates life. That's what I have tried to do.

In the memoirs of older Piotrkow Jews, they often remark on stores that smelled of cinnamon and prunes, and garlands of garlic. Storekeepers gave children handfuls of raisins. When I hear these stories, I try in frustration to remember these sounds, sights and smells. I have read so many accounts of Piotrkow that they now blend with my authentic memories.

I experienced this frustration from my first interview at Yad Vashem decades ago.[1] I know that even memories that seem pristine are often colored by family accounts of events. What exactly we remember is never a simple question. A cemetery of buried memories must exist in my mind and heart, memories scattered along the roadsides of my life, like valises too heavy to carry.

Studies about the memory of us Holocaust children suggest that physical and emotional details are eclipsed by the enormity of the horrendous chapters that followed the early ones.

Recently, my daughter made a post-wedding party,

---

1   Over and over the interviewer grilled me on what I actually remembered and what I thought I remembered.

sheva brachot, for my grandson and his new bride in our large living room. There was a lot to get ready. I'm the grandmother, but here's a bittersweet secret: you never get over missing your mother at a ceremony like this. Seventy close friends and family members filled our apartment on Graetz Street in Jerusalem.

Nearly all of our offspring are Orthodox Jews. How did I keep my faith in religion and manage to pass it on to future generations when so many members of my family were murdered? I had reasons to forget God or to be so angry at God that I might have wanted to jettison religion.

I don't know if my love of God and belief in Judaism is a gift from my birth parents, or if I developed it in the years of survival or my living with my last parents, Leah and Jacob Globe. I am a religious woman who prays daily to the Creator of the Universe, with praise, thanksgiving, and a list of requests for my loved ones and my people. I follow Jewish tradition, keep the Sabbath, observe the dietary laws, and give charity, which we call *tzedaka,* the word for social justice.

I still believe in God even after the Holocaust. How could God have allowed the Holocaust to happen? I simply don't know. We say, "the ways of heaven are mysterious," and I can't really explain how I know there is a God despite the disasters which struck my family. The existentialists might call it a leap of faith.

When I arrived in America in 1946, no one called us "Holocaust survivors." I was a "greener," a war orphan. From 1951, there was a Holocaust Day in Israel, but in America, there was little talk about the death of six million Jews, among them more than a million and a half children. In families where parents and their biological children survived, and where those parents had a community of survivor friends, the stories of the war were often repeated and reinforced. But the average American didn't learn about the concentration camps until much later. I didn't know any other survivors while I was growing up.

I wasn't going to share my past with anyone at school. For "show and tell" I wouldn't have considered bringing in the carved wooden figurine from Sweden that I received in the hospital after the war, although it was one of my few treasures from my past. I wasn't going to show, and I certainly wouldn't tell. No one would know that I was anyone but Rena Globe, a regular American girl, no matter what it cost me. I must have realized that I would have more to lose if I revealed my wretched past.

Of course, children did know I was different and that I was adopted. I wanted them to forget that, too. They must have discussed it among themselves, but they never talked to me about it. I must have broadcast that for all my lightheartedness and outgoingness, this subject was off limits. Also, in the 40s and 50s when I was in school, more subjects were taboo than they are today.

There's a famous photo of a bare-kneed Jewish boy wearing a coat and cap and holding up his hands as a Nazi soldier aims his rifle at him. Books have been published about the identity of this boy, but no conclusions drawn. Most sources think the photo was from Warsaw. Rationally, I know that this little boy is neither of my brothers, but because I cannot call up their faces in my mind, I have long thought of this helpless boy, his hands in a gesture of surrender, as one of my brothers, Yossi or David.

When my New York elementary school and high school classmates talked about their families and asked me how many siblings I had, it was easier to say I was an only child. I didn't feel guilty about it. This was part of my ongoing survival strategy. Why feel guilty?

Those talking about the Holocaust often say there are two lessons to be learned. One is that we Jews can never allow ourselves to be helpless again. The other lesson is that we can never let go of our moral standards and become like our oppressors.

It's often assumed that the victims of the Holocaust became base and cruel to survive in the inhumane world of oppression. I want to say loud and clear: that was not my experience. I found kindness from my fellow Jews wherever I went.

In his book, *If this is a Man*, the late esteemed Primo Levi speaks of the re-emergence of humanity. He was among the survivors of Auschwitz, so weak that they were left to die instead of going on the Death March, as the Nazis evacuated their Polish camps in 1945.

Levi and two others helped light fires to keep themselves and others warm. The grateful prisoners decided to give them a larger share of the bread.

"In the camp, the rule was, eat your own bread and if you can, that of your neighbor," Levi said. The offer of sharing bread "was the first human gesture that occurred among us. I believe that that moment can be dated as the beginning of the change by which we who had not died, slowly changed from *Haftlinge* (prisoners) to men again."

Once again, that was not my experience. I am living proof that humanity was never crushed, not even in the worst situations. Perhaps that's why I still believe in God.

Most of my childhood was spent in purgatory, but I also discovered abundant goodness. How else could an innocent little girl have survived alone in the death camps designed by the Nazis to exterminate the Jewish people? These were places of particular cruelty to babies and children. Our tormentors delighted in silencing children's cries by crushing their skulls. Children are easier to kill and, for those determined to wipe out the future, they are potent targets.

Early on, I learned never to cry. I still have trouble with tears. The pain or joy I feel is coupled with an anxiety about showing my emotions. I hear an internal voice urging me to overcome weakness.

A million and a half children perished. Not having someone to look out for you was almost a guarantee of not surviving. And yet I did survive, thanks to the efforts of good women – those blessed mothers – who reached out to me along the frightening journey.

Recently, Yad Vashem, the Holocaust museum in Jerusalem, held a special back-to-school online exhibit about teachers who saved pupils. Says the text:

"During the Holocaust most people abandoned their Jewish neighbors, turned a blind eye or even participated in the persecution of the Jews. Among them were teachers, who watched as their students were marked, harassed, discriminated against and finally murdered. Only some felt that it was their duty not only to educate and instill values in the classroom, but to live by those ideals, even at the risk of their lives."

The first woman who reached out to me was a teacher. I have always assumed that this noble woman perished, but I will never know. All my attempts to find her have been futile. My dear Mother the Teacher who saved me, if you read these words and are somewhere in the world of the living, please let me know. I want to thank you for making sure I survived and for allowing me to build my family and tell this story.

Did my Mother the Teacher care for me all the way to Bergen-Belsen, or did she pass on my care to one of the women who provided whatever shelter they could to the children there? I believe the latter is the case. It has always been my impression that when I was separated from her, another woman reached out to shelter me the best she could.

Not long ago, I sat in a Jerusalem hotel lobby with Rita Kramer (not the Rita of my childhood). Rita, a survivor from Chicago, also was a child in Bergen-Belsen at the time I was there. We tried to pool our memories of that house of horrors.

How did she find me? She was visiting Jerusalem for her grandson's Bar Mitzvah. She had brought with her a photo from Sweden to look for the little orphan who was going to live with the nice Swedish family.

The tourism hostess at the hotel had heard me tell my story to a Hadassah tourist group, and happily brought us together. There, in the lobby of the Inbal Hotel where well-dressed tourists were gathering, we cautiously exchanged remembrances. We didn't recognize each other, but we slowly began retracing our war history, particularly the time in Bergen-Belsen.

Neither Rita nor I had clear memories of how we spent our days in Bergen-Belsen and how we survived, doing anything other than killing lice. What did we do all day? Did we talk? Did we play? Did we work? Neither of us remembered engaging in any playful activity or doing chores. We were only children. Someone must have helped us to survive.

Rita's savior was her mother. They survived the war together. But my mother was gone. Rita says she remembers me as "the little orphan girl." And she was delighted that she'd found a photo that she was sure was me. It was nice to have someone who remembered me, but I looked at that photo and was certain that I wasn't that girl. But how could I be sure? Like the photo of the little boy with his hands up, it would be hard to be sure about this photo.

This uncertainty caused me a toxic mix of anxiety and shame. Why can't I remember? When I look back at the testimony I recorded in 1989 at Yad Vashem, I see the same discomfort and shame in my body language when the interviewer asked me questions I was unable to answer. How could I have forgotten? We who had survived were charged to remember, not to forget.

I sometimes lie in bed and will my memory to come up with the answers. It won't cooperate with my commands. On the other hand, how could I bear to remember?

After the war, a kind Swedish couple, a Christian man and wife, wanted to take me home from the hospital and envelop me with warmth. Had I gone with them, I might have been a good Swedish Christian woman today. You never know. They might have changed my name to Blix, a girl's name that also means "joy." I will always be grateful to the love that the Swedish mother and her husband poured on me as I struggled to return to life in a strange land. The sunshine of love makes the hidden self-worth inside of us flower. I have written to Swedish websites in their area near the camp to ask them to seek this couple or their offspring. I have turned to friends and acquaintances in Sweden. Not a trace of these good people or their families has emerged.

If that was me in Rita's photo, sitting with that family, posing with my Swedish Mother and Father, then I would have something to go on. I could send the photo to websites in the hope that someone would recognize the couple.

Rita was so excited, and I didn't want to disappoint her. I wanted this to be a photo of me, but there was one problem. I couldn't convince myself that it was me. I was working hard to gather the facts of my life and didn't want to get mixed up with fantasies.

My co-author Barbara Sofer knows an Israeli police intelligence officer named Sharon Brown, whose unit spends its days examining photos of terrorists wearing disguises. I turned over Rita's photograph to Sharon Brown. She happens to be the Israeli police intelligence officer who was able to read Israeli astronaut Ilan Ramon's burnt notebook which fell onto a Texas field when the Columbia exploded as it re-entered Earth's atmosphere.

The police kept the photo for several weeks. They requested additional photos of me as a child and as a young woman. The experts pored over their records and computers. No, they said, the little girl in the photo is not you. She's a different girl. Your memory is true, they said. This was a disappointment, but also a relief. How terrible to think that what I do remember may be confused.

We all know that trauma impacts memory. The end of the war didn't snap my life into place. The Nazis' surrender didn't halt the ravages of the diseases and bodily damage they'd inflicted on us. So many of us died just as the war was ending or in the months that followed. The best known case is the tragic story of Anne Frank, who hid for most of the war in Holland and then, like me was in Bergen-Belsen, where she perished in early March 1945, a month before liberation. She was 16, seven years older than me. We both had typhus.

Psychiatrists have speculated that Holocaust survivors could only begin dealing with their losses when their own children reached the age of their lost parents. I went to my first Holocaust conference in 1981. My oldest daughter was already a young woman.

I'm still searching for my lost mothers. In Israel, where more Holocaust survivors live than anywhere else, there is a radio program called "The Lost Relatives Department." Even after all these years, in 2013, my co-author went on the air to ask if anyone knew a little girl named Fredzia or any of her relatives. *Someone* had to remember them or me, but no one did.

Chapter 4

WAR!

This is how I imagine that horrible day when the war began for me. I'm three and a half years old. I don't go to school yet, but my brothers do. School usually starts on September 1, but because it's a Friday, school won't start today. Everyone gets this Friday off. The first of September, 1939, is a special holiday this year, Momma says. It's a sunny day with blue skies and everyone is out on the streets enjoying the last taste of summer.

I am wearing a pretty dress that looks like a sailor suit with a white collar. We stand in line to buy ice cream. "Be careful not to drip on your collar," Momma reminds me.

The kiosk in front of our house has a long line of children and parents buying ice cream. Music men are out on the street, singing and playing instruments. Momma gives me a coin to put in the box of my favorite juggler who might sing the popular song "Remember Capri." The organ grinder with his parrot plays music, too. Everyone is joyous and expectant on this last day of vacation before the school year begins.

Suddenly, an army truck speeds through town. Momma grabs us and pulls us to the side of the road. The soldiers inside are shouting in Polish: *Wojna, Wojna.* That's the word my brothers use when they play with their toy soldiers. I know it means "war." I don't know what war really means, but I can tell by everyone's reactions that something awful has happened.

I feel scared, too. Momma doesn't explain.

"Let's go home," she says. Her bright smile has been

replaced by a frown and a line sinks deep in her forehead. That's not like Momma. She's always so cheerful and optimistic.

The music stops. We take a detour near Staro-Warszawska Street, the center everyone calls *Yidn Gas*, the Jewish Street. Momma listens as a man says he's heard on the radio that a town called Wielun has been attacked.

"Who attacked them?" I want to know. "Shh. I'll tell you at home," Momma says, touching her lips to quiet me.

"Germans," Yossi whispers to me, as we walk home fast. Too fast. It's hard for me to keep up. I am the youngest. I don't know who Germans are, but I can tell by the way Yossi says it that they are not good.

At noon, the first siren sounds. My heart is pounding. "Come, come, come," Momma shouts. She's holding two pillows and featherbedding from her room. Poppa has come home. He picks me up. We run down the stairs to the cellar. There's a crate of apples there and my precious sled. I've been down here playing hide and seek with my friends but now I'm scared. It's cool. I need the bathroom.

All the families in our building are crowded in the cellar, although each family has its designated storage area. We huddle together, children between parents on the floor. I'm shivering. Momma wraps me in the feather-filled quilt.

I can hear planes flying above, and in the distance a noise like thunder. We wait for what seems like forever, and then go back up to our apartment.

Poppa says we're not going to synagogue tonight. Better to stay home. Instead of the chandelier over the dinner table, we leave only a little light in the hall on. Momma pulls the curtains, but I peek underneath when I hear men singing in Polish.

"Who are they?" I ask.

"They are the Polish soldiers going to fight the Germans," my brother Yossi says. I'm surprised that he seems to know all about this. He says boys in school talk about it.

"The Polish soldiers will protect us," says David. He holds his hands up like a gun, pretending to shoot.

From under the windowsill, I look at the soldiers again. "But some of them don't have shoes," I say. "How will they fight without shoes?"

No one answers my question. We eat quietly and quickly. No one feels like singing. The food doesn't taste the same. I don't fall asleep on the couch the way I usually do during Shabbat dinner. Momma and Poppa let me sleep with them.

When I wake up early in the morning, Momma is at the kitchen table drinking tea. Poppa brings the news. "Some are running away," he tells Momma.

"Where to?"

"East."

But my parents decide it's better to stay in Piotrkow where there is a large family and resources they can make use of. I'm glad we're not going anywhere.

At noon, the noise begins.

It sounds like giant mosquitoes. I put my hands over my ears, but I can still hear it. We run downstairs and hide in the cellar again. Everyone in the building is there except for one family. They've already left. The explosions are louder than thunder. Our building shakes. I put my head in Momma's lap and she hugs me. "It will be okay," she promises. "As long as we're together. It will be okay."

I feel better. As long as I'm with Momma and Poppa, and with Yossi and David, everything will be all right.

On the first day of the attack, many persons are injured and a number killed, among them the star skater

Romek! I think of him whirling around the ice with his sister. Dead, like the kitten in the road. Stiff and broken.

Airplanes appear in the skies. I'm scared. Many Jews in Piotrkow are fleeing the city to the nearby town of Sulejoy, Poppa says. We stay in Piotrkow.

On Shabbat morning, September 2, 1939, the Polish janitor comes around as usual to light the stoves for heat.

On certain Saturdays, we would go to the Great Synagogue on Jerozolinska Street. Often, there are special occasions, like a Bar Mitzvah or *Shabbat Chatan*, the Saturday before a wedding, when the groom is honored. I would sit upstairs with Momma.

Hebrew letters and carved animals decorate the walls. A golden crown is held by two lions, and over the crown, a black eagle spreads its wings, facing the Torah ark with a golden menorah. Two figures that look like little children flank each side. There are beautiful murals of Jerusalem. The ceiling is painted in a rainbow of colors with planets and stars. Gigantic brass chandeliers hang from above. Today we won't be going to the Great Synagogue or to any other synagogue.

On Sunday, school doesn't start on time. It doesn't start at all.

Poppa goes to the shops to buy more rice and beans. I play with dolls and teddy bears. I sit on the floor, trying to watch the street from beneath the curtains. Momma reads us our favorite story, "King Matt the First" about a young boy king. Yossi and David play with their toy soldiers. I don't feel like playing with them. Instead, I play 5-stones, a form of jacks, over and over again.

The planes are back, circling Piotrkow. We run to the cellar. I hear shooting. Yossi says that's the Polish soldiers firing at the airplane.

David wants to play Snakes and Ladders. We play

over and over. The boys play Finagle, which is like rummy and chess.

We can't go out.

On Tuesday, there is the loud roar of motorcycles driving past our home on the street. I sit below the curtain and peek. The motorcyclists are wearing gray uniforms.

Suddenly, there's an explosion. Huge and scary tanks roll through town. I smell fire. I start to cry. I remember a song I've heard. "It is burning, brothers, it is burning. Our poor little town, a pity, burns."

Where do my personal experiences fit into the mega-events that lead to World War II?

A week before World War II began, the Germans signed a non-aggression agreement with the Soviet Union, the Molotov-Ribbentrop agreement, in which Hitler and Stalin agreed not to attack each other. They also secretly agreed to divide Poland. So when the Germans invaded Poland on September 1, they knew the Soviets would give them free rein. German strategy was to attack by air, and then send in the tank corps that would cut a swath through the country it wanted to occupy. Almost immediately, so-called "security forces" followed to terrorize the population. Their primary target was us Jews.

Piotrkow was on the main axis of the Germans' advance on Warsaw. It was the setting for fierce fighting between the Polish 19th Infantry Division and the XVI, 16th Panzer Corps of the German Wehrmacht on September 5, 1939, as the Germans wanted to subdue the countryside and move towards Warsaw. Polish forces were actually successful at repelling the German army, the Wehrmacht, in Piotrkow. But two days later, Marshal Rydz-Smigly ordered the Polish forces to withdraw. The Polish army was overstretched and underprepared.

The 16th Division, part of the German 10th Army, was reputedly the strongest Panzer corps in the Wehrmacht. In the initial period of fighting, 20 Jews in our Piotrkow community were killed.

Chapter 5

SEEKING THE MEMORY OF MY MOTHERS

What do you remember from your childhood? Do you really remember the pleasure of your first bike or the cold pain of falling on the ice? Do you remember your daily cornflakes or the one Sunday your dad tried to make pancakes? For most of us, the past is a mix of personal memory and family stories. Sitting on the couch on a rainy Sunday, looking through the old family photo albums and looking at old movies, we see ourselves as youngsters and recreate memories as we reminisce. At family gatherings, someone always tells about the time a family member fell out of a boat or cried at the family dinner because there was no ketchup. One memory builds on another. Experts say we form memories every moment of our lives and store them away. Memories may be hard to retrieve, but they exist beneath the surface, sometimes refusing to appear. Other times, they arise unbidden.

I have no childhood albums. The last time I saw my father, I was nine years old. He gave me a few family photos. I treasured them, hid them, and nearly wore them thin with kisses. My jailers tore them from my hands, smiling as they ripped apart my last concrete images of my nuclear family.

Think of those torn photographs. That's what my memories are like. Snippets. Fragments. Also scents and dreamlike sequences. I can remember the smell of the soup in Bergen-Belsen but not the face of the woman who covered me with a black coat to keep me warm. I can remember the love I felt for my brothers, but not the color of their hair. With the help of researchers and archivists, there are new, additional pegs to hang my memories on. I reach back in my memory to retrieve missing scraps.

This is a subversive process. While seeking memories my former sound sleep disappeared. Memories long buried wake me. Experts warn that the memories of youth can come crashing down on us in our so-called golden years. I'm already in my golden years. Will I be engulfed by a tsunami of fear and panic if the memories come back like a tidal wave? I realize that I have always been afraid that I'll lose my equanimity if I delve too deeply into my past. Am I ready to take this risk now?

I am also afraid of crowding my memory. I remember those fearsome watchtowers but like every sentient being in a western culture, I have seen so many photos and movies of the same that I worry that I'm superimposing another image on what I really recall. I want my memory to be authentic.

According to psychologist Erik Erikson's famous "Stages of Child Development," preschool years are the time when a child needs to build confidence about testing the limits of individual freedom and group responsibility, of fantasy and reality, of what feels good and what is permissible. There's a need to come to terms with social reality, but in a manner that doesn't frighten the child from believing in his or her self-worth. Erikson says this happens between the ages of three to five and a half. At this age, I was already living in a ghetto where every day's existence became more and more precarious.

After age 5½ until 12 is the next stage, which Erikson calls "industry versus inferiority" – the time when a child learns to function beyond the daily, consolidating his or her inner life in preparation for the unique challenges of adolescence. In this period, I lost both parents and both siblings, all my aunts and uncles. I was a slave laborer and a starved prisoner in a concentration camp.

There have been many studies on child survivors, those of us who were born shortly before the war and underwent persecution with losses, separation, emotional and physical abuse, neglect and starvation during our formative years. Even as kids, we understood that our parents were trying to prevent our annihilation. We witnessed their helplessness to protect us.

Contemporary psychologists have written many scholarly tomes about the difficulty of achieving basic trust for children in war zones, of impeded resolution of autonomy, of damaged concentration. Does the basic trust established in infancy last despite later traumas?

Despite my horrendous childhood, I don't think I experienced these syndromes. Some have said I'm a master of repression, which is, by definition, an attempt to repel desires and pleasurable impulses by subduing the past. Freud, of course, associated this with mental illness. If I repressed the horrors of the past, it was just the opposite. I wanted to overcome the trauma, to experience the joy of everyday life and to have a happy future. Maybe Freud was wrong and repression isn't so bad.

I often think of myself taking part in a Death March in the icy Polish winter without proper shoes or perhaps with no shoes at all. I don't understand how it was possible to survive this ordeal, but here I am, walking on the same two feet that trudged barefoot through the snow. On my most recent trip to Poland, several women in the group I was meeting wanted to go to see a palace in Warsaw. I'd been up half the night. I had just landed. Still, without hesitation, I walked along with them on these old, abused feet. I was fine, delighted with the company and interested in the sites.

I walk up a steep hill to synagogue every Saturday on these same feet. True, one of my toes often hurts.

When I was a child in America, an orthopedist who didn't know anything about my personal story asked me if I might possibly have had a frozen toe in my youth. He was talking about a single toe. I had to smile. A frozen toe. A frozen foot. Frozen fingers. A frozen heart, like Princess Anna in the Disney movie my great-grandchildren love.

My health, post war, has been surprisingly robust, despite the food deprivation, exposure to cold and debilitating childhood diseases before age 10. As part of routine medical examinations, physicians go over my medical history, including family history. I fill such forms with question marks and tell them I have no idea about my family's medical history. I dread this part. If they aren't familiar with my background, they look at me strangely. But then I tell them that my parents and brothers, my many aunts, uncles and tens of cousins were already dead when I was still a child. These relatives never grew old enough to worry about heart disease, hypertension or diabetes.

I carry on the single sample of my nuclear family's DNA, but it's present in my children, grandchildren and great-grandchildren. In Israel, where I live, doctors are used to this, patients without medical records.

Survivors who found one parent or sibling could fill in the gaps in their family history. I met an older cousin after the war, and he told me what my street address was for the forms I needed to fill out. He'd remembered where I lived, but little else about me. I always knew my name. What that cousin told me turned out to be correct and useful when decades later I was searching the archives in Piotrkow.

For me, reconstructing my past has been the work of research and placing distinct memories in a timeline. Sometimes I remembered something, but wanted to know where and when it happened. Barbara Sofer has insisted that we create a chronology and document whatever we can. We are assisted by a researcher/scholar in Poland named Jacek Bednark who has a talent for finding old city records. There have been many surprises along the way.

After all these years, Jacek found a document from the military commission of my father and this is what he told us it said.

"This is a document #1736 from the military commission of Icyk Lichtensztajan. It took place on 31 May 1927 in Piotrkow. His birth date is listed as May 15, 1906. He received the highest military category 'A' and he is able for the military service. His height is 161.5 cm, his weight 54 kg, and the dimension of his chest 79/74 cm. He has no eyesight problems. His education was 2 classes of commercial school in Piotrkow (besides the elementary education). He is a tailor apprentice. He lives on Plac Trybunalski, 10. His parents Jankiel and Cyrla are alive."

Just recently Jacek found a picture of my father. In 1936, soon after I was born, my father applied for a new identity card. We don't know why. In modern Poland, citizens change identity cards every ten years, so that applying for a change might not have been that unusual. Around then, my parents moved from one home to another. We speculate that he used the change of address as an opportunity to update an old card with a new photo. According to my birth certificate, both of my parents were 26. But Jacek found other data. My father, he said,

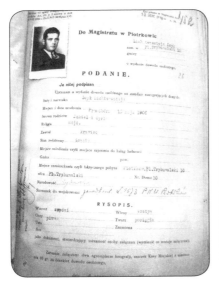 

Rena's father's application for a new identity card in 1936 with his picture. This is the only picture Rena has of her father.

was really 31. My mother was 36. Jacek shrugged when we asked why there were such discrepancies in Polish registries. Inexactitude seemed to be an accepted part of the record-keeping of that pre-war period, and if there were so many errors, that means that the scant facts of my life aren't even certain.

Many Jews in Piotrkow applied for passports to emigrate to Palestine or America. Why didn't my father apply for a passport and take his young family to Palestine or America in 1936 while we could still get out?

This is a heavy question for all Holocaust survivors. I can't answer it for all of European Jewry, but will try for my own family.

Raul Hilberg, author and editor of *Documents of Destruction*, put it this way: "When Adolf Hitler came to power in 1933, a modern bureaucracy set out for the first time to destroy an entire people. The machinery of destruction was not a single organization but a network of offices in the party, the ministries, the army and industry. Its onslaught on the Jews was not planned in advance but developed blow by blow. In spite of such decentralization, few operations could have been more efficient than this singular deed in the midst of a general war."

Even the Nazis themselves didn't understand the extent of their attempts to exterminate the Jews.

Professor Yehuda Bauer of Yad Vashem and the Task Force for International Cooperation on Holocaust Education explains: "There is something unprecedented, frightening about the Holocaust of the Jewish people: for the first time in the bloodstained history of the human race, a decision developed, in a modern state in the midst of a civilized continent, to track down, register, mark, isolate from their surroundings, dispossess, humiliate, concentrate, transport and murder every single person of an ethnic group as defined not by them, but by the perpetrators; not just in the country where this genocidal motivation arose, not just on the continent its planners first wished to control, but ultimately everywhere on earth, for purely ideological reasons."

If, Heaven forbid, such a plan was unleashed today, we would still have difficulty believing that one of the western countries we lived in might endorse it. After all, German Jews fought alongside their Christian brethren on the side of Germany in World War I. Germany was a bastion of civilization, or so it was believed.

Also, please remember that getting out wasn't easy. In the United States in 1936, visas were severely restricted for immigrants from Poland. As far as I know, we didn't have relatives willing to vouch for us in the United States.

If the greatest politicians and strategists in the world couldn't predict the Holocaust, how could my parents? Remember that in September 1938, British Prime Minister Neville Chamberlain signed a nonaggression pact with Adolf Hitler, returning to London in triumph, declaring "peace for our time," and recommending that the good citizens go home and "sleep quietly" in their beds. That was one year before Germany conquered Poland.

No matter what we think of Chamberlain, he was Prime Minister of England, and not a Polish tailor like my father or a businesswoman like my mother.

My parents had a young family, new shops they'd opened with the great expectations and the optimism of a young couple. They were surrounded by loving family members who lived in Piotrkow and the surrounding towns. Looking with perfect hindsight, of course, leaving Poland would have been a brilliant decision. But the horror that was to come was beyond the imagination of any normal human being.

I look back at an essay I wrote in 2007 for a journal published by survivors of my town: "I would give anything to be able to remember the faces of my mother, my father and my brothers. This block in my memory has always haunted me and continues to do so."

What was the strangest about finding the photo of my father was my reaction. Instead of jubilation I had to overcome cognitive dissonance. "That's not my father," I insisted.

When I looked at the handsome dark-haired man, very much different from the daddy I have in my memory, I felt a chill. I couldn't believe this was him.

Even when I had confirmation of the documents, I had a hard time accepting that the image I'd created in my mind was different from the reality of this man who is the age of my grandsons.

It's difficult for us today to reconcile the fullness of Jewish life with the anti-Semitism Jews were experiencing in parts of Poland even before the war. The Jews of Poland built fine schools, wrote beautiful melodies, and celebrated Jewish holidays.

Some wonder how the Polish people could become such vicious collaborators with the Germans in the persecution and destruction of their Jewish community. The roots of anti-Semitism ran deep in Poland, a combination of old-fashioned church condemnation of Jews, with resentment towards any economic success the Jews enjoyed. There had been a better period for Jews under Prime Minister Josef Pilsudski, who led the country from 1926; he actually opposed anti-Semitism and the growing right-wing parties within Poland. Twenty percent of university students were Jews. But when Pilsudski died, a new momentum of anti-Semitism grew. Students were confined to Jewish benches at university lecture halls. They began dropping out of university courses because of the anti-Semitism on campus.

The growth of the right-wing parties in Poland paralleled the popular election of Hitler in Germany. When the Holocaust began, the ground had already been readied for persecution of Jews in Poland. The old Polish anti-Semitism had been notched up and would dovetail with the virulent Nazi hatred of Jews that was a central peg in their identity.

In 1936, in a nearby town called Przytyk there was an infamous pogrom, an attack on the local Jews. When the Jews fought back they were hauled into court and had to face trial. A Jewish carpenter wrote a famous poignant song about it.

s'brent! briderlekh, s'brent!
oy, undzer orem shtetl nebekh brent!
beyze vintn mit yirgozn,
raysn, brekhn un tseblozn,
shtarker nokh di vilde flamn,
alts arum shoyn brent!

It is burning, brothers, it is burning.
Our poor little town, a pity, burns!
Furious winds blow, breaking, burning and
    scattering.
And you stand around with folded arms.
O, you stand and look while our town burns…
Don't just stand there, brothers.
Put out the fire, because our town is burning.

When I hear this song today – there are many versions on YouTube – it makes my heart pound with fear and yearning, even though I no longer understand the language. How prescient was this poet.

If I sat with a hypnotist would I recall all these scenes of childhood? Would I want to? I've considered hypnotism but have rejected it as a strategy.

My memories are black-and-white sketches, scents, feelings. I also have many blanks. Whether they are the result of plain forgetfulness or blocking out traumas I do not know. I certainly had enough traumas. Like many people, I have trouble remembering intense pain. Have I, at some deep level, willfully sealed it off to protect myself from pain that is too excruciating to bear? Even among psychologists, the notion of "active forgetting," my suppression and repression isn't universally accepted.

Recent decades have dispelled the myth of the

memory centers of our brains being static. Today cognitive scientists talk about plasticity. One of their conclusions is that intense activities between neurons – emotionally charged memories for instance – are easier to remember. Balancing this are other theories which speak of a near-amnesia around traumatic events. There's so much literature about false memory that I was relieved that whatever I did remember from my childhood turned out to be documentable.

Branko Lustig, producer of the remarkable movie "Schindler's List," like me, was liberated in Bergen-Belsen. He has said, "I don't want to remember. I think this is the reason I rarely had nightmares."

For a long time, I felt the same way. My husband says he has never once heard me screaming in my sleep. But now I am determined to put the pieces of my life puzzle together.

In a BBC feature on the first anniversary of the liberation of Bergen-Belsen on April 15, 1946, a prisoner of war named Harold Le Druillenec from the Channel Islands raised the question of why we should want to recall these horrors.[1]

Le Druillenec said: "Why not forget? I can sympathize with such a viewpoint. I too often wish I could forget. And yet, at other times, I think that such stories should be remembered. There is a danger that these camps may come to be regarded as part of a fantastic nightmare from which mankind has awakened."

Maybe my forgetfulness is a survival strategy to prevent those nightmares of the deep traumas of war, hiding, death, abandonment, slavery, loneliness, fear. Maybe I just forget my nightmares.

---

1   *Belsen*, 1945, pp. 150-151.

When I hug my great-grandchildren, as I have hugged my grandchildren and my own children, I cannot imagine them going through what I endured. How was it possible for a small, defenseless child to have survived what I survived?

In this memoir, I have supplemented my memory with research and interviews, hoping to recreate the childhood I lost. Lustig, who was in Auschwitz, says that when he reads books describing Auschwitz, suddenly he remembers something. The same is true for me.

I have a huge library of books, collecting history books and personal accounts as I look for clues and fill in gaps that will open the trapdoor of my memory. We have also spent many hours in libraries.

When I was nine, I was transported from among the nearly dead in Bergen-Belsen to a hospital in Sweden. When Barbara Sofer told me that the hospital officials had found my records, I screamed into the phone. "You see, I exist. I really exist!" As if Barbara thought I was a phantom!

So much of my memory is like a sketchy dream. When Barbara asked me questions, I felt acute embarrassment, almost shame when I could not remember. She said she always asks those she interviews the same questions many times. It's her style. Sometimes the first question loosens a lost memory. Sometimes the answers come up later.

I found my birth certificate in 1989. Until then, I didn't know exactly how old I was. I'd taken the birth date of Fannie, the dead girl whose passport I used to enter America. I suddenly became two months older. What a strange feeling that was! At the same time, I was relieved that the two dates were close.

You have doubtlessly heard often that "the Nazis

POLSKA RZECZPOSPOLITA LUDOWA

URZĄD STANU CYWILNEGO w   Piotrkowie Tryb.
Województwo   piotrkowskie

Odpis skrócony aktu urodzenia

1. Nazwisko   L i c h t e n s z t a j n

2. Imię (imiona)   Frajda

3. Data urodzenia   osiemnasty grudnia tysiąc dziewięćset trzydziestego piątego roku /18. 12. 1935 r. /

4. Miejsce urodzenia   Piotrków Tryb.

5. Imię i nazwisko rodowe (ojca)   Icek Lichtensztajn

6. Imię i nazwisko rodowe (matki)   Sura Messer

Poświadcza się zgodność powyższego odpisu z treścią aktu urodzenia Nr 179/1935/VI

Piotrków Tryb.   1989.05.24.—
, data

I - ss KIEROWNIK NIKA
Urzędu Stanu Cywilnego

Ewa Andrzonczyk

263 (740.000) t. A.

Rena's Polish birth certificate was found in the Piotrkow city records.

POLSKA RZECZPOSPOLITA LUDOWA

URZĄD STANU CYWILNEGO w _Piotrkowie Tryb._

Województwo _piotrkowskie_

Odpis skrócony aktu urodzenia

1. Nazwisko _Lichtenszlajn_

2. Imię (imiona) _Josef_

3. Data urodzenia _17-ty stycznia 1931_ _(17.01.1931)_

4. Miejsce urodzenia _Piotrków Tryb._

5. Imię i nazwisko rodowe _Icek Lichtenszlajn_
   (ojca)

6. Imię i nazwisko rodowe _Sura Messer_
   (matki)

Poświadcza się zgodność powyższego odpisu
z treścią aktu urodzenia Nr _23/1931/6_

Piotrków Tryb., data _1989 09 07_

KIEROWNIK
Urzędu Stanu Cywilnego
Cecylia Adamska

OPŁATA SKARBOWA 1000 zł

Pu-M-8 zam. 798/DW/On/88
Sp-nia „Poligrafika" Olsztyn, zam. 263 (740 000) f. A5

The birth certificate of Rena's brother, Joseph, was found in the Piotrkow city records.

POLSKA RZECZPOSPOLITA LUDOWA

URZĄD STANU CYWILNEGO w *Piotrkowie Tryb.*

Województwo *piotrkowskie*

Odpis skrócony aktu urodzenia

1. Nazwisko *Lichtensztajn*

2. Imię (imiona) *Dawid - Mordka*

3. Data urodzenia *23-ci listopada 1932*
   (23. 11. 1932)

4. Miejsce urodzenia *Piotrków Tryb.*

5. Imię i nazwisko rodowe *Icek Lichtensztajn*
   (ojca)

6. Imię i nazwisko rodowe *Sura Messer*
   (matki)

Poświadcza się zgodność powyższego odpisu
z treścią aktu urodzenia Nr *201/1932/6*

Piotrków Tryb., data *1989. 08. 07*

KIEROWNIK
Urzędu Stanu Cywilnego

Cecylia Adamska

Pu-M-8 zam. 798/DW/On/88
Sp-nia ,,Poligrafika" Olsztyn, zam. 263 (240.000) E-5

The birth certificate of Rena's brother, David, was found in the
Piotrkow city records.

were meticulous keepers of records." This is only partly true. For example, I know on which train my father and uncle rode to Buchenwald. I have those records, but I have no documents recording my father's death.

Please bear with me if there are gaps. We have worked hard to fill in whatever we can, no matter the difficulty or pain. I was only 3½ years old when the Germans invaded my city.

Historians say the winters of World War II were all particularly cruelly cold, even for Eastern Europe, as if they were an objective correlative of the political situation. Today I own a down coat and fur-lined boots against the cold. I love cozy warm quilts and scented hot baths. How could I possibly have survived Polish and German winters in the camps in flimsy clothes and no shoes?

Today I serve elegant dinners, with pumpkin soup scented with coriander, served in china. How could I have survived on soup that was no better than the dishwasher water that goes down my drain? The worst punishment in the world was to be denied that soup. It kept me alive.

I lost my birth mother at age seven. How did I become a devoted mother?

According to experts, most people grow up with positive assumptions about the benevolence of the world and with positive self-esteem. But the Holocaust trauma must have shattered these assumptions very early for me.

My father promised to meet me after the war. He never came. Fathers are supposed to keep their promises. How did I become a trusting person? Hundreds of near-strangers have stayed in our apartment. Thousands of men, women and children, Jews and gentiles, have been welcomed into our home and have broken bread at our table.

We begin each meal with a blessing, thanking the God

who brings bread from the ground. *"Hamotzi lehem min ha'aretz."* But bread doesn't come from the ground, wheat does. Bread is the culmination of positive human endeavor and Divine blessing. A single slice of bread was once the difference between life and death in the world I lived.

It's fair to assume that more of my story was accessible in the years closer to the war, had I researched it then. Today, when I meet men and women from Piotrkow, many details that they, too, might have remembered decades ago have faded. At gatherings of Piotrkow survivors, there are a handful of men and women who are older than I am and who would have been old enough to remember more details, but so many years have gone by that I can't count on accuracy. None of them seems to remember any members of my family.

So why did I wait so long to begin this search? For much of my life, I couldn't allow myself to think about my birth mother without being overwhelmed by sadness and terror. Also, remember that I was adopted.

An almost universal comment of adoptees then, and perhaps until now, is that the adoptive family is not eager for their new child to invest energy in finding out about their past. Nor was that an easy task.

In the United States, until today, most states have sealed adoption records. That was true in New York since 1935, coincidentally the year I was born. Today there is often the choice of "open" adoptions.

My case was different, of course. I wasn't the child of an unmarried woman who made the painful decision to give up her baby and whose child couldn't find her. In my case, my final parents had to find out if there were any living relatives who wanted to claim me. When none appeared, they applied to adopt me. Nonetheless, in the

40s, when I was adopted, adopted children or even young adults didn't begin the search for their birth family.

And think of it from my adoptive parents' point of view. They were taking in a child of an unknown past, clothing, feeding, caring for her, building the delicate web of connections that are needed for love and devotion and she is concerned with her family of origin – in a way the competition for their unique connection. They needed all the emotional resources they had to bring me up. Why complicate this with a search for a past that was only full of pain and loss?

And think of me – a ten-year-old who found a safe harbor. Why go out again to the raging seas of uncertainty?

Then, as a teen facing all the challenges of adolescence, why would I have risked discoveries to unbalance the new and wonderful family life that had stabilized for me? After all, I knew what it was to lose parents.

Later, when I married, my husband wasn't troubled by my missing past. He accepted that he had married a woman with chapters missing from her life. With all the challenges of being a young wife and then a mother, I pushed the past away and put my energies into the present.

In their paper "Knowing and Not Knowing, Massive Psychic Trauma: Forms of Traumatic Memory," American psychologists Dori Laub and Nanette C. Auerhahn describe a state where trauma victims are caught between the compulsion to complete the process of knowing and the inability or fear of doing do.[2]

Laub and Auerhahn suggest that one means of coping was a dissociation at the time of trauma in which those like me who experienced such extreme trauma were

---

2   International Journal of Psycho-Analysis, 1993.

able to say "that's not me" and hence not remember it so clearly. The child who was lovingly bathed each evening and dressed in a soft flannel nightgown is standing in a crowded cattle car engulfed in defecation, with nothing she can do about it. It's easier to cope by saying this wasn't her it was happening to. Hence, it doesn't always become part of a remembered life narrative.

Just recently, a young man from Cambodia who was in the audience when I told my story asked if he could call me "Savta," Hebrew for Grandma. He explained that he had lost his grandparents in the massacres of Cambodia and he knew my story in his bones. He wanted to adopt me as his missing grandparent. I was touched and instantly agreed.

In her poignant book, *The Year of Magical Thinking*, author Joan Didion writes about her state of mind after losing her beloved husband, John Gregory Dunne. She said we can fool ourselves by thinking that if we hope for something enough, or by performing the right actions, then we can make changes in painful situations. She couldn't give away her husband's shoes because he would need them "when he came back." This is part of grieving.

Children are experts at magical thinking. The most common example is children who believe their divorced parents will one day get back together again. For those of us who lost so many family members with no specific knowledge of their death, there is no closure. We're always waiting for that happy surprise at the door. Somewhere in the back of my mind I am still waiting for a cousin to surprise me and knock on my door in Jerusalem. "Please come in," I will say. "I am so glad to see you."

Chapter 6

CLINGING TO MY MOTHER IN THE GHETTO

T his is how I picture it. I hear my mother and others saying that the Germans might be in our town for as long as a year, which seems like forever. I do the counting on my fingers. If the adults are right, I will be five by the time they leave. They keep saying that our friends in England and France, and maybe even in America will stop the Germans. How will anyone just sit there and allow the Germans to take over Poland? I don't know who any of these people are. But my brothers do, and they play toy soldiers with English and French troops. All I know is that the real soldiers in our town are very scary. I can feel that the adults are scared, too.

Sometimes, the adults talk in whispers about how the Jews in Germany have been suffering and no one has helped them. They talk about Germany taking over Austria and Czechoslovakia. They say that when Germany took its first bite of Czechoslovakia, the Sudetenland, British Prime Minister Neville Chamberlain thought Germany would stop fighting and there would be peace.

How can one country bite another?

When I first see the German troops marching in their leather boots into our town, even a little girl like me knows they aren't thinking of peace. How can our barefoot soldiers have a chance against soldiers in boots?

Piotrkow was the first ghetto, but the creation of more than 1,000 other ghettos followed ours. Jews were herded behind fences all around Poland, isolated from the general community, making it easier to control and abuse us. With the Jews concentrated in one part of town, it was harder to escape from the deadly net. Workers could be easily conscripted for backbreaking labor.

Putting us in a ghetto was the first step for the totalitarian regime towards the use of the ultimate weapon of mass murder: the extermination camp. By the end, 25,000 people from Piotrkow and the nearby towns and villages were imprisoned in the Piotrkow ghetto. Most of the additional population came from the surrounding towns. Because we were in the first ghetto, the Nazis refined their means of exploitation on us.

The might of the Nazis was unlike anything the people of Piotrkow – or people anywhere for centuries – had ever experienced. The Nazis ruled Piotrkow for six years, enslaving, humiliating, torturing and murdering us.

The occupation began with a show of who was the boss. The Germans displayed their disdain and hate by beating Jewish men, abducting them and sending them off to exhausting slave labor like draining swamps. The conquerors randomly shot and killed Jews. We stayed indoors because it was safer to stay out of sight.

One day, the Nazis ordered the Jews who lived in a block bordered by Staro-Warszawska, (the so-called "Jewish Street") and Jerozolinska ("Jerusalem Street" where the synagogue stood) and Zamkowa Street, to stay home. Then they attacked the homes with fire-bombs. They rounded up any surviving Jews and shot them.

From the beginning of their Occupation, the Germans made it clear that their war wasn't only a military struggle. Equally important to them was their ideological battle to destroy the Jews, on whom Hitler blamed world problems.

They denigrated Jewish symbols in order to

demoralize us. Religious men had their beards and side-curls (payot) torn out. Sacred prayer shawls (tallitot) were collected and used to clean roads and floors. Jews were forced to wash floors and the toilets with pages from the holy books in the synagogue.

A number of Torah scrolls from the synagogues were reportedly buried in the woods so they wouldn't be desecrated by the Germans.

These attacks were clear messages to us Jews that our long-cherished beliefs were going to be destroyed. There was no way out. It was not as if you could pretend to stop observing Jewish customs or convert, as Jews persecuted in the 15th century Spanish Inquisition could do. The Germans didn't care how religious you were or what political party you belonged to. A Jew is a Jew. A Jew is vermin.

Once the Occupation started, fleeing was nearly impossible. Even if you could run away, where would you go? Several families from Piotrkow tried to flee to the Soviet Union. Many of them were killed on the way. Some returned in tatters. Of course, the Nazis often caught up with Jews when other countries were occupied. Jews who fled to Belgium, for instance, were incarcerated and murdered there.

On September 24, 1940, Jewish emigration from Poland was officially prohibited by the Chief Security Office of the Reich in Berlin. The reason? Jewish emigration of Polish Jews might cause a "spiritual renaissance of North American Jewry," which would threaten the Nazis' overarching goal of wiping Judaism from the face of the earth.

The Nazis would soon occupy most of Europe. No one was safe, as this monstrous force began to take over. It would eventually take six years of war, and the strongest armies in the world fighting with all their resources to defeat the power of the Nazi military.

Our lives became worse by stages. That was part of the Germans' strategy to discourage our resistance. You'd get used to one evil decree, and figure "okay – I can live with this. How much worse can it get?" The next decree would be worse and the one after that unimaginable. But then there might be a month or two when enforcing the restrictions was relaxed, so we let down our guard. Subjugation is a physical and psychological process, and the Nazis were experts at it.

The initial occupation by the Germans coincided with the Jewish High Holiday season. In every Jewish community, everyone looks forward to the High Holidays, a unique mix of solemnity and joyousness, when soul-searching is encouraged, and special foods like apples dipped in honey, roasted beef, candied carrots are served.

Try to picture a huge community that's almost entirely Jewish, and in which the community is well-educated in Judaism, and far more traditional than the average Jewish community today, getting ready for the High Holidays. The shofar, a ram's horn, is blown every morning for the month before Rosh Hashanah, and you can hear it throughout the city, a kind of wake up call. There's joyous anticipation.

But then everything changed overnight. Instead of joyous anticipation, we had escalating dread. No one would dare sound the shofar and bring German troops storming up the stairs.

Before the Occupation, even Jews who didn't attend synagogues regularly would come to pray for the two days of Rosh Hashanah, particularly for the evening service of Yom Kippur.

But in that first Occupation High Holiday season

in September 1939, fear already engulfed us. Remember that at the beginning of the month we were all outdoors celebrating the beginning of the school year. Two weeks later, with the holiday of Rosh Hashanah on September 14, we were in the midst of a terrible war. In September, the Germans conquered most of the area in Poland they had agreed on with the Soviets.

The apple dipped in honey – still abundant that first year – symbolizes the wish for a sweet new year, but now, Piotrkow Jews had to contend with the paradox of celebrating, amidst growing fear.

The theme of the High Holidays is personal stocktaking, repentance and new beginnings. On Yom Kippur, from age 10 and above, everyone abstains from eating and drinking for 25 hours.

We Jews believe that our fate is sealed in a symbolic Book of Life. The most solemn prayer is called *Unetanneh Tokef.* "On Rosh Hashanah it is written, and on Yom Kippur it is sealed. Who will live and who will die? Who will come to a timely death and who to an untimely death? Who by fire and who by water? Who by sword, who by beast? Who by famine, who by thirst, who by upheaval, who by plague, who by strangling, and who by stoning?"

Now the future seemed inscribed for doom. The vast majority of European Jewry would die an untimely death, by fire and water and plague and strangling and starvation. Who could have imagined such a fate?

There was a tremendous impetus among the Jews to go ahead with the holidays, no matter what. That's part of our intrepid spirit.

In previous years, as Rosh Hashanah would draw near, the city crier would pass through our streets before dawn and call people to penitent prayer. This year, when

Rosh Hashanah began, the evening of September 13, no one dared to walk the streets in the early morning hours. Rabbi Lau, our city's Jewish spiritual leader cautioned us not to come to pray in the Great Synagogue.

The mail brought New Year's cards from neighbors who had moved to pre-state Israel with pictures of Jerusalem. My parents must have wished that they had moved to Palestine, too. They couldn't have guessed that their little daughter, their grandchildren, great-grandchildren and great-great-grandchildren would live there one day.

On the eve of Rosh Hashanah, Rabbi Lau sent another reminder that people shouldn't come to the Great Synagogue for the holidays because of the danger of a large gathering of Jews presenting itself as a target for a Nazi attack. We should to be careful of all gatherings, because even a small crowd was vulnerable.

The Germans issued a decree on the eve of Rosh Hashanah, prohibiting Jews from being outside their homes after 5 p.m. on penalty of death. Another decree said shops had to be kept open every day of the week, except Sunday.

Rabbi Lau conducted prayer services in the auditorium of an orphanage. In some of the small synagogues, called shtiblach, and in homes, too, services were also held. The Germans burst into one such service, grabbed men, tortured them and then sent them for forced labor.

The Germans were known as a cultured, intellectual people. It was impossible to think of them torturing and murdering millions of adults, children and babies. Yet, we would learn after the war that at the same time my family was living in the ghetto, Hitler began a "euthanasia program" to kill his own Germans who were mentally and physically challenged. Could parents of children with disabilities believe that their government would murder their "imperfect" offspring? Hitler was a democratically elected leader, chosen by the people of Germany, not a despot who came to power because of a coup that enslaved a previously free people. The Nazi party was the only legal political party in democratic Germany from 1933.

In September 1935, a few months before I was born, the Nuremberg Laws ended Jewish freedom in Germany and made "Jewishness" an expression of race. It's no secret that on November 9-10, 1938, the attack on Jewish property in Germany, called Kristallnacht because so much glass was broken, had been organized by the state. This event is often considered the formal beginning of the Holocaust. Still, all of this had taken place in Germany, not Poland. Polish Jews believed the Polish army in which Jews had also served, boosted by the armies of Poland's democratic allies, would protect the Jews from any outside invader.

What was behind the Nazis' attack on the Jews? Some Nazis actually believed in Hitler's ideology of populating the world with their race which they deemed superior to all others. They made the Jews the scapegoats for Germany's economic troubles, resulting from the country's humiliating defeat in what was called then The Great War. The Great War was soon to be renamed World War I, when World War II began.

Still other Nazis and their collaborators were motivated by opportunism, the desire for personal advancement and an easy path to riches by stealing from all those they could conquer.

No one knew what to expect when the Nazis took over our city. No one understood the implications of the ghetto as the Nazis began to enforce their restrictions.

We were helpless to oppose the robbery and abuse, by

the Nazis themselves and their eager Polish collaborators. At any hour, Germans might burst into our apartments and demand anything we had of value: silver ceremonial dishes, jewelry, warm fur coats.

Two days before the holiest day of the Jewish year, Yom Kippur, soldiers entered our Great Synagogue. They tore and trampled the Torah scrolls, chopped down the ark and destroyed the 200-year-old artwork of the eastern wall. They smashed the pulpit, chests, and lamps. Our synagogue was converted to a prison. Jews were ordered to clean up the human excrement from the prisoners with the sacred prayer shawls and synagogue curtains.

The Nazis set up their own government to control occupied Poland: the *general gouvernment.* In charge was *Oberburgermeister* Hans Frank, who declared the establishment of the ghetto on October 8, 1939.

Why was Piotrkow chosen as the first ghetto? There is no clear answer. Piotrkow was easy to turn into a ghetto because most Jews lived in one particular section of town. The Germans were looking for a housing solution for the Poles whose homes had been destroyed in the heavy fighting. Thus, by segregating the Jews they could confiscate houses outside the Jewish neighborhood.

The non-Jews who lived in the Jewish neighborhoods were supposed to move out. Jews who lived in other parts of Piotrkow had to leave their homes. Neither side did this willingly. At the beginning, hard as it is to believe, people weren't afraid to disobey the orders of the Nazis. It reportedly took three months to complete the removal of the estimated 600 Jews who lived outside the ghetto from their homes and to be resettled in apartments in the ghetto. They were allowed to bring in their blankets and pillows.

Some non-Jewish Polish residents actually remained

in the ghetto area. There were even churches that continued services in the ghetto, until 1942.

Jews weren't allowed to own more than 2,000 zlotys ($600) and had to give up their valuables. Our excellent Jewish doctors were prohibited from treating non-Jews.

Ten Jewish men in the city were taken away and held hostage. Each family was entreated to donate ten zlotys plus another zloty per person to save the lives of the captives. Nevertheless, the community wasn't able to raise enough money. Jewelry and diamonds were also contributed.

Rabbi Lau, the most respected Jew in Piotrkow, was deemed by the Germans to be the head of the community. He had to bring the ransom to Hans Drexel, the city commissar. This was the first of many ransoms and taxes demanded of the Jewish community.

We were ordered to create a Jewish Council to serve as liaison between the occupiers and the Jewish community. In Piotrkow, we had a Jewish committee that dealt with neighborhood issues of health, religious services and schooling. A 12-man committee, later expanded to 24, called the "*Judenrat*," or council of Elders, was formed, headed by Zalman Tenenbaum, a former Vice-President of the pre-war Jewish Council. The *Judenrat* had to convey the orders of our new masters and try to ameliorate the decrees.

In addition to the *Judenrat*, Piotrkow Jews were ordered to form a Jewish police force, the *Ordnungdienst*, or OD. Ostensibly to serve as a conduit for providing laborers, the police force became a controversial body. The members wore round hats and arm bands.

At first, the Nazis wanted us to wear yellow Stars of David on our backs, but they changed their minds and decided on white armbands with the blue Star of David.

The entrepreneurial spirit was alive and well, even under such unhappy circumstances. Right away, boys started peddling Jewish star armbands on the street.

A sign was nailed up:

Public Notice!

Mandated by the Fuhrer and by the Order of the Gauleiter: all Jews will wear an identification armband on the right forearm, displaying the Star of David. The armband is to be made of white cloth, ten centimeters wide, and the blue star one centimeter thick and eight centimeters in diameter, which must be positioned in the center of the armband. This order is effective immediately. Jews not wearing identification will be severely punished.

Even little children like me understood that something frightening and terrible was happening around us. Still, I was living in my own home with my parents who gave me as much of a feeling of security as they could. Like the story books they read to us, we assumed today's troubles would have a happy ending. Our parents tried to reassure us.

The ghetto was declared on October 8 and on October 30-31 at night, the Germans surrounded the entire Jewish neighborhood with barbed wire and posted additional signs. Anyone caught leaving the ghetto would be punished by death.

Type the word "ghetto" into your internet search engine. A ghetto is a part of a city in which members of a "minority group" live, especially because of social, legal, or economic pressure. The term was first used in Venice, describing the section where Jews were restricted and segregated. Today, when Jews visit Italy, they're eager to try Italian Jewish food in the Rome "ghetto," today just a Jewish area, or to visit one of the synagogues in the Venice ghetto.

In the United States, the word "ghetto" has come to mean any dilapidated part of a city, a synonym for inner city. But no one ever restricted residents to those streets, guarding them, threatening them with death for the crime of leaving to buy food or to work.

"Ghetto" as used by the Nazis had its own meaning. Most of the Jews in Nazi-occupied Europe underwent the experience of being forced to live in a ghetto. Of the more than one thousand ghettos in Nazi Europe, 600 were in Poland.

Before the war, about 30 city blocks – some 200 buildings – made up the Piotrkow Jewish neighborhood in the same way Chinese Americans made up Chinatown in San Francisco or the North End in Boston was called "Little Italy." Kosher food stores, synagogues, Jewish schools, Hebrew print shops were found in the Jewish section.

In one day our apartment went from being in a Jewish neighborhood to being in a ghetto, with the threat of death for anyone leaving.

The first three months of the German occupation of Piotrkow were a time of chaos. The Germans, together with local thugs, looted and killed Jews whenever they felt like it. There was no one to complain to. A complaint was an invitation for further abuse.

Other families were assigned to live with us, as Jews from neighboring villages or other parts of Poland arrived as refugees.

In November, the synagogue was emptied. Polish people stole the pews for firewood. More signs appeared.

Official announcement about the Piotrkow Trybunalski Ghetto registration of all Jewish property in the city, written in German and Polish.

One said: "Jews Can't Walk on the Sidewalks."

The ghetto rules were often changed. Sometimes we could be outside of our homes from 8 a.m. to 5 p.m., and we could leave the ghetto between 11 a.m. to 1 p.m. Other times we were restricted to our homes except for a few hours when we could buy food. Curfew was called *sperrstunde*. The ghetto got eerily quiet when five o'clock approached.

Public schooling never started, but private educational

initiities sprung up – classes with Jewish teachers in private apartments. Education was illegal, as it was under the Romans 1,500 years earlier. Ironically, in secret classes, Jewish children learned Latin, as well as Hebrew, history and math. The teachers, some from esteemed schools, taught for a low fee. These teachers had a special status in the ghetto. In the Piotrkow ghetto, mothers organized to provide lunch for children who went to school. There were also informal kindergartens.

What optimism such a system of ad hoc schools displayed! The parents didn't want the children to be behind in their studies when the war ended. Few of the students would be lucky enough to survive the war.

I cling to my mother.

Momma reminds us kids to keep our voices down in the apartment. We might be overheard by the Germans on the street. They use extraneous sounds as an excuse for breaking in. I understand the threat and make sure only to whisper.

Children who came from outside the Jewish neighborhood to live inside the ghetto only knew Polish, and learned Yiddish, the lingua franca of the Jewish neighborhood and the ghetto. The Germans hated Yiddish. They saw it as a bastardized form of their revered German.

We adjusted to the new circumstances, hoping these difficult conditions wouldn't last long. At the beginning, even entertainment continued. There were plays and musical performances in the ghetto, not only klezmer but classical music, too. Poets still wrote poetry and songs, even lullabies. Weddings were celebrated with music and dancing. Teenagers organized dodgeball and soccer games in the street. We tried to build a meaningful life even within the confines of our captivity.

Here is the song of the Piotrkow ghetto:

Whither shall I go
When every exit is shut

Whither shall I go
When everywhere stands a guard

Whither shall I go
When I am told to stay put

Wherever I might turn
They tell me – "Jew remain"

At the same time people felt intensely Jewish, everyone wanted to minimize the chances of being picked on and bullied by the Germans. Men shaved their beards and wore European-style clothing. Women dyed their hair blond to be less conspicuous if they came in contact with the Germans.

Piotrkow residents smuggled goods into the ghetto at great risk, bringing home grain from the villages. Bread was rationed, but even in the so-called legal bakeries, the flour had to be smuggled in, with payoffs in bread to the Polish police. There were small illegal bakeries, too. The surrounding towns, at first ignored by the Nazis, smuggled in meat until the ritual slaughterers were arrested. Even brave children would sneak out of the ghetto and bring back potatoes and apples to hawk on the street.

I remember food getting scarcer, but at the beginning not being hungry.

By Passover 1940, we had been under German Occupation for six months. This holiday preparation required even more obsessive cleaning than the average homeowner invests during the year. Before the Occupation, winter clothing was cleaned, and bedding aired in the sunlight. Families that used straw mattresses renewed the straw. Many homeowners made their own Passover wine from raisins, and glassmakers peddled their bottles door to door. Special pots, pans and utensils that had been set aside only for Passover were hauled up from the cellars.

Even under occupation, the Piotrkow bakeries cleaned their ovens, covered the surfaces and began making matzo, the large crackers that replaced bread for the eight days of Passover.

Food was far more precious now. No one would consider throwing any away. The non-Passover food was "sold" for the week to a non-Jew. Despite the deterioration of our lives, it didn't occur to the Jews of Piotrkow that the holiday wouldn't be celebrated. Just the opposite. In the physical and psychological suffering of the ghetto, the week when we celebrated our deliverance from Egypt as slaves, there was still a symbol of hope.

In that first Passover in the ghetto, April 1940, it wasn't yet clear that our situation would become even worse than the slavery of our ancient Israelite ancestors. In the book of Exodus, we read that the Pharaoh ordered the killing of all baby boys. Hitler wanted to kill boys and girls, men and women alike. Baby Moses was sent down the Nile River in a straw basket to save him. The Pharaoh's daughter rescued him. Many Jewish children would be hidden, some would be rescued by righteous gentiles, like Pharaoh's daughter, who had a lot to lose by protecting a Hebrew child.

As food became scarcer, many questions arose about what we should do to observe this holiday. We turned to our Rabbis for guidance. Our own Rabbi Lau didn't survive the Holocaust, but the collection of questions and answers from Rabbi Ephraim Oshry, in the ghetto of Kovno, Lithuania did. He was able to retrieve his notes in 1944 and publish them as *Responsa from the Holocaust* (translated into English). One of the questions had to do with drinking the four cups of wine required at the Seder, when there was no wine at all. A little sweetened tea was substituted. Another question had to do with turning potato peels into matzo.

Although Jews tried hard to keep traditions, there was an understanding that saving lives came first.

In a famous saying, Rabbi Yitzhak Nissenbaum, in the Warsaw Ghetto, admonished Jews to do whatever they could to remain alive. "This is a time for *kiddush hachayim*, the sanctification of life, and not for *kiddush Hashem*, the holiness of martyrdom. Previously the Jew's enemies sought his soul, and the Jew sanctified his body in martyrdom. Now the oppressor demands the Jew's body, and the Jew is obliged therefore to defend it."

On the eve of Passover 1940, you could see men carrying home from the bakery matzo wrapped in spotless white cloths. Rabbi Lau managed to get extra flour from colleagues in other towns for baking matzo.

As the youngest in the family, it was probably my honor to stand and sing the "Four Questions" at the Seder. Today, I try to conjure up that moment: standing on a chair, asking in Yiddish in my sweetest voice, "Why is this night different from all other nights?" For every Jewish family, this is a highlight of the year – the moment the youngest child sings the Four Questions.

I have so many memories of my own children and grandchildren that overlay my own childhood. I try to picture the table. Were my mother's china dishes and silver candy bowl still on the table, or were they already looted by the Germans or turned into money for food?

The hardships imposed by the Nazi conquerors didn't follow in a straight downward line. One of the Nazis' strategies was to ease up on the population after a while and then, when hopes rose, to dash them with far worse decrees. Such it was in the summer of 1940, when I was five. Christians were allowed to come into the ghetto to buy goods and sell food. By then we knew that France had been occupied by the Nazis. In December 1940, for my birthday, I would have been lucky to get a potato flour pancake for a birthday cake. Life was tolerable because I was with my family.

When I'm asked why the Jews didn't fight off the Nazis, I remind the questioners that a country like France that had helped defeat Germany in World War I couldn't stand before the might of Nazi Germany. To humiliate the French, Hitler made them surrender in the same railway car the Germans had surrendered in at the end of the previous war.

A community kitchen was set up for the poor and hungry. Jewish doctors and dentists opened ghetto clinics.

Taxes levied on us in the ghetto eroded any money reserves. My family paid fees for the right to live incarcerated in the Nazi Ghetto.

At the beginning, craftsmen like shoemakers, jewelers and tailors continued to work within the ghetto. Wool, cotton cloth and linen were brought into the ghetto; underwear, hosiery and outer clothing were produced and sold to Germans and Poles. My father was a tailor and could work from home. Polish customers paid by trading goods and food. There were also larger tailoring shops, like the one in Trybunalski Place where my grandparents lived. Their specialty was turning old cloth into new garments.

On one hand, the Germans and Poles ordered items from the Jews. On the other, the secret police decided to enforce the official order against commerce by shooting you.

The frequently-quoted motto was "hold out and endure" in Yiddish, *"Aushalten und durchhalten."*

Typhus was a new enemy. Typhus – the name comes from the Greek word that means smoky or hazy-minded – is actually any of the several diseases caused by the Rickettsia bacteria. Fleas and ticks carry typhus. When you scratch a bite from one of these insects, the bacteria enter your bloodstream.

As the ghetto got more crowded, typhus struck. By my fifth birthday, there were many cases of this dread disease among children. Black wagons carried the dead to the cemetery.

At the end of 1941, fur on coats and jackets was confiscated. Some Jews cut their furs into tiny pieces rather than give them to the enemy. A new edict from the central authorities closed all the open ghettos, threatening Jews who left the ghetto, or Poles who helped them, with death. But with little other choice, Jews, even children, tried to cross the border to get food.

Where were my brothers? In addition to their birth records, the only record we have of my brothers is a report about my brother David being hospitalized. When he was five years old, David was hospitalized in the Jewish hospital. I have a record of his temperature. I've had a dozen doctors try to read the handwriting on the charts to no avail.

Another mystery is the absence of a mention of my mother in the ghetto tax records. On March 20, 1942,

Yitzhak Lichtenstein paid six zlotys for permission to live in the ghetto. Children were not taxed, so we wouldn't have been mentioned. Where was Sarah? Had she slipped out of the ghetto to prepare a hiding place? I think I would have remembered if she had suddenly disappeared.

I remember an SS policeman named Billy. He patrolled the ghetto with his dog that tore chunks of flesh from adults and especially children. Whenever we heard he was coming, we children went into hiding. Polish policemen and Ukrainian guards also joined the sadistic attacks, beating and shooting Jews.

There were orders dispatched by the central authorities and other orders given by the local bosses. Jews over the age of 10 had to wear the white badge with a blue Star of David on their right sleeve. The district captain who controlled Piotrkow required it for children from six years of age. City commissar Drexel, ordered all persons who had even one Jewish parent or who had converted from Judaism to Christianity to wear the yellow badge with the inscription "Jude."

The Germans took over Jewish-owned mills, farm and chemical businesses, and alcohol and vinegar plants. Store owners had to display a white sign marking their businesses as Jewish. Even horse-drawn taxis driven by Jews had to carry the sign. Merchants were required to bring their goods for a general inventory to the city commissar. The goods had to be kept in a warehouse.

As time went on, Nazi exploitation became organized, working through the Council to extract money from the community. Jews were conscripted for life-threatening, back-breaking forced labor. Although the employment office officially supplied Jews for labor every day, homes were broken into in the search for additional laborers, who were beaten and humiliated. Death was the punishment if you were caught trying to escape.

In addition to Jews from neighboring villages, refugees came from the bigger city of Lodz and even Warsaw, because word of mouth continued that life was "better" in Piotrkow than in their own larger, more efficiently closed-off ghettos. They wore yellow stars, not our white ones. Bunks were set up in a square and families slept in the meat market.

By 1942, there were 13,800 Jews officially registered in Piotrkow and another 6,000 who weren't registered. Only the registered Jews received bread ration cards.

The Jewish community organized a welfare office with food and clothing for the growing number of needy. The soup kitchen distributed 3,000 meals a day, including 550 for children. Except for the highly-skilled craftsmen who worked for the Germans, the only source of income was selling personal belongings.

A sanitation committee encouraged cleanliness in the now crowded homes, and helped in bathing of the Jewish residents, and disinfecting clothes. Before the United States' entry into the war in December 1941, considerable help arrived from the American Joint Distribution Committee.

Chapter 7

LETTING GO OF
MY MOTHER'S HAND

I've learned to adjust to the strangers living in
our home, to speaking in a soft voice, to staying
in the house so that I won't meet children with
horrible scabies and catch them, too. My father is often
gone when I wake up in the morning. His hands are raw
and blistered, no longer the tailor's fingers that can lift a
splinter from my toe without me feeling it. I play endless
games of chutes and ladders with my brothers when they
are home. Sometimes they go to lessons, "so you won't be
illiterate when this war is over," Momma says. When she
has her mind on it, she teaches me letters. But mostly, she
is busy having conversations with Aunt Bina.

I already know children who have died of typhus,
and neighbors who have been shot or sent away. "We
are lucky," says Momma. "We are all still together and
in our home."

The High Holidays are once again approaching.
Momma has saved a little bit of meat to be shared by
everyone, and a little bit of honey. There are still apples,
wrinkled like the faces of old people, in the cellar. Rosh
Hashanah used to mean good beginnings. Now it is one
more marker in our struggle to stay alive.

More Jews are arriving in Piotrkow. They are from
Tuszyn. One who is moving into our apartment has
brought a chicken.

I hear people wondering that if we're really being
evacuated to a terrible place, why would the Nazis let

the Jews from Tuszyn bring whole wagons of goods to Piotrkow. Maybe we really will be establishing new colonies in Russia?

Momma just shakes her head. "They are always trying to fool us," she says. "Don't pay attention."

Yossi and David say they have heard from friends that their older brothers want to fight back when the Nazis come to get us. Momma ruffles their hair.

"Even the greatest armies in the world are having a hard time fighting the Nazis," she says. "The teenagers of Piotrkow will be killed in a moment. We have agreed not to fight back. It will be better for us."

The families downstairs are selling their furniture to Polish Christians and packing their transportable goods "so they are ready to go east," the mother tells Momma. "That's what the Germans say. Why should I doubt it?"

"Because everything they say is a lie," answers Momma. "They want us all dead."

What does Momma whisper to Poppa when he gets home? On the holidays, Poppa prays with a small group of men in our building – a short prayer, not all day as he used to.

Momma reads prayers with us at home. "Please God," she says, "protect my family."

Conversations deal with every possible means of escaping the cruel fate that has already come to our brethren in nearby towns of Radom and Kielce, which are now empty of their Jews.

Some Jews are seeking Aryan identity papers and planning to hide with non-Jews. It's an open secret that others are seeking hiding places in the ghetto, building underground bunkers and cutting hidden doors into attic lofts.

Somehow, my father and his brother Aaron managed

Rena took this picture outside the Hortensia glass factory in 1989.

to attain slave labor jobs in the Hortensia glass factory. You had to know someone in a position to help or to pay a large sum of money to get one of these forced labor jobs.

My father was listed as an employee from August 6 to November 9, 1942, at Hortensia, but he may well have worked there longer. In the fall of 1942, I was six and a half years old.

Before the war, working on a glass assembly line wouldn't have been considered a desirable job, but under the Nazi occupation, being employed in a factory was considered a way to increase your chances of survival. Of course, no one knows how fate will turn, but having a job in an essential industry that produced glass items for the Reich meant that the Germans might be more reluctant to kill you. An assumption in the ghettos was that the Germans wouldn't want to kill off their work force.

Working in a factory also offered the opportunity to mix with Polish Christians who were a source of news

The logo of the Hortensia Glass factory.

(all the radios in the ghetto had been confiscated) and food.

Before the war, Hortensia made utilitarian, yet beautiful glass items: art deco vases, serving bowls, candy dishes. A particularly beautiful item in the 1936 catalogue shows a carp, and is likely to have been used for gefilte fish in the Jewish households.

Some of the glass was press-molded and some was blown (such as bottles, carafes, lighting and jars). The (nearby) Kara glass works was used for plate (flat) glass. Like many factories, these Piotrkow factories had gone from household to war-related production.

The work at Hortensia was organized in three shifts. Sometimes workers did overtime. The work was exhausting and often dangerous.

Workers lugged sacks of sand, soda lime, and chemicals, feeding the furnace, and taking off scorching glass from the assembly line. Your skin could burn to the bone from touching such hot glass and you could get terrible burns from the furnace.

My father, one of his brothers, and my cousin Irving Cymberknopf, who was ten years older than me, worked there daily. Young people removed blown glass so it could cool. They had to pick up the glass while it was still molten, and run all day from the belt to the cooling blower. They also carried the petrol-flasks, bottles, and glasses.

Rumors spread of the impending evacuation of Piotrkow, what the Germans called an *Aktion* – an assembly and deportation of prisoners for extermination. These fearful stories were reinforced by news of such *Aktions* in other cities.

According to the rumors, the population in the Piotrkow ghetto would be reduced to ten percent of its size. The other 90 percent would be sent to extermination camps.

On July 19, 1942, Heinrich Himmler, Nazi Reich leader of the SS, ordered the final destruction of the Jewish people.

This was his order:

Herewith is ordered that the resettlement of the entire Jewish population of the Government General be carried out and completed by December 31, 1942.

From December 31, 1942, no persons of Jewish origin may remain within the General Government, unless they are in collection camps in Warsaw, Cracow, Czestochowa, Radom, and Lublin. All other work on which Jewish labor is employed must be finished by that date, or, in the event that this is not possible, it must be transferred to one of the collection camps.

These measures are required with a view to the necessary ethnic division of races and peoples for the New Order in Europe, and also in the interests of the security and cleanliness of the German Reich and its sphere of interest. Every breach of this regulation spells a danger to quiet and order in the entire German sphere of interest, a point of application for the resistance movement and a source of moral and physical pestilence.

For all these reasons a total cleansing is necessary and therefore to be carried out. Cases in which the date set cannot be observed will be reported to me in time, so that I can see to corrective action at an early date. All requests by other offices

for changes or permits for exceptions to be made
must be presented to me personally.
Heil Hitler!
Heinrich Himmler

The factory owners were bribed to take in more
workers. The word in the *Judenrat* was that indeed ten
percent of the Jewish community would be left. Just
imagine a community of 22,000 Jews knowing that 20,000
were going to an unknown place, probably to their deaths.
Influential Jews were trying to increase the number of
those allowed to remain, but they were unsuccessful.

We had already survived the High Holidays of 1939,
1940 and 1941 in the ghetto. But this time, it was different.
Since Himmler's decree, we knew that death was stalking
us. Gloom suffused the ghetto.

Ten days separate Rosh Hashanah from Yom Kippur,
the holiest day of the Jewish year. It's a time of fasting and
repentance. On the evening of Yom Kippur, September
21, 1942, weeping could be heard throughout the ghetto.
A large crowd gathered at the home of Rabbi Lau to pray
with him for the last time. Preparing for deportation and
death, he delivered a goodbye sermon to the community,
speaking about the Sanctity of Death.

The young people in the youth movements still
wanted to resist, but the *Judenrat* had promised not
to resist so that the entire community would not be
murdered.

My parents had three children, 11, 10, and 6-1/2. How
could they possibly protect us? How could they accept
our deaths? They had to take action.

This is how I have pieced together what happened
at this point in my life.

In the second week of October, barracks were

prepared in the Hortensia factory. My father and my uncles came to say goodbye to us.

On October 13, everyone knew that the *Aktion* would begin the following morning. Hundreds of Jews went into hiding in bunkers and attics. At 2 a.m. on October 14, 1942, Ukrainian and German SS troops surrounded and sealed the ghetto. At dawn, Jews were ordered to gather in the *umschlagplatz*, the deportation square, on the premises of the Franciscan barracks. Soldiers drove in many trucks, carrying guns, leading barking attack dogs. Loudspeakers blasted: "All must go outside." Suddenly the whole ghetto was surrounded with German and Ukrainian troops with snarling dogs. The soldiers carried guns, whips, and sticks.

Street by street, we Jews were cleared out. The sick and disabled were loaded onto carts and driven to the square.

Among the deportees were women with newborn babies, who hurried along in the crowd with their infants wrapped in blankets. Many carried rucksacks that had been sewn for the anticipated journey. Ukrainian soldiers reached into the pockets of travelers and stole whatever they could.

On October 19th, German soldiers searched the neighborhood and shot any Jews found hiding. My family's street was targeted for the third transport. The fourth transport included my paternal grandparents' home in Trybunalski Place. Any factory worker present in the ghetto was separated out.

On each of four days, 6,000 men, women, children and babies were jammed – more than 80 people per cattle car – into each of the 52 railway cattle cars. No possessions were allowed.

In his final sermon, Rabbi Lau said "Better a living death than a dead life, and everyone who is killed as a

Jew is a saint." He joined the last of the four transports.

The rain was cold and hard as the last transport drove by the glass factories. Farewell letters were thrown from the freight cars. Christian children collected them and delivered them to the Jewish workers.

At the Hortensia glass factory, there was a rumor that the number of workers would be cut down to half, but the owners reportedly managed to ward off the stern decree and so only a few workers were taken.

The big ghetto of 20-30 square blocks, the entire Jewish neighborhood, was reduced to a small ghetto of 6-8 blocks wide, from Jerozolimska Street where the synagogue stood to Staro-Warszawska Street where we heard the first news of war. Barbed wire ran down the middle of the boundary streets.

There is a man with a club, a gun, and a snarling dog that nips at our ankles. He searches my mother and takes her wedding ring. He marches us to a field, and then into the Great Synagogue, now reduced to a prison. In front of me, a soldier hits a woman holding a baby with his gun. She falls, still holding the baby. Lying in the road are two other women, not moving.

Outside the synagogue, the Germans have brought horses and wagons. The synagogue is surrounded by Ukrainian workers. We are all locked in the synagogue. Those who try to escape are shot. A few people manage to get out because they are tradesmen or are employed in certain factories like Poppa. I don't know how they got there in the first place. Certain Jews are also ransomed by their families; thus, for example, parents gave themselves up in order to save their children.

Many men, women and children are led from the synagogue. People are running and screaming. Babies are crying. They are taken away and murdered in the forest.

I remember the fear and the confusion. In the commotion I hear someone calling my name. Come Fredzia, he says – a command. He motions frantically for me to come. "Fredzia!" But I am holding my mother's hand.

The German guards can shoot me, hit me over the head and push me back. For some reason, they don't. Maybe they think that the next soldier who sees me will kill me. Perhaps a guard is bribed and leaves the door open. Maybe my parents believe the boys have a better chance of surviving than a little girl and have set up my escape. Maybe I have the resourcefulness and guts to respond to a call that will save my life and run on my own. The circumstances are cloudy, but what happens next is clear.

I let go of my mother's hand. I don't look back. I am running. This man scoops me up in his arms and we run for shelter. The heavy synagogue door closes behind me. I remember escaping.

I can still remember letting go of my mother's hand and her letting go of my hand. I am six and a half years old.

My mother's hand, my mother's hand, my mother's hand. How does a little girl let go of her mother's hand? My mother opens her clutched fingers.

She lets me go. She saves my life.

How does a little girl run away from her mother and her brothers when she is so scared? I never see my mother or brothers again. How does a little girl recover from such a loss?

I have so often wondered what my mother thought after we were separated, if she was glad that she had let me go. Did she think, "I wish my little Fredzia was here," or did she thank God that I was safe with my father, at least, in the meantime?

I am unsure when exactly my escape took place. I have always assumed it took place during the week of the *Aktions*, when the 20,000 Jews were being deported. A child might escape in such a commotion.

It could have been my uncle who rescued me and brought me back to my father. He was back living in the ghetto after the workers from Hortensia were returned to the ghetto after the *Aktions*.

Maybe. Maybe. Maybe. My escape could have taken place on October 19, 1942, when our apartment building was emptied. Some prisoners were held in the synagogue that week. But most of those being sent to Treblinka to be gassed had gathered in a public square, not in the synagogue. There, too, I might have managed to get away – a small child could slip through the crowd. In our research, we came across a second possibility. Maybe even a third.

In the short memoir written by my older cousin Irving Cymberknopf, his parents (my aunt Bina and her husband Yosef) and four other families including their children went into hiding in a bunker. He said there were two Rushineks, two Cymberknopfs, two Rimers and four Lichtensteins. I don't know who the Rimers were, maybe neighbors, maybe relatives on the Cymberknopf side – but the Rushineks and Cymberknopfs were first cousins.

My father didn't have to hide because he was in the glass factory, where workers were housed over the course of the *Aktions*. That would mean that the four Lichtensteins were my mother, my two brothers and me.

In a revised version of this memoir, my cousin didn't mention us. But as I learned in a book called *Testimony and Time*, by Sharon Kangisser Cohen, later testimonies often reflect changes, sometimes the streamlining of an earlier account. Perhaps he left us out for brevity or because he no longer remembered who was hiding with them.

So we may have retreated to a bunker that had been prepared for us. I have found another account by survivor Meir Horowitz in which he mentions a larger bunker in the cellar of 2 Czarnieckiego Place which is where we lived. Horowitz's description doesn't mention us by name, just that "several other families" were hiding there. These survivors were older than me at the time this happened, and would have remembered better. Unhappily, they are no longer alive to ask.

According to my cousin Irving Cymberknopf's account, after the *Aktions* were over at the end of the week, we found ourselves outside of the ghetto boundaries and had to smuggle ourselves back in. That would have happened if we had been at 2 Plac Czarnieckiego because our home was within the large ghetto, but not within the boundaries of the small ghetto.

After the deportations, the small ghetto was surrounded by barbed wire, and well-guarded by Ukrainian and Lithuanian guards. Irving Cymberknopf wrote that his father Yosef Cymberknopf, who had military experience in the Polish army, smuggled us into the small ghetto where an Uncle Jankel lived. A second bunker hiding place had been dug there in the cellar. I have no memory of hiding.

Other Holocaust memoirs have recorded the extreme fear of remaining silent and motionless underground. For example, Roman Mogilanski, also from Piotrkow, wrote of hiding in a dark bunker under a corner home. A young mother with a baby they let into their hiding place couldn't keep quiet and they were found. Some were shot to death on the spot. Others were taken first to a temporary jail on

Rena returned to Trybunalski Square in 1989.

Garncarska Street and then to the synagogue, which was larger. Some Jews escape. I may have escaped the initial deportation in the *Aktions* and gone into hiding, but safety was illusory.

The hunt for "illegals" was on. Jewish police took part, and so did the much reviled "Billy" and his dog. He forced someone to yell out in Yiddish that the coast was clear, and when the illegals came out of hiding, Billy was there with his dog. Hundreds of "illegals" were discovered, gathered, tortured.

There are horrible accounts of newborn babies being set on fire and children cooked in basins on a bonfire in front of the synagogue. Some running away were shot.

Testimonies exist about successful escaping from the Piotrkow synagogue, through nearby houses and a water channel.

It is possible that we were apprehended from our

second hiding place within the small ghetto and then sent to the synagogue which now served as a prison.

No matter how many times I ask these questions, I don't have answers. All I know is that sometime between October 21 and December 19, I let go of my mother's hand.

I am not sure if the following is accurate, but this is how I remember it. I manage to get back into the small ghetto where the laborers are housed. My uncle hides me in a bed. When Poppa comes home in the evening, he hugs and kisses me. I will have to hide again, he tells me. He tells me that Momma, Yossi and David have gone away. I will stay with him.

At first he and the other men hide me. When a German comes in, I must lie still under the blanket. But one day they tell me I was very bad. When the German came in, I wriggled under the blanket. They had to put their feet on me to keep me down. I must have been asleep, I tell them. They scold me. Not only could you have been killed, but all of us would have been murdered, too, if you were discovered.

Soon my father and I have a serious talk. To survive, he will take me to work at the glass factory. But I must pretend to be a boy. How will I remember to speak like a boy?[1] With his tailor's skill, Poppa cuts my hair. We practice speaking Polish so that I sound like a boy. Poppa warns me to be careful not to make any mistakes. He doesn't have to tell me why. I don't want them to catch me.

They bring me boys' clothes. My new name is Froim. It sounds a little like Fredzia. It's short for Ephraim, one of the sons of Joseph in the Bible. That Joseph was put in

---

1   In Polish grammar, as well as Yiddish and Hebrew, words have a masculine and feminine form. English does not have this structure.

a pit and he survived. My brother Joseph, whom I call Yossi, has disappeared, too. Maybe he will come home one day like Joseph in the Bible.

Nearly all the Jews of Piotrkow were deported to Treblinka, which was second only to Auschwitz in the number of Jews who were murdered. Sixty-two miles northeast of Poland's capital of Warsaw, 248 kilometers, about 154 miles from Piotrkow, Treblinka was opened in July 1942. On July 23, 1942, mass murder began.

Estimates range from 700,000 to a million men, women and children were murdered in Treblinka. Some reports said that as many as a third of the victims were children. No records were kept of their deaths. Many of the prisoners arrived dead in the cattle cars. Some were shot in the head and pushed into pits that would be lit on fire. Others were gassed with carbon monoxide generated by diesel engines.

Those waiting to be gassed heard the screaming of others as they waited their turn outside. Prisoners who arrived had only a one percent chance of surviving the first three hours.

Ten gas chambers were in operation, and camp commander Franz Stangl, who had trained in the Nazi program to murder their own physically or mentally challenged citizens, boasted that they could murder an entire train with 6,000 Jews between his 7 a.m. breakfast and noon meal.

Unlike Auschwitz, there was no selection and prisoners weren't issued striped suits. Jews went straight to the gas chambers. Their clothes were sorted by a cadre of young people chosen from among the prisoners to be slave laborers.

The transports mostly stopped coming by April 1943.

SS commander Heinrich Himmler visited Treblinka in March and afterwards the victims' bodies were dug up so that they could be burned on pyres. The burning went on through the summer and the prisoners assumed they would be murdered when they finished their work. They copied the key to the SS Armory, took weapons and set the camp ablaze. Killing operations at Treblinka II were ended on October 19, 1943, following the revolt.

Franz Stangl survived and escaped, eventually moving to Brazil where he established a comfortable life with his wife and children until he was extradited to Germany in 1967.

Stangl never even bothered to change his name. He was found guilty and sentenced to life imprisonment, but he died six months later of a heart attack at age 63. I get furious when I think of him living out his life after murdering my mother and brothers and all the others.

When I walk through the Rakow forest in 2015 with the Hadassah group, two flagpoles, one Israeli, and one Polish, mark the massacre. There are pines and oaks, the scent of blooming greenery after a cold winter.

Were my mother and brothers among the dead here, or were they murdered in Treblinka? These may seem like small details to some, but not knowing where and when your mother and brothers were murdered and buried can never be just details.

If they were killed in the Rakow forest, December 19 may be the day of their deaths, a day after my seventh birthday.

My mother and brothers may have been forced onto a later transport to Treblinka. They didn't stand a chance of surviving Treblinka. Nearly everyone who was sent to Treblinka was gassed or shot. The bodies were buried, and eventually exhumed and burned, up to 18,000 at a time, in massive open-air pyres.

It is estimated that only 70 persons managed to escape or survive Treblinka.

I'll never stop wondering what happened to my mother and brothers. Sometimes new material turns up, and sometimes scholars revisit accounts from the past and are able to shed new light on what happened.

Such was the case recently when Holocaust scholar Lea Prais reviewed the wartime account of Yaakov Krzepicki, a Jew who escaped from Treblinka. His account was recorded for the underground archives in the Warsaw Ghetto, written by hand in Yiddish by Rachel Auerbach in late December 1942, until March 1943. He had been deported from Warsaw to Treblinka on August 25, 1942, and escaped on September 13 – so he spent nearly three weeks in the death camp.

I read this account with great interest trying to ferret out information about my mother and brothers.

According to Krzepicki's testimony, even in the death camp, the Germans parceled out scraps of hope. When an SS officer promised the Jews that they would work in their trade, "some people began to applaud the Germans. The majority of the Jews who had heard the honeyed speech calmed down and once again began to believe that they were in a work camp ... and people regained their places, like children in a classroom."

Krzepicki's testimony is sometimes reviled for its bitter sarcasm and his derisive attitude towards the deportees' lack of clarity of their fate. Nonetheless, it does show something of the coping mechanisms of those headed to the machinery of death.

Krzepicki described how the older women met their horrific fate: "Some sought consolation in God and prepared themselves to die with God's name on their lips. Some pleaded for help, prayed for a miracle, a rescue; others had given up all hope ... The women's sobbing was reminiscent of the sobbing that one hears at funerals. Here people were sobbing at their own funeral."

Did my mother cry out, or pray, or stand silently as she met her fate? What about my brothers?

In July 1943, parents and children who still lived in Piotrkow joined a train supposedly taking them to a more benign labor camp in Blizin. At the last moment, the children were removed and shot at an open grave near Piotrkow. Somehow I survived this massacre, too. I don't know how.

Chapter 8

MY FATHER BECOMES MY MOTHER AND I BECOME A BOY SLAVE

I run my fingers over the scars on my knees and think about my day as a slave laborer when I acquired them.

I am only six and a half years old and I am pretending to be a ten-year-old boy.

"If anyone asks you, tell them you are ten years old," my father tells me over and over. I am only a child, but I know that my life depends on doing this right.

"You mustn't cry," my father tells me. "Don't make any extra sounds. Don't talk if you don't have to. I don't want anyone to hear your voice."

I tell myself, "I'm alive. I can think. I can do this. If I don't do it, I will die." I don't want to die.

A whistle wakes me every day. For a second I think my real life is a nightmare. But then I wise up. I am alive and I want to stay alive. We have 30 minutes to get ready each morning. I don't know where he gets them, but my father gives me trousers and a rough shirt.

In Polish, soldiers shout at us *"na zmiane szykowac sie* – get ready for a change."* We march every day from the small ghetto to the factory. We are hurried along by guards who shoot near our feet and dogs that bark and nip at us. I walk as fast as I can to keep up with the others, reminding myself that I am ten years old and a boy.

I know Poppa has to pay one of the supervisors not to see me. Poppa says the supervisor is a decent person. I don't know where Poppa gets the money to pay.

There are trucks that bring sand into the factory. Outside, Poland is unbearably cold, but inside the factory it is hot, very hot. Everyone's skin is red and dripping with sweat. I must bring water.

The Germans have very large dogs in the factory, too. They enjoy terrifying me with their dogs. One day I fall down and cut both of my knees running away from the dogs.

Outside, a war is going on, but inside, this household glass company is still producing beautiful glassware. Hortensia produces both pressed and blown glass.

Pressed glass is a much cheaper way of producing the finished product. The glass is melted in tanks and taken off in individual "gobs," lumps of molten glass that are then placed into metal molds and pressed into shape by a machine. The hot glass items are transferred to the cooling belt.

Like other children, I am a water carrier. In the process of blowing the glass, the glassmakers use wooden tools (paddles and blocks) that have to be kept in water. They have to have pails of water by their sides in which the wooden tools are kept. The water needs constant replenishing. Workers also need water or they will faint from the heat, even when it is freezing outdoors.

I try to stay close to Poppa. Always. When we aren't working, I always hide under the blankets in our bed so no one will see me and question me. Poppa tries to get the night shift because there are fewer guards on the lookout for "illegals" like me than on the day shift.

We are grateful to have factory jobs, but the factory is filthy and vermin hang from the woodwork. One day, I wake up and my face and body are covered with spots. I come down with a fever. I want Momma.

What is wrong with me? Poppa says maybe it is measles, German measles, or rubella. He doesn't know. Momma would have known, but I can't say this.

Poppa doesn't have to say anything. I understand that I have to ignore the spots and the fever if I want to survive. Be strong. You will recover. He doesn't have to say it. I go to work with spots. I do recover. I want to stay alive.

The factory is huge. Poppa says a thousand workers are there. When we work the day shift, it feels longer. My uncles watch out for me when Poppa isn't there.

Poppa and my uncles and other men run back and forth in their underwear, handkerchiefs on their faces, carrying heavy loads of sand, soda glass and chemicals. They pour the ingredients into large mixing drums. Some have to clean the ashes out of the channels. This is very dangerous, Poppa says. It's easy to burn your legs. Careful. Injuries are very bad.

Sometimes Poppa has to dig a huge ditch for a new furnace. Other men sit on ledges inside the chimney, piling the bricks higher and higher.

Poppa says he is most afraid of falling asleep on the job, but I shouldn't worry. He won't fall asleep because he is responsible for me.

Children are also assigned to remove molten blown glass to a cooling blower. Bottles and cups need to cool for three hours. One of my cousins works there. If you don't run fast enough, you get hit on the head with a rod. Others – teenagers – have to push heavy wheelbarrows with sand, old glass and chemicals, which makes the glass colored and shiny. I am afraid I will be asked to do this and they will discover I am not a boy, that I'm not Froim, I'm Fredzia. I bring the water and keep my eyes down.

I remember the fairy story my mother used to read to me about a prince changing into a frog. But was he really a frog? Am I going to be a boy for a long time? I try to remember the end of the story.

I overhear rumors and I am frightened. There are always rumors that we, too, will be sent away on the trains. At least I'll be with Poppa. This time, I won't let go of his hand.

The huge furnace needs to be tended and cleaned. Men are often burned. They cry out in pain. Many children work in the glass factory, but Poppa tells me not to talk to them. They don't try to talk either. I don't talk to anyone except Poppa and Uncle Aaron.

We hear that in the ghetto, a group of men, women and children are gunned down in March. I am more frightened than ever. Many men and women are transferred to the Hasag ammunition factory in Skarzysko-Kamienna. In the summer, we are moved out of the ghetto quarters to housing 500 yards from the factory. Huta, they are called. Poppa says there are 720 of us left. A Polish man named Kutchamer is in charge. He isn't mean.

In July 1943, Piotrkow is declared Judenrein – free of Jews. There's a sign marking the "achievement" of ridding Piotrkow of its Jews at the train station, the Polish workers tell Poppa.

Rumors continue to infiltrate the factory. Sometimes even an underground newspaper gets in. Of course, I can't read it. Poppa says the Germans are losing the war. The Russians are beating them back, reaching the Vistula River in their summer campaign. Poppa says this is good. Will the Russians save us? Poppa emits a strange laugh. The Russians don't like Jews, he says.

We are hungry, but not starving. Poppa buys food from the Polish workers.

Some of the Jewish workers hear from their friends or loved ones through the Polish workers. We don't hear from Momma, Yossi and David. I no longer ask Poppa when Momma, Yossi and David will come back.

We work every day, except Yom Kippur, October 9. Last Yom Kippur we were still a family. I remember the crying from the houses. Momma didn't cry.

This year, I pray hard. I pray for Momma and Yossi and David. I pray that Poppa and I will stay together. I remember the words of the *Unetanneh Tokef* prayer, which feels more frightening than ever before:

> *Who will live and who will die, who by water and who by fire, who by sword, who by beast, who by famine, who by thirst, who by upheaval, who by plague, who by strangling, and who by stoning.*

I beg God to keep me alive. Even here, we Jews believe in and honor God.

Where will we be next Yom Kippur? I can't think that far ahead.

Chapter 9

MY NEW MOTHER,
THE TEACHER

Yom Kippur 1944 comes on September 27. I am still living at the barracks of the glass factory with my father and uncles. I have survived two years of slave labor pretending I am a boy. But on November 25, 1944, the train we have seen in our nightmares arrives in the station. I am a month shy of age nine.

The Russian army is now winning victory after victory facing the Reich's troops. Soon they will conquer Piotrkow.

On November 26, we Jews at the glass factories are moved as the factories in Piotrkow will be abandoned. The Germans decide to move their labor force to a safer place and continue to make arms.

My father knows that as soon as we go to a new camp, we will be taken to the showers. The Germans wash filthy Jews. They check our bodies for valuables. If you are naked, you can't hide what you have.

We realize it is hopeless to continue pretending I am a boy. My father and I will have to split up. I know it. My world is collapsing. My worst nightmare is coming true. I have lost my brothers. I have lost my mother. Now I am about to lose my father.

My father sees a woman we know from Piotrkow. I don't even know her name. I think she is a teacher.

"This is Fredzia. She's really a girl. A good girl. Please take care of her," he says. This good woman agrees.

"Goodbye sweet Fredzia," Poppa says. He calls me by my real name, not Froim. "Here are some family pictures to keep you company. Try to keep them safe. I'll come and fetch you when this is over. Remember your Momma, Yossi and David. They are in this picture. Here we all are. Look how happy we are in the photograph. After the war, I will meet you in our home in Piotrkow."

I tuck the photographs deep in my pants pocket.

My heart is breaking. My father hugs me. I want him to hug me forever. And then he lets go. I hear him catch his breath. I try to memorize his face.

I blink back tears. I know I cannot cry.

The Teacher takes my hand. "Come, Fredzia," she says. "We will be like mother and daughter."

I walk silently with her to the line of women. I say to myself. She will be my mother. I will be her daughter.

I want my real mother. I want my father. I want my brothers.

But I dare not cry.

Instead of work today, we go to the train station near Piotrkow, where we are divided into sections. One group is sent to Czestochowa, the nearby city where many of my relatives lived and where large armaments factories are still functioning. Arms are more important than glass, we are told.

Others are shipped to concentration camps in Germany and in Poland, among them Auschwitz.

I followed the Teacher, but I am not sure where we went.

I don't have a number on my arm, so I know I didn't go to Auschwitz.

Here's what I know.

On April 15, 1945, when I was nine years and four months old, I was rescued in Bergen-Belsen, in Germany, 500 miles away from Piotrkow.

What happened to me in those five fateful months between Piotrkow and Bergen-Belsen? This is one of the mysteries of my life. Even children living normal lives have a hard time going back to a specific month of their childhood unless something important – a special birthday or a tragedy – took place. Try to describe the five winter months of fourth grade, for example.

In those months, I went from being a pretend ten-year-old boy named Froim to becoming a girl again. In this period of my life I was orphaned. I was in concentration camps. I was starving and sick and close to death. Nonetheless, these critical months are missing from my memory. All I know is that sometime at the end of November, I left Piotrkow, Poland.

Look up "traumatic amnesia." I didn't make up this condition. There have been many studies on the memories of Holocaust survivors and those who have survived other catastrophes. They show that former inmates of Nazi concentration camps often can't remember anything of the first days. Experts speculate that our perception of reality was so overwhelming that it could lead to mental chaos.[1] Other survivors share my acute frustration and embarrassment at not being able to recall more than fragments.

Did I stay in Poland at first?

Today, students I speak to often ask me why these major camps were in Poland if the Nazis came from Germany. It was in Poland where the largest population

---

1   See E. Dewind.

of Jews lived before the war. The Germans believed, correctly, that Poland, with its long history of anti-Semitism, wouldn't object, and that Poles would form the large workforce necessary to carry out the extermination.

Chelmo, the first camp set up as an extermination camp, was opened on December 8, 1941, in Poland. At that time, gas vans were also used to murder Jews. Belzec and Treblinka were set up as extermination camps in early 1942. Majdaneck was a combined concentration camp and extermination center. Of course, the notorious Auschwitz, a large complex of labor camps and sub-camps, was in Poland, too. It opened in 1941. The gas chambers were built in nearby Birkenau, also called Auschwitz 2. Many Jews were murdered on arrival, while others – the prisoners who had numbers tattooed on their forearms – were sent to work in forced labor. As the Russians approached, the Nazis began emptying the Polish camps and moving the prisoners inside Germany where they still had more control.

My father was in the group sent to work in Czestochowa. According to the International Tracing Service of Bad Arolsen, I was also sent to Czestochowa along with many members of the work force of the glass factories. It wasn't far away and we were used to factory work.

But here's the problem. I remember Hortensia. I remember Bergen-Belsen. I do not remember Czestochowa, and those Czestochowa survivors whom I have met do not remember me. Of course, I may have forgotten them, and they may have forgotten me.

Nor are the official documents always reliable. For example, the ghetto started in 1939, but if you look at my documents, they don't list the first three years I was there as a small child.

I don't know at which point I gave up pretending to be a boy and had gone back to being a girl. There is also the possibility that I was sent directly to Bergen-Belsen from Piotrkow.

Here's what I do remember. I was pushed into a cattle car of a train. There was suffocating closeness. The train stopped at other factories and more and more people came on. The temperature must have risen. Snow was melting on us. Cold rain and wind is even worse than snow. There was talk of toilet needs. One corner of the carriage was designated as a toilet. I remember hearing about a pail. I remember thinking that I was lucky because I was not in that corner with the pail. But in the end, it didn't matter. No one could get to the corner. No one could move. You had to urinate or defecate where you were.

I remember the first time I had to use the bathroom and there was no bathroom. I remember the floor filling with excrement. I remember people grasping icicles that had formed on the windows to have something to drink. I remember the train stopping and bodies of the dead being thrown outside. I remember feeling filthy, trying to clean myself with the snow when the train stopped. I remember eating the snow. I remember the cold. I remember not crying, even though I was tired, sick, and hungry. I remember someone speaking of "crossing the border" and not understanding. I remember motorcycles with sidecars and men in shiny black boots.

I remember thinking, "I'm still alive. I am lucky. I am alive."

When we cross the border from Poland, some people say they would use Polish money for toilet paper, that it's now worthless.

Did I spend several months in Czestochowa?

SERVICE INTERNATIONAL DE RECHERCHES
INTERNATIONAL TRACING SERVICE
INTERNATIONALER SUCHDIENST

D - 3548 AROLSEN
Tel. (05691) 437 — Telegr.-Adr. ITS Arolsen

Arolsen, 17th September 1981
Bz/Sr

Mrs Rena Quint
74 Wellington Court

Brooklyn, NY 11230

USA

Our Reference
(please quote)
T/D - 361 054

Dear Mrs Quint,

Reference is made to your letter of 16th March 1981 and to our acknowledgement of receipt dated 2nd June 1981. Please be advised that based on the particulars you gave, we made a check of the documents at our disposal.

The following information could be ascertained for you:

LICHTENSTEIN, Fredzia, born in Piotrkow in 1936,
Nationality: Polish, Religion: Jewish, Names of
parents: Icek and Sala nee MESSER, last known
address: Piotrkow,
was in Camp Bergen-Belsen at a date not indicated,
was in the transit camp Lübeck on 24th July 1945
and was evacuated from there to Sweden, aboard the
ship "Kastlsholm" on 25th July 1945.

Remarks: On the DP-2 card is remarked: 1943 in
Ghetto Piotrkow 1 year and Czestochowa 1 year,
thereafter in Belsen.
Further particulars regarding the incarceration
are not available.
Sala = Sarah.

While Rena does not remember Czestochowa, this document from Service International De Recherches says that her DP-2 card indicates she had a one-year stay in Czestochowa.

My friend, the journalist Greer Fay Cashman, grew up in Australia, but her parents were from Czestochowa. From their stories, she feels a close connection to that city, famous for a Black Madonna which Christian pilgrims approached on their knees. When she mentioned it, I searched again and again in my mind for a trace of memory, but without success.

The train ride to Czestochowa would have been a short one. About 50 miles – 81 kilometers. I cannot recall how long I was on the train or how many trains there were.

Czestochowa was a big city. Many of my relatives lived there, but by January 1945, like Piotrkow, most of the Jews had already been sent away on cattle cars and murdered. There was only a small ghetto remaining. At the main factory of Hasag-Pelcery, an ammunition plant, more than 10,000 Jews labored as slaves.

The conditions in the slave labor munitions factories in Czestochowa were worse than in the glass and furniture factories in Piotrkow. Wrote Yiddish poet Franya Kornfield who worked in the Hasag-Pelcery factory, 1943, "Like robots, robbed of life and soul, we stand at work and think of revenge." Here's a fragment of the poem "Hasag" by Dovid Zisman, in the same camp, 1944.

A Hasag Jew has no solution,
Like a dog, he carries a number attached to his back,
He is treated just like an animal,
Yet he still fights for a new world.

The late Naphtali Lau-Lavie, whose biography is *Balaam's Prophecy: Eyewitness to History, 1939-1989*, lived a short distance from me in Jerusalem. He didn't remember me from Piotrkow or Czestochowa, as a girl or as the boy Froim.

The Czestochowa children were going to be disposed of in Auschwitz. According to some reports, a bribe of a diamond from Rabbi Lau's sons allegedly saved the children in Czestochowa from extermination in Auschwitz.

I found a transport list with the names of Naphtali Lau and Israel Meir Lau, and my father. The transport list confirmed that my father was deported to Buchenwald from Czestochowa. There's no mention of me.

I have a clear, horrendous memory of the parting from my father. I simply don't know where and when it took place. It could have happened in Piotrkow, but it might possibly have taken place later in Czestochowa.

Even for laborers, like my father, Czestochowa was a short stay, a month or two, before deportation. On January 15-17, 1945, SS troops appeared and gathered the Jews of Czestochowa to dispatch them elsewhere. Was I among them or already in another camp? I'll never know unless one day my amnesia from this period goes away. But then, could I trust new and unfamiliar memories?

A second group that left Piotrkow went directly to the German concentration camps. The men and boys went to Buchenwald and women and girls were sent by train four days to Ravensbruck. Among the women and men in Ravensbruck, some were sent on to Bergen-Belsen.

Based on everything I have read and discussed with experts and other survivors, this is what I guess happened:

Soon after leaving Hortensia in Piotrkow, the Teacher and I are sent to Germany.

When we cross the border from Poland to Germany, the doors of the trains are flung open. We jump down into the snow. We eat the snow. We drink the snow. We use the light reflecting on the snow to see who is still alive. While we are adjusting, Germans come on motorcycles with sidecars. They have beautiful shiny black boots and clean uniforms. We are filthy. They make an announcement on bull horns for women to line up on one side, and men on the other. Now I will have to go with the women.

Why did the Teacher take me? Her goodness? Maybe her own desire not to be alone, even if she was the one who had to provide care?

A mother myself today, I know that sometimes the act of mothering provides our strength and preserves our humanity. I also know how much of a responsibility it is.

Had she lost children of her own? Was she single and yearning for a child like me? Was she simply a kind person who couldn't bear the idea of a child on her own in a world gone mad? The relief I felt was coupled with the fear and horror of leaving my father.

I know that many people describe the inmates of Nazi slave labor camps as having sunk below the level of animals. Humanity, they said, was crushed in the competition to survive. That was not my experience. I was a little, scared girl who needed to eat and who needed care. The Teacher was the first of the new mothers who took responsibility for me, despite the hardships and dangers. The Teacher was willing to risk her life, and sacrifice for me.

I remember my father's words. I remember his promise. I do not remember his face. He promised. He promised. But he didn't keep his promise. Fathers are supposed to keep their promises.

The months that followed are a blur. I cannot

assimilate the loss of my father.[2] I am hungry and cold. I was hungry before, but there was always a source of some food.

In Hortensia, on the walk to the factory, my father could buy bread and apples from the Polish people along the road. We worked among non-Jewish Poles who would tell us what was happening outside of the camp and who could help with supplies. He bought bread, onions, and sugar. We were hungry, but we weren't starving.

As soon as we leave the slave labor camp of Hortensia there is no longer any opportunity to buy food. Rations are sparse.

Going with the Teacher, did I feel disloyal to my own mother? Did I feel guilty? I knew she would have wanted me to survive.

Did I stay with my Mother the Teacher or was this just a short stop from which I moved by train with her to Bergen-Belsen? There was no mention of me on the train records and I don't remember being there. Women prisoners were usually sent out to one of the huge Buchenwald systems of sub-camps.

In this blurry period of my childhood, I had to have arrived in Bergen-Belsen sometime between January and April 1945.

There is also the possibility that my journey included the Ravensbruck concentration camp. I have no memories of Ravensbruck. Either I wasn't there or have repressed the experience so much that I don't remember it.

---

2   According to a 2014 Danish study, adults who were children when their mothers died are 55 percent more likely to die young – and that's not in the Holocaust. Losing your father in childhood is connected to a 50 percent greater risk of premature death. As many as four percent of children in wealthy countries lose a parent while growing up in normal times.

Many little girls were imprisoned there. Ravensbruck was about fifty miles from Berlin near the town of Furstenberg. It was another version of hell on earth that was part of the Holocaust. There are testimonies about children thrown alive into the crematory, buried alive, and drowned. Hundreds of little girls were sterilized by direct exposure of genitals to X-rays. Children who survived had to work day and night with the women in the workshop and help them with the heaviest labor. Very few of these children survived the war. According to historians, in December 1944, over 32,000 women and children were in the camp, with three or four in a bunk and many lying in the dirt.

I have looked for records. The camp's expert historian, Rochelle Saidel, advised me not to expect to find any. The Nazis destroyed the records as the Soviets approached.

My arrival – if I went to Bergen-Belsen by way of Ravensbruck – would have coincided with Ravensbruck being transformed into an extermination camp. Gas chambers were constructed. Around 5,000-6,000 prisoners, mostly women, were exterminated in three months. Could I have escaped this new horror?

On January 15, the separate children's camp in Ravensbruck was closed. If I was at Ravensbruck, I could have stayed with my new mother and gone to the women's camp. There were 20,000 women prisoners who were evacuated on a Death March to Germany at the end of March. Many of them went to Bergen-Belsen. I might have been among them.

Might, might, might. How many times have I tried to reconstruct my personal history? These days I lay awake at night and try to force myself to remember. No records and no witnesses and no experts have been able to go beyond speculation.

I share this frustration with other child survivors.

In his autobiography, *Sevek and the Holocaust, the Boy Who Refused to Die*, my fellow Piotrkower Sidney Finkel, who was four years older than me, also says his memory of the transition period for him from the factory in Piotrkow, to Czestochowa, and then to Buchenwald is vague, that his memory must have shut down in order to remain sane. I know exactly what he means.

I also identify with the account by Dutch sociologist G.L. Durlacher, a survivor of Birkenau, who interviewed other child survivors from this camp.

"Misha ... looks helplessly at me and admits hesitantly that the period in the camps is wiped out from his brain ... With each question regarding the period between December 12, 1942 till May 7, 1945, he admits feeling embarrassed that he cannot remember anything."

Chapter 10

WHY CAN'T I REMEMBER MORE?

To those around me, I know I seem different from a typical Holocaust survivor. I have become a true American. The outgoing, positive Mrs. Quint, who drives a Cadillac or Town Car full of children, who is the first to volunteer for the PTA and to hold class parties at her big home couldn't possibly be a survivor. No accent. Not bent over. American-educated. Athletic. A lover of good food and classical music.

At age 78, I go to see a psychologist.

Since the 1960s, there has been a widely publicized concept that Holocaust survivors suffer from a syndrome called "survivor's guilt." Anxiety, nightmares, depression, and mood swings are the symptoms. Survivor's guilt is based on the idea that survivors irrationally feel guilty for not dying and believe that they somehow caused the death of their loved ones. Just about everyone has heard this.

These were early conclusions about the psychosis of survivors made by the few who sought out psychiatric care. Even those who did seek psychiatric care might have been directed to psychiatric clinics because this was part of the overall check-up necessary to receive war reparations.

The majority of survivors, like me, weren't interested in talking about our childhoods or our suffering. Nearly all of us assumed we would die in the Holocaust, and when we didn't, we wanted to grasp this gift of life with both hands.

We wanted to revive our dreams of what we wanted to do when we grew up, now that we had a chance to grow up. We children were encouraged by those who took care of us after the Holocaust to do this, in the hope that we would grow straight and tall and not be disfigured emotionally by the trauma. For those of us who were adopted, new parents had an additional motivation to see the past put behind us.

After the first wave of psychologists came up with theories based on the survivors they met in their practices or in hospitals, others began to rethink and revise the initial conclusions about us. They found that post stress factors, like adequate health, a social life and enough money could correlate with good mental health, despite a terrible past.

As early as 1975, Paul Matussek, the German psychiatrist otherwise famous for his ideas on delusion, concluded that, in contrast to earlier theorists, for the majority there were no concentration camp syndromes. And in his foreword to *Medical and Psychological Effects on Holocaust Survivors* in 1997, the late Nobel Laureate Elie Wiesel complained that certain "psychiatrists have invented theories, for the most part, poorly founded and even absurd about the guilt-feelings of Auschwitz survivors whom they treat as mentally ill."

There are hundreds, maybe thousands of books about our mental health. We Holocaust survivors rightly continue to make a fascinating subject to study, particularly because the question of how to overcome abuse and trauma still looms large in our times. How should a psychologist approach a ten-year-old schoolgirl in Nigeria who had been captured by the Boco Haram if she could get free?

If you read the research, you'll see that the questions psychologists and sociologists ask have changed. They now openly wonder how so many of us did so well in life after the experience of loss, pain, and multiple separations.

Half-a-century-old studies by Joel Shanan and Orna Shahar showed that contrary to expectations, we Holocaust survivors tend to be more task oriented, cope more actively, and express more favorable attitudes toward family, friends, and work than others.

Shanan, a Holocaust survivor himself, concluded an eight-year follow-up study in Jerusalem of mid-adulthood and aging to determine characteristics of 25 survivors of concentration camps (aged 46-65 years) as compared with a control group of 25 persons who had spent World War II in Israel. He found that even under adverse conditions of the Holocaust we managed to cope in a way that safeguarded our subsequent development into old age. He concluded that we revealed "age-appropriate cognitive functioning and a basically active coping style," as opposed to earlier researchers who found us cognitively impaired.

An interesting study published in the *Journal of Abnormal Psychology* in 2005, compared eating habits of Holocaust survivors decades after the Holocaust with a control group. Some had theorized that severe food restrictions would result in eating pathologies that would last nearly forever. But the study disproved the theory. We Holocaust survivors eat as heartily as the rest of our brethren. I certainly love cooking and eating. Nor are we fatter than our brethren.

Holocaust survivors reputedly exhibit more severe reactions when facing life-threatening stressors, such as major illness or war. Some of this research was done after the 2001 Gulf War in Israel. My daughter Naomi claims that I would get up every day of the Gulf War and put on my jewelry, "in case I had to flee." We are indeed more on our guard than others who haven't undergone what we have.

What about obsessions? I'm sometimes very thrifty. Friends tease me for pumping my own gas despite arthritis. On the other hand, I never stint on the lavish meals I serve. I like to keep my pantry full. Is this a result of the Holocaust? I have many friends with similar habits who haven't had traumatic pasts. I love to give away possessions. I once gave a cousin of my husband's my mink stole because she wanted one and I hardly ever wore mine. Go figure.

So why go to a psychologist? Because I feel self-conscious that while writing this book I often can't remember details of my past.

In all the 70 years from liberation to beginning the writing of this book, I never went to a psychologist. I was never troubled with sleeplessness and nightmares.

But since we have begun working on the book, I don't sleep well. I am torn between trying to remember and trying to forget.

I seek my mothers' faces. I want to be able to answer Barbara Sofer's questions, but I can't.

Barbara suggested that we make an appointment with the psychologist at Amcha, an organization for Holocaust survivors. We need to get some perspective on this issue and to figure out how to proceed.

Amcha was established in the 1980s because certain Holocaust survivors who had gone decades without expressing a need for psychological help were now seeking assistance. The name Amcha means "your nation" in Hebrew, but it's also a code name. When two Jews hiding in the Holocaust met each other, they only had to say the word "amcha" to assure the other of their Jewish identity. I'd heard about Amcha's services of course, but never saw a reason to go. In addition, because we were financially secure, I didn't want to take advantage of organizations that were more important for financially-strapped survivors.

But after a discussion with the organization head, we are offered an appointment to see the psychologist Elisheva Van der Hal.

Amcha is located in a nondescript office building in downtown Jerusalem. In one room, a group of Holocaust survivors has gathered to watch a film together. We are directed to a waiting area near the organization offices. Another woman is also waiting.

When Holocaust survivors meet, there is a quick exchange of the outline of their experience – the country, the camps, where they live now. When they hear my American accent, there's always a moment of confusion.

Nonetheless, I swap the difficult information with a survivor from Czechoslovakia before it is my turn to see the psychologist.

For 25 years, Elisheva Van der Hal has worked with Holocaust survivors, particularly those who were small children like me when the war started. She has published numerous studies.

I wouldn't have wanted a psychologist without experience of the Holocaust. I couldn't bear a psychologist asking me, "Are you angry at your mother for letting go of your hand?" for instance, although that might be the sort of clichéd script you would expect in a usual session.

Dr. Van der Hal is a neat, slim, attractive woman with incongruous unruly, curly salt and pepper hair. She is a child of war herself. When the question of Barbara Sofer's presence comes up, I insist that she stay. After all, coming here is her idea. Barbara has told her about our working on my memoir.

Why have we come? "It's my inability to remember," I tell her. "I can't recall all the details of my life."

I give her a brief recap. She listens and then says, "But you do remember. You remember what you need to remember. When you were a child, you needed to act quickly to survive. There was no time to brood. You had to deal with life and death and you did. You put aside the pain in order to preserve your life."

The vast majority of Holocaust survivors are okay, she says. Somewhere between 10-20 percent have sought out psychotherapy, and they are in countries in which psychotherapy is readily available. That's less than the number of non-Holocaust survivors!

I have read so many Holocaust memoirs where parents made their children swear they would remember. Even though no one extracted such a promise from me, I feel guilty that I can't remember.

Van der Hal speaks in a soft, soothing voice. What I remember is bad enough. What I have forgotten may be much worse. You remember enough, she assures me.

What about guilt? Why don't I feel guilty that I am the only family member to survive, that perhaps my family's strategy to save me worked, but failed for all the others?

Van der Hal smiles. She doesn't think much of survivor's guilt. "Of course you're happy you survived. You should be."

It has been her experience of interviewing child survivors over two and a half decades that they don't feel guilty for being alive.

"You were happy to survive. You are happy you survived. You should be thankful to have survived."

Her research shows that having a feeling of protection in the early years is important for mental health later in life. She has found that the most important factor in overcoming a terrible past is having a positive attitude. That seems to be the key to my healthy survival. Either

I was born with positivity, or my birth mother or other mothers did such a good job that a natural tendency to be optimistic was bolstered, she says.

My psychologist believes another protective factor is a "sense of coherence," a perception that the world is comprehensible, manageable, and meaningful. This belief buffers the impact of traumatic Holocaust experiences for the fortunate survivors who have it.

When the late Judith Kestenberg, a Holocaust survivor and psychiatrist who became the expert on children in the Holocaust, was speaking in Jerusalem at the Children in War Conference, she told the story of a young woman survivor who was so depressed after the Holocaust that she had decided to kill herself. In the meantime, survivors in the DP camp were showering. There was a long line. One of the women in line saw the young woman's unhappy state and said she should take her turn to shower. That act of kindness broke through the sadness and gave her the will and desire to live.

Through all the chaos and trauma I experienced, the kindness of strangers touched my soul.

I am welcome to come back, of course, Dr. Van der Hal tells me. However, from her perspective, I remember just as much as I need to. I feel relieved.

Chapter 11

MOTHERS ON THE DEATH MARCH

Rumors penetrate the camp. Somehow we know the Germans are losing. Inside the concentration camp, we become even more vulnerable. Our cruel masters show no signs of giving up their efforts to annihilate us, to hedge their bets, so that if tables turn, we won't be able to testify that they are such monsters.

There is a new demonic twist in their oppression: the death marches. On the death marches, when we are no longer confined behind barbed wire, the circle of potential murderers grows larger.

They don't know our names, and on the whole, we don't know their names. They are forbidden to talk to us, and we certainly don't attempt to talk to them. Who are these men and women who so abuse us?

I am standing on a steep hill looking down. Two men are lying in the snow. Their pants are pulled down. After everything I have been through, I am still shocked to see these men exposed.

If a Jewish woman runs away, maybe she can pretend she is a Christian. When a Jewish man runs away, circumcision is a giveaway – a dead giveaway.

Why were the Germans putting so much effort into moving us prisoners at this late stage in the war that they were clearly losing? There are different theories. The march of prisoners might slow the Allied attack by airplane, some believed. We might protect the Nazis from bombings because they thought the Allies wouldn't want to kill us.

But where did this take place? Have I merged several moves into one? Cold, death, fear, filth, hunger: it blends into a numbness of mind and soul.

As the Russians approached Poland, the Germans moved prisoners from Poland to Germany, from one camp to another. We remembered all those rumors in Piotrkow that we were being "moved east to Russia." In the end, they moved us west, from Poland to Germany.

In Poland, the death camp of Majdaneck was liberated by the Russian army in August 1944, nine months before we came to the end of our march in Bergen-Belsen. The Soviets found survivors, bodies, gas chambers.

A Polish-Soviet commission was charged with investigating and documenting the crimes against humanity. In the fall of 1944, a museum was set up on the grounds of Majdaneck. The Nazi crimes were fully documented. This undercut the often repeated claims that the death marches were the Nazis' last attempt to cover up.

And yet another theory is that industrial workers were being shipped east, to create a stronger Germany so that terms of surrender would be less harsh. But there was already a surplus of workers in Germany for the factories that were still operating.

Another theory is that the need to move the prisoners was an initiative of the guards – no matter their rank – who would then have an excuse for not taking on more dangerous assignments at the front.

Still another theory is that Heinrich Himmler, head of the SS and responsible for the concentration camps, wanted a final reserve of Jews as a bargaining chip.

In his book *The Death Marches, the Final Phase of Nazi Genocide*, author Daniel Blatman asks: "Why did the men in charge decide to transport hundreds of thousands of prisoners along the retreat routes of the Third Reich, with no apparent advantage or clear purpose in view? Why did so many groups and individuals take part in their liquidation? Even if we take into account the vast dimensions of the Nazis' murderous lunacy, the death marches are still an inexplicable chapter in the annals of the genocide they perpetrated."

Another author, Daniel Goldhagen, claims that the motive for the killings during the death marches was fanatic and murderous anti-Semitism, linked to the "Final Solution."

But Daniel Blatman says that the thousands of brutal killers of prisoners on the death marches were not necessarily anti-Semites or proponents of some orderly racial ideology.

"The killers were the product of a society that for 12 years had promoted a certain ethos, which transformed many of them into Nazis, though they might not define themselves as such. The combination of the Nazi beliefs with the circumstances that prevailed toward the end of the war turned a considerable number of them into murderers. As long as the transportation of prisoners to the destination camp answered their need and served as insurance that they wouldn't be deployed on the front line, they continued to do their jobs. But the moment the prisoners became a liability, as often occurred, they did not hesitate to butcher them mercilessly. Actions that were ostensibly driven by zealous ideological motivation were, in fact, frequently fueled by solely opportunistic considerations. Although mass evidence couldn't be wiped out, guards wanted to liquidate the witnesses who could point a finger at them after the war."

Author Blatman says no one can claim these murderers

on the death marches were just following orders. These men and women murderers were determined to kill as many Jews as they could before the war ended and they would go back to their regular lives.

Think of it. Piotrkow was liberated in January, but Bergen-Belsen, where I was last incarcerated, wasn't liberated until April 15. Auschwitz was liberated on January 27, 1945. Three and a half long months would go by before we, the slaves of Bergen-Belsen, would be emancipated.

The winter of 1945 was very cold, even by Polish and German standards. I was nine years old, walking through the snow in wooden clogs.

To march miles in the snow, today you would wear boots and thermal garments, and you'd still worry about getting frostbite, when your flesh freezes.

Along the way, the march halted and Jews were massacred. A woman was protecting me. Was this my Mother the Teacher or was I with another good woman who held my arm if I stumbled or lagged behind? No child could have survived this frozen trek alone. Who were my mothers on the death march?

I remember looking at the forests, wishing I could escape. Where would I run to? Who would let me in? There was no escape. I stopped thinking of running.

Hundreds of thousands of prisoners trudged along the roads and were being murdered at the whim of the guards. There was a trail of blood and bodies.

If someone sat down, he was shot. If someone fell, he was shot. If someone looked the wrong way, she was shot.

Everywhere, everywhere were blood and bodies. I never looked up in fear that a guard would catch my eye and kill me for fun. Somehow I survived.

Chapter 12

AMONG THE DEAD
IN BERGEN-BELSEN

Our body lice are the size of sesame seeds. They feed on our blood. They carry typhus. I am covered with lice that fill my scalp, eat my body, lodge in my clothing and the straw I sleep on.

All day long, I try to clean the lice from my body. Those children who fall behind on this job turn black from the insects boring into their skin. The lice crackle as I crush them between my thumb nails. You have to crush them, but they are always laying more eggs and more and more are always hatching. I am grateful that I have hair. No one has shaved it off.

My lice-killing is interrupted by a daily torture called *appel*, German for roll-call. The very old, mothers, and children under three are counted inside the huts, but the rest of us have to be counted outside. The sums never seem to match what the overseers think is correct, so we are counted again and again, no matter what the weather is. The idea of the roll-call seems absurd to me. No one can escape the ten rows of electrically-charged barbed wire surrounding us. The only way out of Bergen-Belsen is by dying.

I stand in the snow, frozen and paralyzed from the cold. I can't feel my feet. My legs hurt. "Just do it," I tell myself. The guards taunt and punish us for even the tiniest infraction. The soldiers in their black boots shout at us. If you fall over, they hit you hard. I do not fall, no matter how tired and cold I am.

I can't tell time, but we wait for what must be hours before the counting begins. The daily count always includes beating prisoners.

The older prisoners say that having a strong will helps survival. Something inside me impels me to keep trying to stay alive.

Every day there are corpses dragged out of the tents into the huge piles of bodies that begin to decay. Tangled heaps of limbs, bulging eyes, and twisted faces lie together in mountains.

The lice are winning. People around me are burning up with fever, eventually becoming delirious and dying.

The air smells of burnt and rotten flesh. I get used to it. Everyone does. I don't smell it much anymore.

More bodies are tossed into a deep ravine. I get used to that, too. Deeper ditches are being dug.

I am in the women's barracks, with one of my adopted mothers, close to the tents where pregnant women give birth. A woman is screaming and suddenly there is the cry of a baby. I see a baby come out of a woman. The woman curses in Polish. I am nine years old, and despite everything I've witnessed, this is surprising and shocking to me. I don't know where this baby came from. The next day it is gone.

Later I will learn that many pregnant women were shipped to the women's camp in Bergen-Belsen. According to Dr. Thomas Rahe, the museum historian, "sick and pregnant women whom the SS classified as unfit for work were also transferred to Bergen-Belsen systematically from other camps, so that the number of births in Bergen-Belsen started to rise. At least 100 babies were born in Bergen-Belsen. The majority of these new-born prisoners had zero chance of survival."

I'm sitting at my Jerusalem dining table with my books and papers on Bergen-Belsen spread in front of me. I open the albums of photos from Bergen-Belsen taken by photographers with the British army which liberated the camp in 1945.

The photos show mountains of dead. Men, women, children. Dirty and twisted and broken. Skinny as the skeletons in biology class in high school.

These dead bodies once were human beings, Jews, who were moms and dads, teachers and doctors, scientists and singers. One of them doubtless played the violin as well as Jasha Heifetz. Perhaps he or she hailed from Heifetz's hometown of Vilna. Another might have been

Dead bodies were everywhere in Bergen-Belsen.

Sign reminding drivers about typhus in Bergen-Belsen after liberation.

a second Albert Einstein, born not far away in Ulm, Germany.

American broadcast journalist Barbara Walters' family came from Lodz, near Piotrkow. Former US Secretary of State Madeline Albright's family came from Czechoslovakia. Artist Marc Chagall was rescued by American journalist Varian Fry and American diplomat Hiram Bingham IV from the south of France. Google founder Sergey Brin came from Russia. More than two million Jews in the former Soviet Union were murdered in the Holocaust.

Antek (Yitzhak) Zuckerman, Deputy Commander of the Warsaw Ghetto uprising, told the story of a boy who approached him with a request. What could a six-year-old boy want, wondered Zuckermann.

"I have a violin and love to play it. My teacher was taken away. Could you find me a violin teacher?" the boy asked.

Zuckerman smiled. Despite the appalling conditions of the ghetto, and more pressing requests for food and medicine, he found the boy a violin teacher among the many talented Jews in the ghetto.

Years later, after the war, Zuckerman saw the teacher he'd found. "What ever happened to your student?" he asked.

The teacher didn't know if the boy had survived, but doubted it. He remembered his student's enormous talent. "He was such a genius, such a progeny! Had he lived, he'd be famous on world stages today, like Itzhak Perlman." Itzhak Perlman's parents were from Poland, too. They managed to get out of Poland in the 1930s.

How many violinists, cellists, lawyers, doctors, plain people did the world lose in the mountains of bodies in Bergen-Belsen? I look at the photos of the dead in the memorial albums, in the museum and on the internet. You can see a collection photographs of Bergen-Belsen by the great British photojournalist George Rodger on the Time-Life site.

These dead are old acquaintances of mine. I walked among the dead. I look at photographs and I don't weep. I look for myself.

The faces of the dead were always distorted in wild grins. Was this relief or agony, I wondered back then, sure that I would know.

I think something inside of me died there, too. Otherwise I couldn't look at these pictures today without collapsing.

Bergen and Belsen were small, unimportant towns, located between strategic German cities: Hanover, Hamburg, and Bremen. The campgrounds were first built by Hitler to train army units in the mid-1930s while he was still hatching his plan to take over the world. Later the buildings were used to house tens of thousands of Russian, French, and Belgian prisoners of war captured by the Nazis. Conditions were reportedly so terrible that the prisoners ate grass, and each other. Then Bergen-Belsen became a misnamed "convalescent camp."

By 1943, the Nazis were losing the war on all fronts. Faced with defeat on the battlefield, they continued with their primary goal of eradicating the Jews. Their soldiers were fleeing the Russians, the Americans and the British.

A child walks down a road lined with dead bodies near the Bergen-Belsen concentration camp, 1945.

Allied bombers ruled the skies, but the Nazis still had the power to murder Jews, so they did.

The Nazis came up with the idea of segregating certain Jews who would be useful for exchange purposes, to release Germans held in internment camps or to gain foreign exchange. In March 1943, Heinrich Himmler ordered the establishment of a camp for prominent European Jews or Jewish citizens from neutral states. Concentration camp prisoners were dispatched to build additional housing for this group in Bergen-Belsen.

"Exchange Jews," those with Latin American passports, for instance, might be exchanged for German nationals in Latin American countries. So might Palestinian Jews, those with Palestinian passports. There were also German nationals being held in pre-state Israel, under the British protectorate who might be released.

The Bergen-Belsen concentration camp was therefore organized in eight separate sections, held under different conditions. Those in one section weren't supposed to fraternize with the others. There was the so-called "Neutral Camp" where Jews with passports from Spain, Argentina, Portugal and Turkey were imprisoned, and the "Special Camp" which held Polish Jews with passports to South American countries. There was a Hungarian camp where Himmler wanted to trade Jews for money or goods. Back-channel negotiations were going on.

Dutch Jews and certain other nationals wearing their own clothing with the star marking them as Jews were held separately and had somewhat better conditions. Because of the stars on their clothing, this part of Bergen-Belsen was called the "Star Camp."

In her book, *The Children's House of Belsen*, Hetty Verolme describes spotless barracks and a dental clinic. These children had arrived directly from their homes in

Holland in February 1944, and were about to experience the Holocaust for the first time. Some were called "the diamond children" because they were the children of the valued diamond experts. The Nazis needed diamonds and suddenly realized they couldn't just assign laborers to cut and polish them. There was no replacement for the skilled artisans whom they forced to work for them by holding their families hostage. Powerful Nazis hoarded eminently portable diamonds to make their escape with stolen riches.

In March 1944, sick and exhausted prisoners from other concentration camps were dumped in Bergen-Belsen, not that they were to receive medical treatment or better food. Prisoners would find only disease and starvation waiting for them. Nearly all of the sick men and women who were brought to Bergen-Belsen died soon after arrival. I don't know why the Nazis bothered to move them.

In the late summer and fall of 1944, a camp in Bergen-Belsen was created for women and girls evacuated from Poland. A large tent camp for approximately 8,000 women was set up. They came in many transports from Auschwitz.

In January 1945, a larger women's camp was built. Women and girls of the Sinti and Roma race, pregnant women who were close to giving birth, and many orphaned children (in hut No. 211) were housed together. As a result, it was called the "children's barracks." Some sources say that 2,000 children under the age of 15 lived in the camp.

I have gone into so much detail about these different camps because I have discovered, in my personal research for information about this period in my life, that there are many different descriptions of Bergen-Belsen. All were awful, but certain parts of the camp were worse than others.

For instance, compared to the others, the conditions of children in the Star Camp looked relatively good, but as you read in the memoirs of survivors these were terrible times for them, even though the Germans were interested in keeping them alive. When the Red Cross came to inspect in March 1945, the inspectors were taken to the barracks with the healthier children.

We heard that the children received a thick slice of white bread with butter and a box of chocolates. A slice of white bread with butter sounded like heaven.

It's important to be aware of the false impression of some of the propaganda photos of the camp. Some of the children weren't skinny because they'd only left their own homes a short time before. "They are going to trade us," they would say to us other children without such hope.

Anne Frank, the Dutch teenager who became posthumously well known for her diary of hiding from the Nazis, died in Bergen-Belsen shortly before liberation. She reportedly had typhus. Reportedly. As if there are medical records for this brilliant, talented girl whose story has touched millions of souls.

January and February 1945 were among the coldest winter months of the 20th century in Europe, with blizzards and temperatures as low as 13°F. Until the middle of March, temperatures were well below freezing. I have to smile at the understatement of Wikipedia about the evacuation of prisoners. "Most of the POWs were ill-prepared for the evacuation, having suffered years of poor rations and wearing clothing ill-suited to the appalling winter conditions."

Ill-suited? When you entered a concentration camp, your clothes were taken away. Prisoners were issued wooden or leather clogs. No socks. The rough material rubbed against your skin.

One of the most emotional moments for visitors to Auschwitz and Majdanek, and the Holocaust Museum in Washington, is seeing the huge piles of old, graying shoes that were taken from us. Some of the prisoners came walking on their knees into Bergen-Belsen.

Piles of shoes.

My images: A long road into the camp. Tall pine trees. Barbed-wire fences. Growling dogs. Sentries with rifles. So many people everywhere. Barracks lined up in rows. Sand, grit, dirt, snow, sleet, mud, grime. More and more people entering a camp that seems so crowded that I can't imagine squeezing in more.

When I arrived at Bergen-Belsen, we were sent to showers, not make-believe showers with gas spigots.

Later, water would become a scarce commodity in this camp. In April, at the end, there was no regular water supply. The Germans claimed that the pipes were damaged. Prisoners drank from puddles after the rain. When you're that thirsty, you'll drink anything. That meant that I probably arrived in January or February, soon after my father was sent to Buchenwald. I can only estimate my arrival date.

After the shower, all our personal belongings were gone. There were piles of clothing. I got a brown dress like a bag. My "mother" risked her life, leaping forward and grabbing a black coat. I held my breath. No one shot her. Her body heat, and the coat, saved my life.

Women slept on planks, body to body. The barracks were so crowded that prisoners often slept sitting up. In the tents, the covers flew away, leaving prisoners soaking

Women in the barracks in Bergen-Belsen.

wet and cold from the rain and snow. The ground was sullied by urine and feces.

Beyond the high wire fences surrounding Bergen-Belsen was a strip of land about 50 feet wide. The skull and crossbones signs that I first saw as a three-year-old in the ghetto were posted around this area. Watchtowers were perched over the high fences.

Rutabaga is a grey turnip. Farmers from the surrounding areas grew these for the camp. The soup came in the middle of the day. There was a brown substance to drink in the morning and a dry piece of bread in the evening. A muddy potato peel floating in my bowl was a treasure. The bread that tasted like sawdust was life-sustaining. Later, even that was gone.

You will never find a turnip in my kitchen. I can't stand them. Today, no matter how dressed up I am for a family celebration, if I happen to walk behind the hall or restaurant on the way in, the stench of dirty dishwater, similar to the soup, makes me nauseous.

It's pointless and banal to try to figure out which of the concentration camps was the worst. In terms of numbers, the death camps near the major Polish cities, Auschwitz near Krakow and Treblinka near Warsaw, claimed the most lives.

At Bergen-Belsen, some of the prisoners came from Auschwitz. They told scary stories of mass murder by gassing. Prisoners at Bergen-Belsen told the newcomers from Auschwitz: You were lucky before you came here. In Poland, there was food every day.

In Bergen-Belsen, the Germans didn't have to expend money on gas chambers. The camp killed you with hunger, thirst and disease. You knew you would die. The only question was when.

At first, people went over to a ditch to do their bodily functions. Then they didn't bother. We were afraid of falling in and drowning.

The guards were fat and powerful. They ate their meals in front of us. They came to Bergen-Belsen from other camps where they had polished their sadistic methods.

On the first of December, 1944, shortly before the liberation of Auschwitz and four and a half months before the liberation of Bergen-Belsen, the infamous Josef Kramer left Auschwitz and became Kommandant of Bergen-Belsen. In the four and a half months he ruled the camp, Kramer earned the epithet "The Beast of Belsen," and his guards would be remembered among the cruelest men and women in history. Many were known to be criminals in the real world, wherever the real world was.

At the women's camp we had to contend with the notorious Herta Bothe, who might shoot you for fun. And there was the wicked Irma Grese, who strutted through the camp with a riding whip. She was young and pretty, so everyone called her "The Beautiful Beast." They reminded me of the wicked witches in the stories my mother used to read me.

The worst moments were when these Nazi women in their uniforms and whips came into your barracks. Who would they strike first?

There were 15,257 prisoners recorded at the time of Kramer's arrival. That number quadrupled as the Polish camps were evacuated. In the next four months, from January to April, another 35,000 inmates were dumped in Bergen-Belsen. The camp became a main center of exterminating prisoners who had no further economic value. By March 31, the number of prisoners reached 44,060.

I was nine years old in Bergen-Belsen. My last memory of life before the Nazis was six years earlier.

I couldn't have survived without a mother. But whether she was my Mother the Teacher, or a new mother I cannot say. I have a strong memory of living in a tent with a woman who acted as my mother, but I don't know which of my mothers she was.

Today, we use the term "hunger pangs." When we've missed lunch or have a later supper, we're hungry. That's not what real hunger means.

Ironically, in America with its abundance of food, during the war in 1944, Dr. Ancel Benjamin Keys conducted experiments on the impact of starvation on 36 conscientious objectors in what was called the Minnesota Starvation Experiment. Conscientious objectors were first placed on the three-month baseline diet of 3,200 calories after which their calories were reduced to 1,800 calories a day while expending 3,009 calories in activities such as walking.

Obviously, the patients lost weight. Doctor Keys' experiment also showed that starvation causes the victim's heart rates and temperatures to drop.[1] Another effect, called Marasmas Kwashiorkor, caused by the deficiency of calories and protein, is "a condition in which there is a deficiency of both calories and protein, with severe tissue wasting, loss of subcutaneous fat, and usually dehydration.[2] This results in fatigue, decreased muscle mass, and increased chance of disease due to a decaying immune system. Iron deficiency causes mental grogginess. Pernicious anemia causes confusion. Severe malnutrition impacts your level of self-initiated intellectual activity.

---

1   Tucker, 135.

2   Dorland's Medical Dictionary.

We were in a state of chronic malnutrition, far more severe than those in the experiment. According to Bergen-Belsen historian Dr. Thomas Rahe, from the end of 1944, food rations were barely enough to survive. If you were lucky enough to have a mother, she might sacrifice by sharing her own food with you.

There's a famous story written by the great Yiddish writer I.L. Peretz called *Bontscha the Silent*. When Bontscha dies, he is judged in the heavenly court. His guardian angel tells how Bontscha never cursed or complained to the Almighty, even though his life was heavy with sorrows. When Bontscha got to choose whatever pleasure he would like in the World-to-Come, he opted for a fresh roll and butter. At this point in the story, the devil laughs at the choice of such a modest reward. I can imagine asking for such a gift. The ultimate, almost unimaginable gift in a concentration camp was a slice of white bread and butter.

I look for myself also in the memories of others. I scour literature for any mention of children in Bergen-Belsen. Josef Rosensaft, a survivor who was 34 in 1945, wrote of the children of Bergen-Belsen.

"The number of children in Belsen was so small, you scarcely noticed them. These young shoots could not survive in the Hitler soil. The Nazis cut them down more rapidly than the older victims. And yet, by some miracle, a number were snatched from the jaw of death, not always by their mothers, who frequently were not among the living. Small, pitifully small, was their number. Every now and then one saw them in Belsen, brought here by the Germans a year before liberation. There were several hundred of them, Jewish children from all German-occupied lands."

In the *Diary of Bergen-Belsen*, Dutch lawyer and writer Abel J. Herzberg says, "Quite a few young children were deported by themselves. Here in Bergen-Belsen, too, there are young children all alone."

I can't find any mention of a little girl called Fredzia. Was I invisible? Was being invisible an advantage?

The March weather turns first spring-like, and then to sleety rain and wind. We hear nearby bombings day and night. I am hungry, always hungry.

The Nazis laugh at us and boast that they will never surrender. No one will defeat the mighty Reich.

Snow is back. I'm cold and I'm starving to death. It may be spring, but not a flower or blade of grass grows in Bergen-Belsen. Nothing grows in this place of death.

News has drifted into the camp that the British are a hundred kilometers away from Bergen-Belsen. I don't know who or what the British are, but when people say "British" I know they are good.

By April 1, there is no running water. Excreta is everywhere, as are decomposing bodies.

On April 6, 1945, the SS and police authorities "evacuate" the prisoners from four subcamps of the "Residence Camp" of Bergen-Belsen. The Special Camp, Neutrals Camp, Hungarian Camp and Star Camp prisoners begin leaving. They are being moved towards Theresienstadt, near Prague. Others go back and forth on trains until the American soldiers eventually catch up with them.

By April 9, there is no food at all. My mind is blank. When you are so tired, desperate and hungry, there's little energy to think.

I am just waiting to join the dead. I seek the shelter

of a tree and lie down to await death. There are others already dead around me.

Prisoners who can still walk are forced to move corpses to mass graves. Will they pick me up? Above me, planes are flying. Can the pilots see me? If the planes bomb us, there won't be any shelter, but I don't have the energy to get up.

By now the fences are lined with bodies which makes a second separation between our world – the world of those who have to be imprisoned for a reason I know not – and those who live outside.

The piles of bodies are higher than a standing man. I am tired and sick. I am ready to die. Is this my time to join them? Some of the men and women and children lying here are like me: not dead yet. We are waiting and watching. I close my eyes. Then something happens that makes me open my eyes and look around. I do not know the date.[3] Men and women who never walk faster than a shuffle are running. I watch them but I can't stand. Suddenly, people who never talked louder than a whisper are shouting.

Soldiers in khaki uniforms enter the camp. I can tell these aren't German soldiers. Some of the soldiers are throwing up. Nazi soldiers never throw up. How strange.

I know that instead of fear among the adults, there is surprise and joy and hope.

"*Ihr seid frei*, you are free," I hear on a loudspeaker. "We are the English Army. Be calm. Food and medical help are on the way."

"*Frei. Frei.* We're free," shout women around me in Yiddish. What does "free" mean? I do not understand. I am too tired to move.

---

3   Today, I know it was April 15, 1945.

LICHTENSTEIN	Fredzoa		· 1936	Piotrikov	7872
LIEBESKIND	Genia	27.I0.I9I8	Lcdz		7I66
LEWIN	Rachela	20. 8.I922	Wieno		

Rena (Fredzoa Lichtenstein) is listed on an official document from Bergen-Belsen.

But now there is a different feeling. Looking back, I'd call it hope.

Today I know the American poem by Emily Dickinson that we learned in school.

> *Hope is the thing with feathers*
> *That perches in the soul –*
> *And sings the tune without the words –*
> *And never stops – at all.*

I feel the flutter of the feathers of hope as I lie there under the tree. The British soldier whispers something to me in a language I do not understand.

The soldiers are lifting me onto a stretcher. I can't understand what they are saying, but I know they are trying not to hurt me.

Next I am in a hospital tent. I feel lucky. I'm so sick they'll take care of me right away. What an odd thought.

I later learned that on April 12, the Second Army crossed the Rhine and the German Military Commander at Bergen-Belsen approached 8 Corps to negotiate a truce and avoid the fight over the area of Bergen-Belsen. There were 800 Wehrmacht, 1,500 Hungarian soldiers and their

Piles of the dead bodies in Bergen-Belsen.

families, plus SS prison guards.

Today, there is a forestry museum in Bergen, and advertisements for Lower Saxony feature gorgeous photos of trees: beech, and oak and sycamore.

The great filmmaker Alfred Hitchcock was recruited by his Jewish friend, director Sidney Bernstein, to document the story of Bergen-Belsen. The images are difficult for the average person to look at, and to imagine what we lived through. Hitchcock shows where human beings starved and died inside the barbed wire, so close to the rich farmlands, well-fed cows and self-respecting German townspeople.

Corpulent, arrogant Germans show no remorse for their actions, now that the victorious British soldiers have taken charge. The 30,000 twisted bodies go beyond any imagination of Dante's inferno. The world didn't want to see this movie or face the horrors. It was abandoned and shelved for 70 years because it was considered politically sensitive.

When I watch Hitchcock's movie, available on Youtube, I am not repulsed. I watch with a particular interest for the children. Hitchcock was surprised that any of us survived.

There's a lovely scene of children eating soup after the liberation. They eat so carefully, not to miss a single drop.

Milk is brought into the camp in big metal containers. I remember running my finger around the rim to get an extra taste of milk. I remember climbing inside.

The 11th Armored Division of the British Army liberated us. This is how Vice-Director of Medical Services Brigadier Hugh Llewellyn Glyn Hughes described the scene on April 15.

> The conditions in the camp were really indescribable; no description nor photograph could really bring home the horrors that were there outside the huts, and the frightful scenes inside were much worse. There were various sizes of piles of corpses lying all over the camp, outside the wire and some in between the huts. The compounds themselves had bodies lying about in them. The gutters were full and within the huts there were uncountable numbers of bodies, some even in the same bunks as the living. Near the crematorium were signs of filled-in mass graves, and outside to the left of the bottom compound was an open pit half-full of corpses. It had just been begun to be filled.
>
> In Hut No. 208, which was close to the pile of corpses, there were dead women lying in the passage, which was so full that no women could lie down straight.

The main room on the left of the passage was one mass of bodies and you could not get another into it. The inmates were in a state of extreme emaciation and women were dying frequently.

The Nazi officers who surrendered explained the starvation: there simply hadn't been enough food or water for us. But the British found abundant food.

In that camp there was any amount of food which could have been distributed – A fully-stocked bakery in the Wehrmacht Camp with a terrific grain supply and capable of turning out 60,000 loaves a day which it did immediately afterwards and continued to do so with the same staff and from the same stock of grain.

There were vast quantities of medical supplies which weren't exhausted yet. You will hear that in the administration block in No. 1 Camp there were about 100 wooden boxes of tinned milk and meat which were in SS quarters marked "Hungarian." They were Red Cross parcels which had been sent to the Hungarian internees by the Hungarian Red Cross and had been stolen by the SS guards. With regard to the water supply, although the camp had been without water for from three to five days and that all there was were these foul concrete tanks with bodies in them, as soon as somebody started to try and do something, within two days, with the equipment which was already in that camp and with no addition to it, there was an adequate working water supply laid on to every kitchen, and within five days, with the assistance of only the local fire brigade, there was a complete and proper water system running throughout the camp. So much for the story that this was a breakdown of organization due to war conditions. You will hear that there was nothing lacking to provide full water and sanitation in that camp had anybody wanted to do it at all.

British soldiers immediately took control of the food. There were rumors that the Germans were cooking poison to finish us off in the final days, so all the pots had to be scoured.

The dying didn't stop. The soldiers offered us their rations. Fortunately, I was too sick to eat. The food might have killed me. Around me, starving men and women ate some of the tinned corned beef/pork rations. Many died.

The word went out. Don't eat the food or you will die. You cannot tolerate such rich food in your emaciated bodies.

The Nazis weren't quite finished. Four German Focke-Wulf fighter aircraft attacked the camp in the morning, killing three medical orderlies and damaging the water system and field ambulance.

On its website, The United States Holocaust Museum provides a summary of the period after liberation from the report of Major General James Alexander Johnston of the Royal Army Medical Corps.

Upon arrival, Bergen-Belsen was divided into two distinct camps. Camp I, frequently referred to as the "Horror Camp," housed approximately 22,000 females and 18,000 males. It had no running water or electricity, poor sanitation, limited clothing and infrequent and insufficient burial of the deceased.

Camp II had less sickness, a lower death rate, more clothing, and better means for burial. Internees in both camps experienced severe cases of physical and mental sickness.

An estimated 15,000 survivors suffered from typhus fever and nearly all suffered from diarrhea brought on by dysentery and starvation. Severe malnutrition reduced inmates to base survival instincts which, in some cases led to cannibalism. In an effort to limit further starvation, disease, and death, British units established four priorities: providing regular meals, preventing the spread of disease, removing survivors from the Camp I, and burying the deceased. Efforts to provide regular meals were hampered by limited mobility, limited staff, and the emaciated condition of the internees. Many suffered so severely from malnutrition that they were incapable of walking from their hut to a central food distribution center. However, limited staff impeded transporting food to the huts. At first, each hut designated a member to gather food and deliver it to the remaining inhabitants. Unfortunately, this system failed to equally distribute food.

The presence of 11 Light Field Ambulances provided increased staff and alleviated some of the food supply problems by helping to equally distribute the food among the huts. Finally, due to prolonged periods of malnutrition, survivors could not digest normal rations. Some survivors could not even digest milk without first diluting it with water. Therefore three different dietary scales were created of 800, 1,700, and 3,000 calories until survivors could absorb a normal diet. To prevent the spread of typhus, the source of the virus first had to be identified.

Although there was no cure for typhus, eliminating lice helped prevent the transfer of typhus from one individual to another. Therefore all clothing and huts of infected persons had to be either cleaned with delousing powder or burned to ensure that all of the lice were killed.

The United States Typhus Control mechanically operated a multi point D.D.T. sprayer. Additionally, treating the effects of starvation enabled the internees to fight typhus if it was contracted. Before survivors could be removed from the Horror Camp, British troops had to prepare an alternate facility in the nearby Hohne Barracks. This entailed preparation and staffing of the reception building, removal of existing furniture, procurement of necessary furniture (i.e. hospital beds, etc.), organization and staffing of the wards, kitchens, stores, etc., and organizing a route from the Horror Camp to the Hohne Barracks.

The task of clearing, cleaning and equipping the Hohne Barracks was carried on just ahead of the transfer of patients. Staffing problems were alleviated by using German prisoners of war including 35 medical officers, 130 nurses and 140 male orderlies. Before entering the Hohne Barracks, survivors were washed and deloused in a converted stable. The patients arrived to the stable via ambulance cars, then were placed upon tables and washed with hot water and soap, and finally dried and dusted with D.D.T. powder. Long, thick hair was initially cut off to ensure the elimination of lice, but later was dusted with D.D.T. powder and retained due to the psychological impact of losing hair. Upon completion of this process, internees were placed upon clean stretchers and moved to the Hohne Barracks. This process was known as the "human laundry."

Removal of the deceased proved to be a difficult task due to the sheer number of bodies and the lack of available personnel. The remaining SS guards were assigned to this task and buried over 26,000 victims in two months.

On April 21, 300 patients relocated to the Hohne Barracks after first undergoing cleansing and delousing; eventually this number increased to 670 patients per day. The 11th Light Field Ambulance, assisted by the American Friends Ambulance Unit, a Quaker organization, handled the evacuation. At first, the internees in the camp were divided between those with serious cases of typhus and those recovering from typhus, designated by either a "T" or a "PT" on their forehead, dividing transportation based on physical health. Psychologically, this was difficult for the patients because it separated groups of people and relationships that were formed. Eventually, the process was changed to admitting patients upon the hut they were in to retain the personal attachments formed, although this did prove more difficult for the medical personal to treat the patients.

In an effort to protect the staff, all were vaccinated against typhus and wore protective clothing. Of the twenty that contracted typhus, all of them fully recovered. Six detachments of the British Red Cross Society, composed of eight women assigned to the medical field and four men in the Military Government, and 97 British medical students arrived, supervised by the dietician Dr. R.A. Meiklejohn of N.N.R.R.A., arrived to help ward off starvation and improve upon conditions before the patients in Camp I to prepare for the transfer. This resulted in a decreased death rate and an increased morale as conditions improved.

Between April 18 and April 28, the dead were buried. At first the SS guards were made to collect and bury the bodies, but eventually the British needed bulldozers to push the thousands of bodies into mass graves.

A week after liberation, the evacuation of the camp began. We were moved from the women's camp to what was called Camp 2, where patients were somewhat less ill.

On May 19, evacuation was completed. On May 21,

flamethrowers arrived. The ceremonial burning of the last barracks brought to an end to the first stage of the relief operations. By mid to late May, Bergen-Belsen assumed the status of a displaced person's camp. The British General Hospital, a 1,200-bed hospital, was transferred from Eekloo, Belgium, to the newly-liberated Bergen-Belsen concentration camp.

Who was taking care of us? Nurses from the British army's Queen Alexandra's Imperial Military Nursing Service, from Quaker groups, and from Australia, New Zealand and the USA. Later on, other organizations, among them the Jewish Relief Unit, arrived to help rehabilitate survivors. We spoke many different languages. Some of the patients, even adults, screamed when the nurses gave us something intravenous, afraid of being the guinea pigs for new medical experiments.

Certain nurses were very kind. Others weren't, like the German nurses forced to help us. Their hostility was transmitted in their rough touch.

I loved the feel of clean sheets. Even the stretchers they carried me on had clean white sheets.

I didn't have the strength to wash myself. I was too sick and in a delirium.

The nurses and medical staff who treated us had to scrub the excrement from our bodies and spray us with DDT to kill the lice. All the scrubbing didn't get rid of my typhus.

People kept saying we were lucky to be free at last, but no one seemed ebullient. Now we had to confront the deaths of our loved ones. I didn't feel like celebrating. I had no idea what the future might bring. How would I survive without a family? I was too tired and sick to think this through.

According to Dutch psychologist Krell, himself a

hidden child, no one was asking us children what it was like for us, what we saw or how we felt.

Wrote Krell: "Adults assumed that children were lucky. Lucky not to have memories. Lucky not to have suffered unless they were in concentration camps. Lucky not to have understood what was happening. Most of the assumptions proved to be wrong.

"The pre-war mental health professionals, who had been preoccupied with even a single trauma experienced by a child, were nowhere to be seen. Jewish children subjected to a relentless series of traumas for months and years received little help. Perhaps the problems of brutalized children were simply too overwhelming even for the healers. We remained silent. It was expected of us.

"Therefore we were alone, struggling with fragments of memories that were painful and made little sense. Most of us thought we were a little crazy and kept that belief, as well as other secrets, to ourselves. The reality of being hunted left many with a sense of shame. Who but the guilty are pursued with such ferocity? But we hadn't done anything.

"The Jewish people were the target of a genocidal assault on their existence, and genocide demands the killing of children. The Nazis and their legions of enthusiastic collaborators achieved near success. In the countries under German occupation, 93 per cent of Jewish children were murdered."

Recently, I went to the dentist to repair a chipped tooth. A molar. He said I was lucky that this was a "nice, thick tooth." When did I get such a tooth? I asked. "Oh, that's a six-year molar," he said.

I thought of all the advice on healthy eating and good

Removing the dead in Bergen-Belsen.

Bulldozer pushing the bodies into mass graves.

Mass burial of the dead in Bergen-Belsen.

oral hygiene. When I got my six-year molars I had already been in the ghetto for more than two years.

How do I have a nice, thick tooth that would make it with me into my 70s? I went years without brushing my teeth. I had a low protein, low carbohydrate, low vitamin diet. In a study of starvation, the lack of Vitamin C and B12 is considered seriously detrimental. But I lived on near-starvation rations until I actually began to starve to death.[4]

I experienced dehumanization, which experts say leads to overwhelming paralysis of the adaptive and recuperative mechanisms of the psyche. Given my experience, according to the early experts on survivors, I should be suffering now from Concentration Camp Syndrome – depression, anxiety, and sleeplessness.

Some studies predicted we children would be intellectually impaired. We'd be aggressive and have difficulty forming relationships as a result of "catastrophic psychic trauma." Yet we have adapted to new lands and started new lives.

We survivors of all ages underwent both personal and collective trauma, perpetrated by persons who belonged to a highly regarded culture. It was never clear to me as a child why we Jews were the object of their persecution.

No matter how you look at it, according to these theories I should have been psychologically impaired. But I don't feel impaired. How is that possible? My only explanation is the quality of the mothering I received, both from my biological mother and from those who took over her job. Their parenting must have given me the strength and confidence to survive. I'm so grateful.

---

4   Under ration scales imposed by the Germans in Warsaw, rations for Jews were a mere 183 calories a day, as compared to Germans at 2,310 calories a day (Martin Gilbert, *Atlas of the Holocaust*).

The buildings in Bergen-Belsen were burned by the British to prevent the spread of typhus.

An interesting theory presented by Scottish-Israeli psychologist Shamai Davidson who spent 30 years working with survivors in Israel, suggested that those of us who experienced gradually worsening conditions while still protected by a parent developed resistance to the trauma. Dr. Davidson interviewed children who survived the Holocaust as teens – a little older than I was. Davidson concluded that those like me who had a long exposure to Nazi brutality, years in the ghetto, forced labor and then concentration camps, had developed a protective mechanism – in contrast, for instance, to those Dutch children who went straight from their homes to Bergen-Belsen.

He concluded: "Before their deportation to the concentration camps and separation from the family unit, the majority of these youngsters had spent periods of one to three years in ghettos and other specially designated areas for Jews under the Nazi regime. In this early pre-camp exposure to fear, death, brutality and hunger, they were to some extent protected by family and other supporting social bonds and went through an important preparatory process in learning 'adaptive behavior' to the Nazi persecution and terror together with parents, older siblings, friends and others in these closely knit communities. Family bonds were often strengthened during this period; manual skills were learned; and guiding precepts and models for dealing with stress acquired, which were utilized later in reality and fantasy in the struggle for survival in the concentration camps, and indeed throughout their lives ever since. This preparatory stress period, undergone within the family unit, served to some degree as a 'toughening' experience for many, which helped to mediate the impact of the initial acute, overwhelming trauma and shock upon

arrival in the concentration camp and increased their chances of 'adaptation' and survival. In contrast, those torn from their families later in the war adapted less well."

That would, of course, apply to someone like me.

What happens to feelings? Students often ask me to recall how I felt back then. This is a hard question for me. Surviving was such an overriding challenge that my feelings must have been deeply repressed. I didn't let myself feel or I would have been engulfed in a lethal tsunami of emotion. That effort of repression may explain the difficulty of calling up the most painful memories.

Another theory that relates to me was proposed by sociology Professor Elmer Luchterhand, an American who served in the US army in Germany from 1943-46, which included liberation of the concentration camp victims. Like Davidson, he spent more than two decades of his professional career interviewing Holocaust survivors in depth. He believed that pairing was an essential part of survival. You did better if you were part of a twosome.

A pair, of course, could be mother and child. And, his most chilling sentence to me, "When one partner died or was removed, replacement was swift." It sounds so callous.

I was fortunate to find those who wanted to help me. If these psychologists are right, although it might seem counterintuitive, the need to take care of me, paradoxically, might have helped my mothers to survive. I certainly hope so. I owe these women my life.

April 15, 1945. For me, the war is over. I am nine and a half and alone in the world. All my mothers are gone.

But how can I live with this extreme loneliness? Everyone is searching for loved ones and struggling to make a new life.

Did I actively seek a new mother, consciously or subconsciously? I think of myself as a cat seeking a new home.

Chapter 13

MY SWEDISH MOTHER

I ride in the ambulance train from Bergen-Belsen to Lubeck, a major ferry port, where we are treated at the Cambria Barracks, renamed the Swedish Transit Hospital.

Our treatment includes more washing with hoses. I don't mind. I am so happy that the Swedes are willing to have us. I embrace their ethic of cleanliness, glad to be beyond the years of imposed filth in cattle cars and starvation camps.

Group portrait of the staff of the ambulance train that took survivors from Bergen-Belsen to Sweden for recuperation. Sunday, July 1, 1945, Photograph 41271, courtesy of Charles Rennie, US Holocaust Memorial Museum.

Soldiers and health care workers place me on a boat called "Castlehome" which sails from Germany to Sweden. The dock leads to a long boardwalk. Walking is so difficult that even a few hundred feet feels like a marathon. In the end, I am too weak to walk, so I am carried.

I am transferred to the so-called "aliens' camp" in Bjarred, a coastal town that's part of the Lomma Municipality in Skane County. It's about 12 miles (20 kilometers) north of Malmo, six miles west of Lund.

In late May 1945, Sweden offered to take the sick children from Bergen-Belsen, and to give us six months of treatment in Swedish sanatoria. After several weeks of medical treatment in the hospital barracks in Bergen-Belsen, which was turned into a displaced persons camp, the staff began transferring us by ship to Sweden for recuperation.

Several of the parents who have permission to go to Sweden because they're accompanying their survivor children are from Piotrkow, like me, and are friendly towards me. I don't think they really know me or my family, but my being from Piotrkow is enough for them to reach out to me. This feels good.

In Sweden, we're given pudding and jelly to fill our shrunken stomachs. The nurses know about those who died from eating the wrong food in Bergen-Belsen. We eat bland potatoes and fish balls, fruit, and berries, sweet cream and sour cream. We have to drink fish oil, and we comply even though it tastes bad. We get thick pancakes for breakfast. We're encouraged to play outside and to bask in the sunshine. We get new clothing, including warm wool coats.

How lonely I am. Throughout the war, I hoped that my parents would somehow return. I was waiting to

List No. 1

ABOUT JEWS LIBERATED FROM GERMAN CONCENTRATION CAMPS ARRIVED IN SWEDEN IN 1945

WORLD JEWISH CONGRESS   THE JEWISH AGENCY FOR PALESTINE
RELIEF AND REHABILITATION DEP.   RESCUE COMMITTEE

GREV MAGNIGATAN 11
S T O C K H O L M

Lewkowicz, Josek, 6/6/18, Dom-
   browa.
Lewkowicz, Kajla, 20/4/21, Lututow.
Lewkowicz, Kalman, 12/5/12, Sob-
   kow.
Lewkowicz, Manila, 15/10/23, Lodz.
Lewkowicz, Matka, 5/8/26, Lodz.
Lewkowicz, Matka, 5/9/26, Lodz.

Liebhaber-Futerman, Helene,
   10/3/07, Warszawa.
Librach, Jadzia, geb. Librach,
   15/4/12, Radom.
Lichtensztajn, Ajzyk, 3/1/24, Sosno-
   wiec.
Lichtenstein, Fredzia, 1936, Piotrkow.
Lichtenstein, Genia, 10/4/22, Wilna.

Rena's name is found on the official list of Jews liberated from concentration camps and sent to Sweden for recuperation. On this list, she is listed as Fredzia Lichtenstein, from Piotrkow.

tell them everything that had happened to me since we parted. They would want to know. They would want me to unburden myself. Poppa promised to meet me after the war. He surely must be coming. I just have to wait, if impatiently.

Like other orphans, I fantasize that my parents might somehow be safe in Palestine, so I tell myself that coming for me will take a little longer.

But this hope is tempered by the acknowledgment that the trains carrying nearly everyone from Piotrkow brought my mother and brothers to Treblinka, where all the "passengers" were murdered.

In my heart of hearts, I think I know they aren't coming back, and that I am alone in the world.

According to psychologist Hans Keilson, who spoke of "sequential traumatization" there were three stages of traumatization for us Holocaust orphans: separation from family, survival during the war, and returning to "what no longer exists" at the end of the war. Keilson believed that the last stage was the most traumatic, because it was then that the orphans like me understood the irreversibility of what happened.

Knowing that everything once dear to me is lost is an unbearable reality.

The typhus, which I somehow avoided during most of the war, has a firm hold of me. The lice are gone, but I am so sick that in Sweden that I am transferred to a hospital in Hassleholm, a nearby town for treatment.

I am diagnosed with both typhus and diphtheria, potentially deadly diseases.

While researching this book, Barbara Sofer contacted this hospital where the staff was kind enough to forward my hospital records. Let me remind you how exciting it

Rena (circled), in Sweden with other survivor children.

was for me to find records. Everything I know about my early years is sketchy memory. I remember being in the hospital. I remember that I had typhus. But suddenly here is my hospital chart with the doctors' notes on it. (A Swedish-speaking physician at Hadassah Hospital in Jerusalem kindly translated it.)

Typhus means severe headache, high fever, stupor and delirium. The mortality rate can be as high as 60 percent. Antibiotics weren't available for us, but with vastly improved nutrition in Sweden, the removal of the lice that caused the disease, and overall care, I pull through. Once again I miraculously beat the odds.

My mind is fuzzy. In the hospital, there are Swedish families who come to visit. They are so healthy looking and attractive: blond, neatly dressed with round faces and bright blue eyes. Sometimes their eyes get teary when they visit me. Someone tells me they have seen the photographs of Bergen-Belsen.

There was no war in Sweden. I don't understand how that can be. Children here went to school, had birthday parties, enjoyed thick pancakes with syrup while we were starving. Now these nice men and women want to help me. By the time I am well enough to think clearly, months have gone by.

Sweden has a mixed Holocaust record. Sweden remained neutral in World War II. On one hand, Jews who could get in, particularly from the other Scandinavian countries of Norway and Denmark, were given asylum. Some 8,000 Danish Jews crossed the Oresund Straits and escaped to Sweden in October 1943. Hero Raoul Wallenberg, a Swedish diplomat in Budapest, managed to save thousands of Jews by offering them protective passports. On the other hand, Swedish-based German companies could fire their Jewish employees. But most of all, the hundreds of thousands of Jews who could have had shelter in Sweden found the country's gates closed, and went to their deaths.

During the last few weeks of the war, the Swedish Red Cross launched its "White Buses" program, to rescue Scandinavian concentration camp inmates. The Swedish negotiations were led by Count Folke Bernadotte. Estimates differ on how many prisoners were saved, somewhere from 15,000 to 30,000. The Swedish Red Cross took a major role in these end-of-war rescue efforts, setting up some 150 rehabilitation centers for survivors.

I can never judge Sweden. I was reborn in Sweden. I will be forever grateful to that country and its people. The Swedes are energetic, straight-forward, and punctual. They have a sort of no-nonsense approach to getting things done, combined with a warm human touch, which I'm sure was beneficial for us. I thrived under their care. They saved my life when I was so sick.

Among the Swedish people who come to visit me are a sweet man and woman. They bring me red and white candy canes. The man is particularly kind. He carves me a folk figurine of an old man and woman. The couple takes me and other friends to the movies. The Swedish couple also brings me a doll,[1] with a fragile, porcelain head and eyes that moved up and down. One day the leg of the doll falls off. I feel terrible and don't want to show them the

Rena's carved folk figurine.

---

1   Today, this doll is what we'd call an antique China doll.

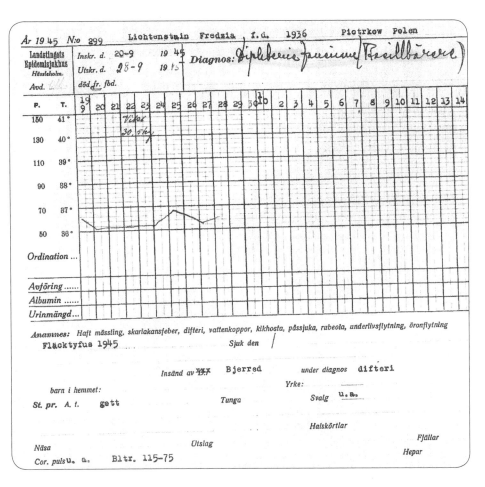

This chart is from Rena's (Fredzia Lichtenstein's) 1945 hospital records in Sweden. Her temperature is not normal, and she is diagnosed with Fleck typhus, which is an acute febrile disease with eczema, caused by the bacterium Rickettsie prowazkii. It is transmitted by lice.

broken doll. The man sees it and, without saying anything, fixes it. I am grateful and relieved. I'm also surprised that something can be so easily repaired. I've lived in a world of unrepairable brokenness.

I am ten years old, and ten-year-olds don't usually play with dolls, but I have missed my childhood. In some ways, I am like an old lady in a child's body. In other ways, I yearn to return to my protected childhood when I was just a happy little girl.

The Swedish man and woman live in a wooden house near the hospital. They want me to go home with them. They want me to become their daughter. I tell them yes. I like the Swedish man and woman. I am ready to be their daughter. Then I will be safe. They want to make arrangements to adopt me, but the people I have met from Piotrkow stand in the way.

How could these Swedes take this little Jewish survivor to a Christian home? In the end, the negative voices prevail. I have to stay with the Jews and go to the Jewish place they called Palestine. They keep saying that my parents might be in Palestine and I might miss seeing them forever.

I am very sad and disappointed. I am so lonely, but I make friends in the hospital with other children. Even after all the evil that has happened to us, we children have retained the capacity for friendship.

By the time I leave the hospital, I look different from the girl who was lifted from among the dead in Bergen-Belsen. I have gained weight and my skin is pink, not grey. The filthy rags are gone. I have skirts and blouses and a woolen coat, thanks to the help from organizations and charity of neighbors. Ironically, I look like a little Swedish girl. I look like the natural daughter of the Swedish woman who has offered to be my mother.

I meet relatives for the first time since I separated from my father. Yitzhak Hirsch (Irving) Cymberknopf, Aunt Bina's son who worked with us in the Hortensia glass factory is ten years older than me. He is in Sweden, too. He tells me that only four of us cousins have survived, and that 144 aunts, uncles and first cousins are dead. The numbers don't mean anything to me. His confirmation that my parents and brothers are not among the survivors feels like nails in my chest. He tells me what my address was in Piotrkow so that it can be properly recorded if anyone comes to look for me.

Another surviving cousin is Yitzhak Rushinek, my Aunt Leah's son, who is also older than me. My Aunt Rachel's son, Joe, is alive, too. I am the youngest member of the family and the only girl to have survived.

Looking back at it, I would have expected an overwhelming feeling of joy at finding a few of my many cousins alive. I don't recall feeling that way. It was clear that my cousins were struggling to create new lives themselves and couldn't possibly volunteer to take care of me.

There was also a female relative, a distant cousin, I think, who knitted me a blue sweater. Oddly this Jewish cousin knitted reindeer onto the sweater. She later disappeared. I have no idea who the woman relative was. Later, when my American adoptive parents searched for relatives who would have first claim on me, no one stepped forward.

When I am strong enough, I discover the joys of a swing. My legs pump up in the cool Swedish air. The breeze feels pleasant on my cheeks.

When I got to America, I learned the poem, "The

Swing" by Robert Louis Stevenson. "Oh – I do think it's the pleasantest thing, ever a child can do!" But none of my classmates would ever know what it meant to go "up in the air and flying again" after being an abused and terrified slave.

After the hospital, I am sent to another survivor camp in a town called Tinsgryd.

Look up Tinsgryd today. The municipality of Tingsgryd is eager to absorb immigrants.

Here's their ad:

> Move to Tinsgryd Commune! In our municipality, nature is always right next door. Colorful fruit orchards stand shoulder to shoulder with calm forests and you're never far from water – several hundred lakes offer exciting fishing, relaxing canoeing or a swim.

In Tinsgryd in 1945, we are a gaggle of Jewish children who have spent most of our early years figuring out strategies to survive. We can hardly believe our good luck coming into this beautiful countryside. The trees are heavy with crisp apples.

We are determined to gather those apples. Partly it is the game and the challenge. Partly it's our lingering food insecurity that makes those apples such an appealing prize.

I climb on a fence. I can reach the apples. I pull them off, one after the other until I have six. I can carry six apples in my pockets and in my hands.

I hear the farmer shouting, "Get away, you children. Thief! Stop stealing my apples."

I begin to run. I hear his footsteps running behind me. I need to hide. There is a wooden outhouse. I run in and slam the door. I throw all of my apples into the outhouse toilet. There is no flush, of course. There is no way to redeem them. The farmer will find them and ask who has stolen them.

I am so stupid, I think. This is terrible. You can't be stupid to survive. You can't be stupid. Sharpen your wits! The farmer never comes after me. I don't know when he finds the apples. No one seems to care. I am never punished.

Close to seventy years later I can still remember my heart pounding. I remember my fear. I remember thinking that you can't be stupid if you are going to survive.

We recovering kids enjoy the Swedish winter. The snow in Sweden seems different from the snow in Poland. Here it's a source of fun to make snowmen and throw snowballs. Before, it was one more barrier to survival. The Swedish snow is so high we have walls like a tunnel around the path. But now we have warm clothes and warm, plentiful food.

There are always adults arriving in Sweden seeking missing children. I still have illogical hopes that someone will come looking for me. It's not as if I don't believe my cousin that all my family is gone. I'm hoping one aunt or uncle might have survived. Even in Tinsgryd there are children with one parent or an older sister or an uncle who made it through.

No one comes for me. I am alone in a world in which most children belong to families. I live in a small house, probably what the Swedes called "hytte," sort of a cottage vacation home. I share it with a girl named Lucia,[2] and her mother. I am also friends with a girl a little older than me named Helena, who has come to Sweden with her

---

2   Today she is Sara ben Ari and lives in Haifa, Israel.

father's girlfriend.

Helena is older and learned to read and write before the war, but for me learning to count and memorizing the alphabet in the camp school is a new experience.

After the war and clean-up, Bergen-Belsen became one of the largest Displaced Persons camps in Europe with Jews arriving from all over Europe, seeking shelter and seeking surviving relatives. Almost immediately, these emaciated survivors began to revive Jewish life with prayer services and schools.

Among them was a woman named Anna Philipstahl who would play a critical role in my life. Philipstahl wasn't her real name. Somewhere, sometime she had acquired a passport with that name. This good woman was born, Anna Paine, on August 18, 1903, in the city of Ochtendung in the western part of Germany. She was a bookkeeper. She married a man named Baumgarten who was in the oil business. They lived in Druhobycz in Poland (today in the Ukraine). He was sent to Siberia by the Soviets as a counter-revolutionary. She, her two sons, and her daughter Fannie all survived the war, but only her son Sigmund and Fannie are with her.

Anna's son Sigmund is 14, and knows several languages. He's young and hardy enough to serve as a translator with groups of children going to Sweden. He insists that his mother come, too. And so Anna (Baumgarten) Philipstahl arrives in Sweden when I do, and is also relocated to Tinsgryd, with Sigmund and Fanny.

I know she'll be leaving soon. She is waiting for papers to immigrate to the United States. Her older brother David (like mine!) moved to the US before the war, and is serving in the US army in Europe. He has applied for visas for Anna and her children.

At last their visas arrive. But by then, her daughter Fannie, a girl close to my age, has died. Like so many other children and adults whose bodies are weakened and who harbor unknown diseases from the concentration camps, she hasn't really survived the Holocaust.

In her grief, Anna turns to me and whispers an offer that will change my life forever. "Why don't you come to America as my daughter? Would you like to be my daughter?"

Rena (at the time of this picture in 1946, she is called Fannie) with her new mother, Anna Philipstahl, in Tinsgryd. Anna is circled in the second row. Rena is circled in the bottom row, arm-in-arm with Lucia.

I cannot believe my good fortune! My answer, of course, is "yes!"

I am thrilled to have a new mother. This kind and elegant woman wants me! I don't know anything about America except that it is where so many survivors want to go.

Joy curls around my heart like a purring kitten. I am ready to attach myself to a new protector. I will have a new mother. This time, no one is going to stop me. I am Anna's little girl now. I am not alone in the world.

Chapter 14

MY MOTHER ANNA

On March 26, 1946, I leave Sweden. From the moment I board the ship, I feel safe. I have a new mother and a new name.

Anna Philipstahl is my mother. My new name is Fannie Philipstahl.

I don't think twice about taking on a new identity. I don't think about it being odd or illegal to pretend to be a dead girl. No one suggests this behavior is wrong. After what we've been through, formalities are luxuries we can't afford. I have a new birthday and a new place of birth. According to Fannie's documents, I was born on February 15, 1936, in Germany. These will remain on my formal documents forever (even today when I know that they aren't correct).

For me, it's simple. I am not alone. I have a nice woman who wants to be my mother. She is going to a place totally unknown to me, but one which seems to be desirable for all of us displaced persons. Any survivor in Sweden who gets a visa to America literally dances with joy. They don't seem to be disappointed that they're not going to Palestine.

We sail away from Europe on the SS Drottningholm. The ship has been chartered by the United States from the Swedish American Line to carry special passengers – prisoner exchanges and family reunions – across the sea during wartime. The ship is grand, at 538 feet long and 60 feet wide with two masts and one funnel. There are 1,712 passengers on this voyage. I am given a green pants outfit

TO WHOM IT MAY CONCERN

This is to certify that Fredzia Lichtenstein, born 1936 in Piotrkow, Poland, entered Sweden 1945-07-26 in a transfer sponsored by the Swedish Red Cross from German concentration camps.

1945-07-26 she was transferred to an aliens camp in Bjärred
1945-08-10 she was transferred to a hospital in Hässleholm
1945-09-28 she was transferred to an aliens camp in Tingsryd.

1946-03-26 she left Sweden for U S A.

Ex officio

Harriet Johansson

Harriet Johansson

No charge
Rena Quint b. Fredzia Lichtenstein

This document was provided to Rena from the Swedish immigration office. It shows that Rena (Fredzia Lichtenstein) arrived in Sweden on July 26, 1945, and left Sweden on March 26, 1946. It also documents that she lived in Bjarred and Tinsgryd, and also her time as a patient in the Hassleholm hospital.

and a red dress for the ship. My wonderful new mother has a flare for color!

On board, abundant and delicious food is served. We kids have fun running around the ship, playing hide and seek, and other games from a childhood we missed and want to reclaim. I'm officially listed as passenger 901759624618. My age is listed as 10.

I feel elated leaving Europe with Anna. I watch the

churning water as the sea separates me from Europe, far from the ghetto and slave labor and concentration camps.

Aboard the ship, none of us kids talks about the Holocaust. No one shares tales of rats in the ghetto, hiding in sewers, watching executions of siblings. We children are sailing off to a new life and we don't want to recall the horrors of yesterday. Truth be told, no one exhibits sadness. We don't let ourselves dwell on loss. We have music, food, new friendships, and we're going to America.

I feel no ambivalence about leaving. By now, I've understood that no one is coming for me. I've internalized that my parents and brothers are dead. I am alone in the world except for Anna, who has decided to become my next mother. I feel so fortunate to have someone to love and care for me. I, too, am eager to sail off to a new life, with a new start and to forget all the terrible things that have happened to me. I know I am lucky that Anna has chosen me. Other girls wanted to be her replacement daughter, too and were disappointed that she chose me.

I stand with Anna and all the other passengers who enter New York Harbor. The Statue of Liberty comes into view.

Of course, I have no idea what is written on the pedestal of the great statue, Lady Liberty. Emma Lazarus, a Jewish woman, penned her immortal sonnet that was chosen for the statue.

> *"Give me your tired, your poor, your huddled masses yearning to breathe free, the wretched refuse of your teeming shore..."*

We are processed, and our health is checked in Ellis Island. Our names are compared with those on the ship's manifest. Despite all our past illness and our name changes, we pass muster. Anna, Sigmund and I are among the 15,535 Jewish immigrants who come to America in 1946, and the 10,870 who come to New York.

Next to my name, Fannie Philipstahl, in handwriting, a clerk adds that I am Anna's daughter!

Anna's family is waiting at the dock to take us home. Her brother David is still in Europe with the American army, so Rabbi Louis and Molly Goldberg come to greet us: Anna, her son Sigmund, and me, make-believe Fannie. Rabbi Goldberg signs that he will be the official guardian of the Philipstahls.

Soon after arrival, the Goldbergs move us out to a house in Lindenhurst, Long Island. I am enrolled in public school. Since it's so close to the end of the school year, the children are given extra time on the playground. They are very nice. They try to teach me English – one day "tree" and then "house" and "hat." It feels as if a new word is born every day. My favorite is "etc." They think it is sweet that I don't know English and I enjoy their affection.

Sigmund is now using the name Stanley, and I get a new American first name, too. My new name is Frances. No more "Fannie."

I have no toys, so someone brings me a doll and a baby carriage. I'm ten, but I'm delighted with these toys. I feel comfort in pushing my carriage and playing with my doll.

On Friday nights, for Shabbat dinner with the Goldbergs, Anna, Sigmund and I eat chicken soup and chicken fricassee, a mix of necks, belly buttons and meatballs. Sigmund and I complain that we always have the same dinner. We're bored.

Just imagine. A year earlier, I was eagerly awaiting dirty gruel, and here, I am fussing over repetitiveness in food. I guess that's healthy – a reassertion of our personalities.

After the Exodus from slavery in Egypt, the Israelites also complained about the sameness of the manna that sustained them in the desert. I remember that after liberation, survivors, who had been starving not too many weeks before, complained that the restorative food provided by the British was too treacly.

In the summer, we join a group of the Goldbergs' friends in a Catskill bungalow colony somewhere in the mountains. For all intents and purposes, I'm a full member of the family. We have one room and Anna cooks in a communal kitchen with the other moms. A built-in summer camp offers arts and crafts, a swimming pool, and blueberries to pick. I learn how to swim, how to ride a bike, and how to play jacks, similar to the games of my early childhood. Life is very good.

Then one day my mom Anna isn't in the kitchen when I come back from camp. I ask where she is. I am told that she isn't feeling well and has gone back to Long Island. The other adults say they'll keep an eye on Stanley and me. What would I like to eat?

Then the Goldbergs appear. They look very sad. "Gather your things, Frances," they tell me. "We're going back to Long Island."

They drive, without talking, to a place called Farmingdale. I'm scared.

When we get there, I understand. Anna has died. I only get the news that my new mother is gone at her funeral. I have no time to absorb this.

To make this even harder, I am attending my first funeral. I see a casket for the first time. What is this box? I see a cemetery on a beautiful grassy field for the first time. There are flowers and glossy stones. Is this a park?

All around me, well-dressed grown-ups are crying, wailing, saying what a shame it is, how she didn't get a chance. It reminds me of the crying at the beginning in the ghetto. In the concentration camps, we learned never to cry.

No one has prepared me for the funeral. I am totally confused. Either they think I will not understand or that I know so much of death that I don't need preparation. I have no mother to turn to. No one takes my hand.

My mother is dead. Maybe they think I don't love her because she isn't my real mother, but I do. On September 18, 1946, Anna Philipstahl, who isn't really Anna Philipstahl, gives up her earthly existence in Manhattan County, New York. She is 43 years old. She joins the thousands of so-called survivors, like Fannie, who died after the war.

I would learn later that many so-called Holocaust survivors hadn't really made it past the finish line. They were already harboring the diseases and physical incapacities that would end their lives earlier. Even advanced American medicine couldn't cure Anna.

Anna survived the Holocaust and, out of extreme kindness, took me under her bandaged wing and volunteered to be my mother forever. She foisted me on her relatives, willing or not. She gave me the gift of her daughter's birth date, her name – and her visa.

Sigmund has relatives around to comfort and shelter him. I am not their real relative. I am only a make-believe Fannie. I am a child who needs to be clothed and fed, sent to school, and treated as a child. Anna was willing to do all this for me. Now that she isn't here, who will be my mother?

I can tell they don't want to keep me. They just want Sigmund, but he says he doesn't want to stay with them.

How am I going to survive? Now I am alone once more, and, to make it worse, in this strange country where I barely speak English.

Men with beards dig a deep hole in the ground. Everyone is crying. I am bewildered and frightened, but I don't cry. I never cry. I don't remember how. Moreover, I don't understand why everyone is crying. Only one person has died. I have lived among the 30,000 dead in Bergen-Belsen. My mother, my father, my brothers, my cousins, my aunts and uncles, my Mother the Teacher have all died. Why fuss so much over the death of one person? I don't understand. I am filled with need for a mother, but I can't cry.

No one explains to me when and why Anna died. It will take decades before this mystery is revealed.

Many years later I met Sigmund's wife Marsha and daughter Nancy who were sad and angry that he never told them about me – the family they had always missed.

Nancy shared the following letters with me that her late father had written (Edward was Sigmund's older brother who was still in Europe after the Holocaust):

(Letter 1)
Dear Edward,

I know this letter will cause you sorrow. But that's what happened and no one could help it. Our beloved mother has died. Somebody did everything that was possible. He took her to the best doctors in New York. Momma was getting shots, every shot cost $40 every hour and penicillin every 10 minutes but it didn't help. It was meant to be.

Beloved Dziunek (her brother David Pane) did everything that was in his power, as if a saint.

Now I have one request. I want you to come as soon as possible because, you, Dziunek and Milek are the closest to me. I think that Dziunek is going somewhere and when he calls you, don't give him any pain because he now is my father, my mother and everything that I own. Therefore get here as soon as possible.

We have a small apartment, me and Fredzia (Fannie). I and Fredzia will go to school and you will go to the university.

Try to come because I'm waiting for you.

Kisses,
Your brother Stanley

⌘⌘⌘

(Letter 2, from Anna's brother David (Dziunek)

Dear Edward,

Your mother is not alive anymore. I want you to know I did everything I could to save her. And if I didn't do everything I could then I didn't know what to do. I am not able to write anymore today.

Love,
Dziunek

⌘⌘⌘

(Letter 3)
September 18, 1946
My dearest brother,

Unfortunately, I don't know how to begin this letter because it's very difficult to write to you after so many unfortunate things that we had to make. We have today to add one more sad news and I never expected that I would be the one who has to inform you about the death of our mother and father.

I must today add one more information about our dear sister and the only one we had. Our dearest Anja (Anna) died today at 1 in the morning. She was fighting like a lion to try to live. (Reference to the lion was because of a city in the region in Poland called "lion city.")

After I learned about her illness I went quickly to America. When I came she was feeling better and I was sitting with her in the hospital. I was convinced everything was fine. That's why I sent a telegram. She was very happy I came and we made plans and I went to the apartment she was renting. I arranged so she would have everything she needs when she comes from the hospital.

Unfortunately, on Friday she felt worse again. I had doctors take care of her. Unfortunately they couldn't tell me anything what is wrong with her and they couldn't find the reason for her illness.

I moved her to the biggest hospital in NY, I gave them all the money I had to move her. I had the best surgeon in the world and they started from the beginning. She felt better on Sunday. Unfortunately, on Monday it was worse again. On Tuesday, at 5 in the afternoon she was in a coma. I asked for the children to come but she could not recognize them when they came. At one in the morning, she died. She was fighting. She didn't want to die. She was begging me for life and I was broken up because I couldn't help her.

The doctors couldn't find anything. One thing they are claiming that she may have been in a basement and a rat may have bitten her or she ate pork that was spoiled.

From eating that, she got some sort of bacteria which attacked her gall bladder and then the liver, which was rotting inside of her. They could deal with that but she developed complications. She got pneumonia. She got better but then a clot in her lungs, all due to the bacteria.

I was trying by all means I had to keep her alive. She was receiving penicillin and we did everything that was possible but nothing could help.

The children are doing well. Lusio (Stanley) was behaving like a grownup man but I fell apart like a little child. The first time in my life I couldn't handle that after all these years of surviving Hitler that all the money I had couldn't save her. I spent $5000 to save her and it didn't work. It's a curse that after finding her I couldn't save her.

It's after the funeral and she is buried in Wellwood Cemetery. I decided to keep the apartment and the children will live there and maybe I'll live there, too.

As I said in the telegram, I have a visa to enter Poland and I hope that then I will tell you everything in person.

I will do everything to keep the children in good life and we will see what will happen when we see each other.

After losing our beloved ____, I thought that

would be all but it didn't happen like that. My heart is bleeding. Milek, remember that I did everything I could but couldn't save her but I cannot write to Edward because I'm so broken up. He asked Lusio to write to Edward but to tell someone else to write what you feel is difficult.

Love,
David

Chapter 15

MY MOTHER LEAH

My instincts are right: Anna's relatives are not going to keep me. I hear them talking. With all due respect, I am not their relative. While Anna was alive, they were willing to humor her. But this child is not their responsibility.

What are they going to do with me? There are orphanages in America, of course. I dread the thought of being alone in an institution. Who will have power over me there? I feel vulnerable.

I hear Louis and Molly Goldberg talking about Leah and Jacob Globe, a couple they know that lives down the street from Louis's brother and sister-in-law, Max and Esther, in Brooklyn. The Globes have no children. Perhaps they would want a ten-year-old who has gone through the Holocaust and who now calls herself Frances Philipstahl?

They call the couple and explain my situation. I understand that the man and woman are interested. They are willing to meet me. The Goldbergs tell me that I have an invitation for Shabbat from a nice couple named Mr. and Mrs. Globe.

To say I am nervous doesn't quite cover how anxious I feel. I don't want to show it. I want the people I am visiting to think I'm a cheerful little girl.

The Goldbergs drive me to the front door of a big house on Lincoln Road in Brooklyn. They ring the bell. The wide wooden door opens. A woman with dark hair and hazel eyes like mine opens it. "Come on in," she

Max and Esther Goldberg, with their daughter-in-law.

says and smiles. "We're glad you've come, Frances. I'm Leah Globe."

I step inside. The door closes behind me. The house smells wonderful.

Something moves and catches my eye. A dog! They have a dog living in their home. I hold my breath. An image of the Nazi dogs snarling at me goes through my mind and I begin to shake.

Then I realize that this dog is little and it's wagging its tail. Leah reaches down and pats him under the chin. To my surprise, I want to do the same but don't dare. He follows us into the kitchen. I don't want to show I'm afraid. Maybe liking this dog is one of the qualifications for being adopted.

Leah offers me something to eat, but I tell her I'm okay, even though I'm a little hungry. I don't want to appear too needy or greedy.

Chicken soup is simmering on the stove. There's a bowl with thin noodles to go into the soup. On the counter sits a lemon meringue pie, with waves of meringue like a fancy hairdo.

On the counter is a blue metal box that I've seen in other homes. I can read the letters: JNF, but I don't know what they stand for.

A tall handsome man with a mustache joins us in the kitchen. "This is my husband, Jacob," Leah says.

Jacob takes my small suitcase and I follow him up to the room they have for me on the second floor. "I'll show you around," he says. The house has two living rooms near a big kitchen.

The dog follows us. "Don't worry, he doesn't bite," Jacob reassures me, sensing my nervousness. "His name is Buddy *Hakelev*, that's Hebrew for dog."

Upstairs there are four bedrooms. The man shows me my room. It's huge, with a mahogany bed with a soft mattress and lots of blankets. Jacob opens the door of a big closet to show me where to put my things. Best of all, there's a desk that Jacob shows me opens with a mirror that pulls up inside.

Before I unpack, he shows me the third floor, "the pool room," he says. I think at first they have a swimming pool, but they don't. There's a big table with a game with balls and a place to keep the sticks. "It came with the house," Jacob says. I'm not quite sure what that means.

He lets me unpack. From the first hour I meet the Globes, they give me time to be by myself. Either they understand that I need privacy, or they are used to time by themselves, too.

I'm not entirely alone. While I'm unpacking, Buddy, the dog, comes and sits on my rug and looks at me. His tail whacks the wood-paneled floor. I'm breathing fast but don't want to call Jacob.

I open the vanity, keeping an eye on the dog. I look at myself in the mirror. My hair has grown thicker. It's blond and wavy. My cheeks are round now. They no longer sink into the bones of my face. I remember that the Goldbergs warned me I should be polite and smile. I smile at myself in the mirror. Be friendly, I coach myself. Either these people take you or you're going to an orphanage.

Leah calls from downstairs. "Frances, come down. We're going to light Shabbat candles." Buddy follows me down the steps. A new friend.

Leah offers me cookies. "We won't eat for a while," she says. "I don't want you to be hungry."

I am hungry. There are two kinds of cookies: gingersnaps and chocolate. I take a chocolate cookie. It's delicious. The chocolate melts in my mouth. Leah watches me eat and smiles. Leah gives me a puzzle with many pieces. "You can get started on Shabbat," she says.

Then she gets ready to light her tall, silver Shabbat candlesticks in the dining room. Leah covers her eyes to light them and doesn't speak for a long time. I wonder what she's saying to herself or to God.

God is a mystery to me. I know He has kept me alive, but why has He taken my father, my brothers, and so many of my mothers. Will he take Leah and Jacob?

Leah and Jacob. My biological mother's name is Sarah, like the Biblical matriarch who was married to patriarch Abraham. Their grandson Jacob married two sisters, Rachel and Leah. In the Bible, Leah is the more fertile of the two sisters.

But Leah and Jacob have been unable to have children. This is what I've heard the Goldbergs say. She and Jacob are both 46. That's too old to have babies I guess. What do I know about such things? I remember women having babies in Bergen-Belsen. I remember the screams.

Jacob owns a plumbing supply business, which sells sinks and pipes for houses, he says. Leah was born in Poland, like me, but she seems totally American. Cousins and friends come to the house for Shabbat dinner. I wonder if they always come or if they want to meet me and check me out. They speak English too fast for me to follow.

The back of my neck tenses up. What do they think of me? I'm quiet and I try to eat nicely and to smile a lot.

One of the guests is a little girl named Rhea Mandelbaum.[1] Her mother is a friend of Leah's. She smiles back at me and says I can come to her house to play. She says she has a lot of toys. Will I be here long enough to play with her toys?

The food is delicious. I like the way the noodles swirl in the soup. The potato kugel is hot and filling. Leah makes gefilte fish like the kind they served in the synagogue in Long Island and there's a big salad with lettuce and tomatoes. The pie is the most delicious food I've ever tasted, sour and sweet at the same time.

At dinner, Jacob and two friends talk about the news from Palestine. My ears perk up. I understand that they are very interested in what is happening there. I wonder if they will send me to Palestine where many of the children in Sweden were going.

I sleep through the night in my big bed. I hope I'll be able to stay here. I pull the quilts close over me and feel good, but I don't want to let my guard down.

Leah says we're going to the synagogue.

I love the singing in the synagogue. It feels nice going like a family to synagogue, sitting with Leah like mother

---

1   Now Rhea Israel, who lives in Rehovot, Israel.

and daughter in the women's section. I don't let myself think about my childhood. There's too much at stake for me to become gloomy.

In the afternoon, I work on my puzzle and play with Buddy, whom I'm getting used to. Dogs can be pretty nice, I decide.

At the end of Shabbat, Leah and Jacob ask me if I want to stay with them and to be their little girl. Just like that! My heartbeat speeds up. I am engulfed with relief and joy.

Yes, yes, yes!

For me, the answer is obvious. Of course. I need a new mother, and this mother comes with a new father, too, with a big house, and pies, and a dog named Buddy.

I tell them yes, thank you very much. They smile and say they're happy, but they don't look fully happy. They don't hug me yet. That's okay with me. I'm uncomfortable with hugs.

The Goldbergs drop off my few possessions. I still have the carved figures from Sweden. I put my things in my new closet.

I meet Jacob Globe's sister, Rose, and her children, Judy and Jonathan. They are nice to me, but I have a feeling that they are not so glad that Leah and Jacob will have their own girl now and pay less attention to them.

"The school year has already begun," Leah says. Just like regular moms and daughters, we go shopping for back-to-school clothing. Leah buys me a pea coat and brown lace-up shoes. All of this is happening so fast.

I have a problem. No one ever taught me to tie laces. I'm so embarrassed.

Leah just smiles and sits with me until I get it right. She doesn't make me feel stupid.

Nearby is a neighborhood New York City public school. They're all called PS and then a number. PS 92.

The Globes suggest that I change my name before registering! I've already been Fredzia, called Freidel in Yiddish, and then I was the boy Froim, back to Fredzia, then Fannie of blessed memory and the so-called American Frances.

Leah says that since Frances and Fannie are not my real names, and Fredzia sounds European, that I should use the Hebrew named Rena, which means joy and is easy to pronounce. I agree easily. Why not? So I become Rena. They give me the wonderful feeling that I am their joy and I want to return their generosity and love. What's a name?

I am 10 years old, now Rena Globe. I practice saying it. Rena Globe. Rena Globe. Rena Globe. A girl with blond hair and green eyes. I put myself to sleep with it, tucked into a soft bed with clean sheets and a cozy blanket. Rena Globe. Rena Globe. Rena Globe.

Benjamin Nachami, the son of Drs. Nachami, she a pediatrician, and he an obstetrician, agrees to walk with me to school. He is a very smart boy, everyone says.

I, on the other hand, am not smart. I don't know how to read, write or spell. I don't understand numbers. This makes me miserable. I want to fit in. No, I want to be among the smart kids.

My teacher, Miss Dutney of the third grade, loves to give spelling tests. I fail them all. I hate failing. I don't know what to do when she calls out the words I can't spell and all the other children are bent over their papers writing.

Miss Dutney sees me looking around. She thinks I'm cheating. She sends me the principal! All the children in the class look at me as I leave the room. I walk down the hall terrified, with my head hanging down. What will my punishment be? What did I do?

I try to explain to the principal. In my broken English,

I tell the principal that I couldn't cheat. I'm too dumb to cheat.

He calls my parents. Soon, they come rushing into his office. I look at Leah's and Jacob's faces. They don't seem angry, but I am worried they will send me away.

I am a mix of repentant and defiant. There is a lot of talk. The principal is smarter than Miss Dutney.

The next day I am moved up from third to fourth grade. There my teacher is Mrs. McKinney. She seems nicer. In addition to reading, writing and 'rithmetic, we have singing classes and music appreciation. We must sing "Country Gardens," a song which is popular with school orchestras. The English folk tune is unfamiliar to me. The words are too long. "How many kinds of sweet flowers grow in an English country garden?" we sing. The lyrics include such words as flox, lady smocks, bobolink and thrush. I have no idea of what I'm singing, but I try to sing along. I do love music.

This class is better, but one day at a school assembly, I'm in trouble again. I am looking around, and supposedly not paying attention. Once again I am sent to see the principal.

I am mortified. But now I'm defiant and not so repentant. I haven't done anything wrong and I know that in America the punishments are bearable.

I say that I wasn't afraid of the Nazis and I'm not afraid of the teachers. The local educators are stumped.

No other European children go to my school or live in my neighborhood. I don't even know anyone else who was adopted, let alone anyone who has been through the Holocaust and lost her family.

Leah and Jacob are new at parenting, but they realize that the situation in public school is hopeless. I'm not going to fit in. Leah and Jacob follow their instincts and take me out of public school.

I may act defiant, but the feeling of pain and helplessness that I experience in the American public school system eclipses the pain and fear of my past. I am singled out to be humiliated. That is something I never had in the ghetto or Bergen-Belsen where we were all treated like trash.

The Globes seek private Jewish education for me. Unhappily, the first private school my new parents approach for me, the Yeshiva of Flatbush, immediately rejects me. It's a rather prestigious Jewish school where the children's achievements are bragged about. The principal assumes their curriculum, which is half English and half Hebrew and Bible, will be too hard for a little refugee girl who hasn't mastered English. (Maybe he is right.)

(Ironically, my husband will one day become chairperson of the board of the school that rejected me. I reminded the administrators that they rejected me.)

Later I am rejected by the Yeshiva of Crown Heights.

Another school principal agrees to take me as a student. In 1927, a Conservative school called the Center Academy was established as a coeducational elementary school in the Brooklyn Jewish Center, which was an Orthodox congregation that practiced Conservative Judaism. It even has a woman principal. Leah thinks teachers in this Jewish school might have a more sympathetic attitude towards a mixed-up, defensive little girl who has been through loss, forced labor and concentration camps.

There are only ten children in the class, so the teacher has time for all of us. Indeed, the new school works out well.

In addition to the small classes and empathetic staff, I get a private tutor to help me overcome the language barrier. Everyone knows I'm adopted, although the process hasn't yet finished. Polite children are taught not to mention it. I never talk about adoption, or about anything that happened to me in the Holocaust, or the difficult start of my life in America.

Leah and Jacob are trying to get permission to adopt me. They have to make sure there are no relatives who could suddenly claim me. They send out search letters to agencies around the world. Maybe they will find my parents and my brothers. I never stop hoping, even though I know in my head that they are all dead.

On February 15, my new parents make me a birthday party, even though we know that the date we're celebrating is really Fannie's birthday! I don't know my real date of birth.

Leah bakes cupcakes and frosts them. She buys hats and puts up banners. Girls from school and synagogue are happy to come to this party. I'm delighted to be the center of all this attention.

No word about my biological parents has come from all the agencies they have contacted. I push this out of my mind.

Leah and Jacob take me skating. I'm a good skater. I learned to skate in Sweden, or perhaps relearned the skill I'd had as a preschooler in Piotrkow.

One day, I put my foot through the ice in Prospect Park. I go to a friend's house to change, not to tell Leah who will be upset. I need to protect her from the naughty Rena.

On the whole, Leah and Jacob give me a lot of freedom. That's their personal style – they aren't "helicopter parents," hovering over their children. I learn to use roller skates. Jacob teaches me to ride a bike. Leah and Jacob allow me to bike on my own, visiting friends or just to take an evening ride. Their confidence in me gives me a feeling of self-confidence.

Soon it's summer. The oaks and elms in the yard are covered with green leaves. I love the scent of the purple lilacs. Pansies and yellow daffodils line the walkways.

Leah and Jacob want to send me to a sleepaway camp! That's where the boys and girls in the neighborhood go. I know this is considered a treat. The girls in my class who are going are considered very lucky. I pretend that I'm happy about this, too.

The idea of sleeping in a bunk of girls makes my stomach hurt. I put on a happy face as Leah sews labels with my name, Rena Globe, on them.

The camp is in the mountains. The first nights, girls in my bunk cry for their parents. I don't let myself feel unhappy, even though I would rather be in my room in Brooklyn, but I won't cry.

The second year in school is much easier. I speak English now and understand the habits of American children.

Now that I'm in a Jewish school I wonder for the first time about being Jewish. I didn't think much of being Jewish throughout the Holocaust or its aftermath. We were being persecuted because we were Jews, but I didn't think about the implications. There are those inside the barbed wire and those on the outside.

Now I am in an all Jewish school which instills pride in our peoplehood, teaches Hebrew and English, and celebrates, with great joy, the establishment of the Jewish State on May 15, 1948, two years after I arrive in the United States.

Both at home and at school, we follow with great pride and interest as the Jewish State comes into being. Jacob is a member of a club of Zionists who support the new country. I think of Lucia and other friends who are living there, and sometimes I fantasize that my parents and brothers are there, too, although I know they are dead. I shut down such thoughts. Why look for trouble? I have Leah and Jacob and a nice room in a big house. I am doing better in school. I have friends.

Every week, there is competition in class as to who can recite a certain daily prayer, *Ashrei,* the fastest. I still come in last. The words mean "Happy are those who dwell in Your House." One line of the prayer resonates. "The Lord supports all who fall, and raises all who are bowed down." I hope God will also help me read faster.

Even as the kids get to know me better, no one asks me to tell the class about the Holocaust. Just the opposite. The class is going to see "My Father's House," a film about Jews driven out of Poland who reunite in pre-State Israel. The teacher doesn't think it would be a good idea for me to go, and Leah and Jacob take this advice. Instead we go to see "Pinocchio." I don't complain. I am trying hard to put the events of my childhood behind me. That is Leah and Jacob's strategy, too. They encourage me to look forward, and not to dwell on my too-horrible-to-confront past.

I desperately want to be accepted. I never had a real girlfriend before coming to America. Now I have a best friend named Janet. Another girl seems jealous that Janet is my best friend. We are part of a group of six girls who are a close friendship circle. We're invited to our first Bar Mitzvah party. The boy's name is Barry.

The following summer Jacob's business has a setback. Expensive summer camp isn't an option. Instead, together with a neighbor who has a daughter my age, Leah hires an art tutor to give me lessons. I have neither talent nor much interest, but Leah herself is fascinated and becomes a skilled painter. That summer, she also teaches me how to sew. I don't even know how to thread a needle or sew on a button. These are skills I've missed growing up and Leah has wonderful instincts about helping me fill in the gaps without making a big deal of it.

More letters are sent through agencies to countries around the world to see if any relatives have first dibs on me. A cousin is found in Canada, but no one there is able or willing to take on an orphaned girl. They have their own challenges and say they would be overwhelmed by adding my expenses and needs. In short, no relatives want me. That's the bad news, but also the good news. Now Leah and Jacob are free to adopt me.

Not that taking care of me is so easy for two nearly 50-year-olds. My mother Leah confides to a friend that I am not easy. They have to deal with a strong-willed little girl who doesn't accept authority.

And when they are displeased because I misbehave, I threaten to leave them and run away.

Jacob Globe, a businessman, writes out a contract in which he and Leah agree to love me, and care for me forever, and I have to agree to be their daughter. No more running away. No more threats. They never like to go head to head with me in a fight, which is smart.

Growing up, I admire Leah, who always stands ram-rod straight and dresses so nicely. She has a large collection of bright jewelry pins. She never goes out without a handkerchief and often sews a pocket into her skirts and dresses so that she can carry one.

We both like parties. For one birthday party I wear curlers in my hair for three days before the party, and then can't get the tight curls out, until she comes to the rescue.

Not all is perfect. When I get my period for the first time, I am totally unprepared and think something terrible is happening to me. Leah has never mentioned that it would happen one day.

Despite my determination to close the door on the Holocaust, I have flashback moments of extreme fear. One day driving on a long deserted road with my parents, I am overwhelmed by terror. Where are they taking me? They are getting rid of me! I panic. Of course, nothing of the sort is happening. This is a family outing. But logic doesn't always rule my soul, as hard as I try to overcome emotions.

By the time I am in high school, I have become an excellent student, except for typing, math, and handwriting. With a little help from Jacob's brother-in-law Jack, I am admitted to Thomas Jefferson High School, on Pennsylvania Avenue in the Brownsville district of east Brooklyn. I play the cello in the school orchestra and join the Hebrew club. The girl who  didn't know a word of English at age 10 is elected to the Arista Honor Society!

My close friends know I am adopted, but no one makes a big deal of it.

I get my first pair of high heels for a Passover present, as part of the search for the "missing" piece of matzo at the Passover Seder.

At 16, I celebrate my Sweet 16 with a lavish party at our home. When I am 17, I am finally called to the immigration authority to take my citizenship test. I line up with other immigrants from all over the world. By

Rena, between her parents, Jacob and Leah Globe, August 1952.

then I speak fluent English with an American accent, and I know that George Washington was the first president and that Abraham Lincoln freed the slaves.

On December 30, 1952, Rena Globe proudly becomes a citizen of the United States of America. I am fully American.

By 17, no one can guess that I'm anything but a typical American teen. I wear bobby socks and a pony tail. I know the lyrics to popular songs particularly those by Eddie Fisher, whom we had a special affinity for as Jews. I go with friends to the movies and see "April in Paris" starring Doris Day and Ray Bolger. I like rock and roll.

At 18, my father teaches me to drive. I pass my registry of motor vehicles test the first time. Jacob hands me the car keys that night and lets me go out by myself. He and Leah are the perfect parents for an independent teen like me.

With my good Jewish background from going to religious school, I become a Sunday School teacher. When I'm home too late at night on a date or at parties, Leah substitutes for me so I can sleep in.

Jacob Globe has many biological cousins whom he's sponsored to leave Europe for America. Now I am able to teach them about American money and how to use the subways. I tutor them about Abraham Lincoln, George Washington, and the 48 American states for their citizenship tests.

Like other New York teens who are invited to take part in an accelerated program, I finish high school in three and a half years. In my graduation picture, I have a round face, thick wavy hair, and a wide smile.

Unlike most high school graduates in 1953, I am confident enough to go with a friend on a biking trip through Europe.

Europe! For my classmates, it's exotic and sophisticated. For me, it's the continent that nearly killed me. Yet, I am ready, even eager, to go on this adventure. I am so identified with my American friends that I almost forget my past.

My girlfriend and I sail on a ship from Canada to Southampton, England. We have an arrangement where we can stay on ship on Shabbat, so we won't violate our religious principles. Bikes are waiting at the ports. We meet the other members of the group. We bike first in Normandy and Paris, bike into Belgium and Holland. Only when the group takes the train into Germany, do I refuse to go. I don't explain why.

We meet up with the group in Denmark, then Sweden(!) and at last Scotland. I put my past experiences in Sweden out of my mind, as hard as that is to believe. I know that not too many teenagers would undertake such a trip. I am away for ten weeks with the total trust of Leah and Jacob! What a fortunate young woman I am to have such supportive and indulgent parents.

Even if as a teen, when others are mopey and share stories of unhappiness, I don't tell anyone about my tortured past. I don't want anyone to think of me as a victim. I don't want to expose myself to either the skepticism or sympathy towards "those who were in the camps."

I begin Brooklyn College in the fall. When I am 20, I become quickly engaged, but later break it off. Leah and Jacob seem relieved.

My major is psychology with a minor in education. On a whim, I take the teacher's qualification exam and pass it. The idea of earning my own living as a teacher appeals to me. I become a teacher. I will come back to psychology later I tell myself. I get a job teaching in a public school.

Chapter 16

MOTHER RENA

I take a summer vacation group tour to Israel in 1958. We sleep in the Rehavia Gymnasia in Jerusalem, travel around, take an old bus to Eilat, and sleep on the warm sand. I make a new, good friend in the lovely Eveline Rudolf.

Israel is the place where more survivors settled than anywhere else, but I don't go on a search for relatives. I do visit Lucia, a friend from the Swedish DP camp, now using the name Sarah Ben Ari. She lives in Haifa. She doesn't want to talk about the old days in the Holocaust. She is angry at God and doesn't want to have anything to do with religion, while I am deeply religious.

In the first week of October 1958, back in Brooklyn, we celebrate the holiday of Sukkot which, somewhat like Passover, marks the story of the Exodus from Egypt. In the desert, after Egypt, the ancient Israelites lived in thatched huts. So for eight days in the fall, observant Jewish families build these huts outside of their homes if the weather is mild enough. No desert here, just the scent of autumn leaves.

We enjoy long meals and singing and socializing. We young adults go from sukkah to sukkah. I am with my new friend Eveline and her brother Sheldon in their sukkah in Crown Heights in Brooklyn. One of the other guests is Emanuel Quint, who everyone called Manny. Not that I pay him much attention. He's just a skinny guy in a brown suit. He surprises Sheldon by asking for my phone number. Sheldon warns him that I am very popular and independent-minded. Eveline warns me that

Manny is much too serious, religious, and quiet for me. He is a bookworm and I love to dance. I socialize at parties while he spends most evenings at home studying Jewish texts. We are traditional Jews, but Manny has studied in a yeshiva, a religious college that seems old-fashioned to us and is very strict in his personal observance. Manny doesn't have a pulpit, but he is an ordained Rabbi, as well as a lawyer. Eveline and Sheldon can't imagine fun-loving Rena with Manny, the Rabbi.

Sometimes a warning can be intriguing. I am busy the first time Manny phones to ask me out, but he perseveres. At last, despite the warnings or because of them, I agree to a date.

On our first date we go to see the controversial film with Brigitte Bardot, "And God Created Woman" – ironically a risqué film about an orphan girl!

> "My only mistake was not asking Rena to marry me on the first date."
>
> ... *Rabbi Emanuel Quint*

Maybe it's a test. Is he too stuffy for me? He seems okay with the movie. We actually have a lot to talk about. He is a starting-out lawyer. I am teaching school. It's clear to me immediately just how smart he is. He's widely read and knows much more about so many subjects than I do. He was born in the United States, but both his parents were born in Eastern Europe, like me. He's 29. I think I'm 23.

Next is a double date with his sister and his brother-in-law to see the movie "Around the World in Eighty Days." It's a rainy night. Manny is driving a Pontiac. We have a flat. He changes it with ease. I'm impressed that this studious, nerdy man can change a tire. What an interesting combination, I think.

In the movies, he whispers to me, "Practice saying yes." I'm a little taken aback. I don't practice saying yes (about what?) but I agree to see Manny again.

I like to travel and talk about foreign places. He hasn't traveled as much as I have, but he's read more. He's knowledgeable about the places I've visited, without having been there.

There are, of course, areas of potential conflict. He is indeed hyper-studious. I am an honor society student and an avid reader, but he goes into depth in everything. I think he's nice and special, but I'm not sure he is right for me. I've already been engaged once, and don't want to make a mistake.

I do indeed like to go out dancing – both social dancing and Israeli folk dancing. He has never done any of this, and I can't imagine him flying around the room in a "hora" circle.

Another area of potential conflict is his greater religiosity. I, for instance, think that an essential rite of American life is to go out on New Year's Eve. I always have a date and sometimes I make the New Year's party.

So on New Year's Eve, I am ready for a party to toast the arrival of 1959. I have a new steady boyfriend and don't have to think about a date. I have my gorgeous clothes picked out.

Manny announces that he won't go out on the 31st of December. He doesn't think it is proper to go out on New Year's Eve, a non-Jewish celebration of the secular year.

He reminds me that New Year's Eve for religious Jews is Rosh Hashanah, the Jewish High Holiday. It's a happy but serious time. The first of January is no more than a calendar changer and bank holiday at best. At its worst, it's a pagan ceremony.

Pagan ceremony. Right. New Year's Eve at the eve of 1959 falls on a Wednesday. Manny adds insult to injury by saying he is in fact going out. He's attending night class on the medieval Jewish scholar Moses Maimonides. He never misses that class.

It's just one class, I argue. He's never going to be tested on this material. He's studying for study sake. He's studying for fun. A 12th century philosopher can wait. It's important to me to go out.

I don't believe he'll really pass up an evening with me. He keeps saying how much he loves me. I get dressed and wait, sure he'll surprise me. He doesn't. I'm furious and sick with disappointment.

I'm also practical. I realize I've hit a potential deal breaker. I have to make a decision about a possible future with this man who will never go out on New Year's Eve and who thinks medieval Jewish Rabbis are more important than a date with me.

There will be no more New Year's parties with confetti and champagne. I think hard about it, and decide he's worth the sacrifice. There is something exceptional and deep about Emanuel Quint.

He calls me "princess" and looks at me with admiring eyes. He begins a mantra of "marry me." He says he won't stop saying it until I agree. He's warned me to practice saying "yes." So I do.[1]

---

1   According to author Helmreich, at that time 83 percent of survivors were married, 80 percent married other survivors, compared to 62 percent of American Jews in the same age group. His research shows that early negative assessments of the marriages proved to be faulty. Like much of the early psychological theory about Holocaust survivors, generalizations are based on studies of the small number of survivors who sought psychological help. Writes Helmreich, "Although evaluating the quality of the relationship for the average survivor is difficult, it appears

Very formally, Manny asks Jacob Globe for permission to marry his daughter.

Leah and Jacob, who strongly objected to the man I was engaged to before, adore Manny. Nonetheless, they ask around. Jewish Brooklyn isn't that big. Everyone who knows Manny says the same thing: quiet but nice. We meet his family. Soon Jacob starts wearing a yarmulke in respect for his soon-to-be son-in-law, the Rabbi.

Manny's father emigrated from Bialystok in Belarus to the United States in 1928 after studying in the prestigious college of Judaism in Slobodka. He works as the secretary to the revered Lubavitcher Rebbe, Rabbi Menachem Mendel Schneerson. This is unusual because he isn't a member of the Chabad Hassidim. He worked for the previous Rebbe in the dynasty, as well. Manny's mother is the former Menucha Diamond. They met when Manny's father lived for a period of his life in pre-State Israel. It was a time of great unrest, especially in the city of Hebron where there had been a massacre. They have a greater understanding of my history than American-born parents might have.

Manny says his parents loved me the minute they met me. I don't know if this is true. They are such nice people they wouldn't ever say anything bad about anyone.

Manny is just starting out as a lawyer, so after we marry, we can live on my salary. I am earning $4,000 a year as a teacher.

One unpleasant question does come up. Jews are divided into three groups based on ancient distinctions. Most of us are "Israelites" but some are descendants of the priestly class, *Kohanim* and *Leviim*, who served in the

---

that the majority were at least as stable as those in the general population, if not more so."

central Temples in Jerusalem thousands of years ago. Many of the persons with last names of Cohen and Levi are descendants of the original priests. The distinction is passed through the father, and *Kohanim* even have genetic markers that tie them to Moses' brother, Aaron, the first *Kohen Gadol,* the High Priest.

Kohanim have certain restrictions in marrying. They can't marry a divorcee, for instance. There is also a question of a *Kohen* marrying a captive woman. Manny is a *Kohen,* and the question arises whether I am considered a captive because of my being in concentration camps. I don't like the question. I feel insulted. But fortunately the Rabbinic authority Rabbi Yisroel Zeev Gustman[2] quickly dismisses any question, and we get the go-ahead to plan our wedding.

In a sense, that rabbinical decision put my past behind me. It isn't as if I would deny my life as a Holocaust survivor, an orphan, an adoptee, but it won't have bearing on the rest of our lives.

We also receive a blessing from the very famous and highly respected Lubavitcher Rebbe, Rabbi Menachem Mendel Schneerson. Manny arranges a meeting at the Lubavitch Center at 770 Eastern Parkway in Crown

---

2   There are many stories of the greatness of Rabbi Yisroel Zeev Gustman, a great scholar and personality who also survived the Holocaust. My favorite was his ability to comfort Professor Robert J. Aumann whose son was killed fighting in the IDF in Lebanon. Rabbi Gustman, whose Talmud class the professor attended, came to console him when he was sitting *shiva,* the Jewish mourning period of seven days. Said the Rabbi, "I too lost a son. He was murdered in the Holocaust. He is waiting to receive your son. My son was killed because he was a Jew. He is a righteous martyr. But your son died while trying to save others. He will lead the prayer service in heaven." His words were a great comfort to Professor Aumann.

Heights in Brooklyn. I am a little scared and awed. Manny assures me that the Rebbe is welcoming. He's right. The Rebbe wants to know about me and says it's wonderful that I am teaching children (even though he is Orthodox and I am working for a Conservative Day School, the East Midwood Jewish Center).

That is the period of time when many Jews are moving into Crown Heights to join the community around the Lubavitcher Rebbe. Manny is entrusted with handling the legal side of the real estate purchases. His law practice will receive a boost from this, as he gradually becomes an expert in real estate law.

We go shopping together, and in one store I buy six pairs of high heeled shoes at the Sid-and-Mac store on Flatbush Avenue. This is an expensive store, not a discount outlet. Each pair costs $16, a lot of money in those days. I am used to living in a well-to-do family in which I am the only child. I am earning a salary and I am getting married to a wonderful man. I shop with ebullience and largesse.

We look for wedding halls. At the Saint George Hotel the banquet manager advises us that "we only do kosher dinners." I wonder what we are wearing that makes him think we might not want a kosher wedding. Maybe there is something lighthearted about me that undercuts our religious appearance. We assure him that we only want kosher food.

Having a religious wedding isn't only about the choice of officiating Rabbi and food. Would men and women sit together at the same tables? Would there be social dancing, or would men and women dance separately, in circles, with line dances and entertainers?

I have never been to a wedding where men and women sit separately. Manny doesn't even suggest it. He knows he's marrying me, somewhat less religiously

Rena and Manny's wedding in Brooklyn, at the Saint George Hotel.

observant than him when he could have aimed for a woman from a more religious background. He does veto social dancing. Men and women will sit together at the dinner, but dancing will be separate.

I have never been to a wedding like this, either, but I agree. I realize that there is a certain amount of adjustment I'll have to do to make my marriage work. After all, I am good at adjusting.

I go shopping for a beautiful white gown with Leah. I am a self-absorbed bride like most young women. I am caught up in the planning and wedding details and my husband-to-be who wouldn't be kissing me publicly after the "I do's" like the characters in movies. I don't think much about my mothers who wouldn't be with me under the wedding canopy. I don't think about my biological family and my horrible childhood. All of this is firmly locked away in a vault in a chamber of my heart. However,

Rena and Manny Quint, after the marriage ceremony. To the left is Louis Goldberg, who became Rena's official guardian after she arrived in the United States in 1946, when she was known as Fannie Philipstahl.

Leah makes sure that Louis and Molly Goldberg, who helped me come over with Anna, are there.

On March 15, 1959, I walk down the aisle with Leah and Jacob Globe on either side of me. Jacob's father, Morris Globe, walks in the wedding procession. Leah's sister's daughter is a flower girl. I am being launched by my loving family, just like any other lucky American Jewish bride. Manny's parents walk him down the aisle, and his sister and brother-in-law, with whom we've double-dated, are Best Man and Maid of Honor. We have more than 250 guests because I have so many friends. Manny and I invite four bridesmaids and four ushers – all unmarried to be part of the wedding party.

Most of the young women wear sleeveless evening dresses, and this is considered modest enough. My father, Jacob Globe, is wearing a top hat. My mother, Leah Globe, is wearing a short-sleeved dress with long white leather gloves.

My own wedding is the first wedding I'd ever been to where men and women don't dance together. The wedding lives up to my fantasies. My dress is gorgeous, with long lace sleeves, a bouffant skirt with a crinoline. I feel magical. I wear pearl earrings given to me for the wedding by a dear older friend named Martha Cammerman whom I frequently visit on Shabbat. The Shabbat before the wedding I visited her in the hospital where she was being treated. My heart soars as I dance all night in a circle of women friends and relatives. I dance with Leah in the center, and then, in turn, with each of my women friends – some of whom will remain my friends for life.

Manny does the same with his friends and family on the other side of the room.

Amateur entertainers do somersaults and balance bottles on their heads to amuse the bride and groom.

The only time Manny and I dance together is when we're both lifted high on chairs and hold a handkerchief between us, but that's fun, too.

Manny and I spend our wedding night at the Saint George and fly to Miami for our honeymoon the next day. I bring so many clothes that we have to pay overweight, especially for those stiletto heel shoes. (On the way home, someone will tell me that Rabbis don't have to pay overweight.) My father-in-law has booked us into a kosher hotel called the Strathaven. We are served oatmeal in the morning with low salt for easy chewing and not to raise our blood pressure! It turns out that Strathaven is a favorite hotel for senior citizens. We realize we are in a less than ideal venue for a honeymoon.

I might have agreed to the separate dancing, but the drab hotel room with frayed carpets and octogenarian residents make me – shall I say – the opposite of ebullient.

Manny knows he's in trouble. He takes the initiative and says we're moving from Fourth Street to the Ritz Carlton, a luxury hotel. I let out my breath. Now this is more like it!

What will we do for entertainment? Certainly not nightclubs. Manny has found all sorts of free events. We go to watch tennis matches. We go to visit a Miami serpentarium, where Manny volunteers – showing off to his bride – by putting a snake around his neck. We take buses instead of cabs. Manny raves about the bus system in Florida, but I don't think it's special.

It doesn't occur to me that Manny is seriously worried about money. He tries to be conservative in spending, but to show me a good time. At some level I am worried that married life will be less fun than single life. I have lived a blithe existence since moving in with the Globes and here is married life with old-age hotels and fume-filled buses.

Have I made a mistake?

When we get home to New York, Manny confesses. Before the wedding, he worked long hours on a big case. When he was paid, the client's check bounced. The money he was counting on for the honeymoon and initial living expenses was no longer certain. He was ashamed to tell me, and thought he could work around the problem.

I take a deep breath. I don't like his hiding the truth from me, but I like the honesty of his admission.

"Okay – we'll use my money," I say. I have a steady if modest income as a teacher. When the boiler breaks, I take out my pension fund from the Teachers' Union. My parents have faith in Manny and are glad to help us out financially. They provide the down payment on a small two-family house. The price is $19,000, and we rent out one of the apartments to add to our income. I, too, feel cautiously optimistic that we're going to be okay and, despite my past, imagine that I'll have a storybook marriage.

Of course, like all young couples, we have adjustments to go through – maybe even more than the average, if there is such a thing. Practically speaking, maybe we should consider waiting before starting a family. But I won't consider this. I desperately want a baby.

Why desperately? I am young, and I am the breadwinner. A couple needs time to get to know each other and work out their differences. A baby will come along soon enough without the desperation. But that isn't how I feel. I suppose I am carrying within me, curled inside without ever being spoken of, the survivor's desire to bring more life into the world.

On the whole, survivors have had more children per family than American Jews. This is partly because there are more Orthodox Jews among us and Orthodox Jews tend to have larger families, but it also reflects our burning desire to replace our missing family members and to replenish the number of Jews in the world. There's another reason that might have been part of it. Having children is the Holocaust survivor's ultimate victory over Hitler.

Six months after the wedding, I'm pregnant. I'm delighted. How lucky I am. A baby!

But then I lose the baby. A miscarriage. Manny drives me to the hospital on a Saturday, our Shabbat. "I've failed you," I tell him over and over. I tell him that if he wants to divorce me that's okay. I am overwhelmed by grief and defeat.

The doctor says it's common to feel a sense of bereavement after a miscarriage, the sudden cutting off of expectation, love, and joy. He tells Manny to expect moodiness and unpredictability that is a common reaction to miscarriage. Miscarriage is nature's way of dealing with imperfect babies, he says.

He doesn't know how these words hurt me. How could he? He knows I am Rena, but he doesn't know I'm also Fredzia, who has seen so many dead babies, and who barely escaped death as a child. I am not seeking a perfect baby.

The doctor doesn't know that repressed and submerged in this weeping woman is profound loss and acquaintance with death. I've lost my mother, my brothers, my father, the replacement mothers. I need to focus on staying alive. Now I've lost my baby, powerless to save it. Death follows me. Despite all my efforts, I haven't managed to slam the door on the leering angel of death. I have brought that doom into our marriage, as irrational as that might sound.

Manny had better get away fast. I'm a failure. I am not the perfect wife and mother that I promised to be. The

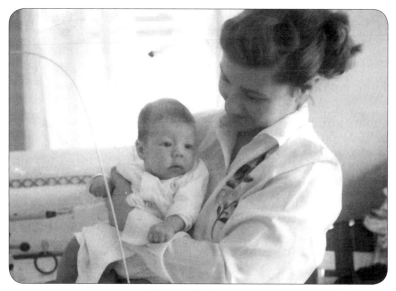

Rena and Menucha.

storybook wedding was a sham.

No one suggests counseling. Fredzia never allowed herself the luxury of grieving, but Rena is grieving.

Manny is loving and supportive. We'll have another baby, he says. He loves me and I'm wonderful, he keeps telling me. He only regrets not asking me to marry him on the very first date. His total approval and love help me get through this crisis.

Several months later I'm pregnant again. This time I see a specialist.

This is a time when American women are taking a new and highly recommended drug called thalidomide[3] to prevent nausea in pregnancy. I shake my head. I don't want anything to suppress the feeling of pregnancy. I want morning sickness and afternoon sickness. I want to feel

---

3   Thalidomide is later found to cause horrendous birth defects.

nauseous to prove to myself that I am really pregnant. I love being pregnant.

I am not scared to go into motherhood. I have an odd confidence that I will know what to do. I can't wait to shower my love on a baby.

The pregnancy and birth go smoothly. In my arms is a beautiful baby girl. I already love her. I promise to keep her safe.

I don't suggest the name of my birth mother or the mothers who have nurtured me along the way. I don't want to hurt Leah. We name our baby Marlene, Menucha in Hebrew, after Manny's mother who has died recently. It means "resting place" or "peace."

I love being a mother. Leah loves being a grandmother. Manny loves being a father. Jacob loves being a grandfather. Menucha is engulfed in love.

Leah has never had her own baby, and is beyond excited to have a grandbaby, to fuss over, for whom to buy frilly outfits, and to walk with me around Brooklyn with the high baby carriage. Leah and Menucha develop a very close relationship. The satisfaction and joy of every mother is amplified for me in the relief of being able to build a new family. Here I am, a woman who had benefited from so many mothers – able to mother a child, too.

Manny's law practice is growing, and we're the typical American family. I stay home with the baby and he leaves in the morning with a kiss and comes home for supper, warm on the stove. He continues his serious Jewish studies and we both are involved in Jewish community activities.

Two years later, I give birth to Naomi Rachel, and then two years after that, Jodi Miriam is born. She's named for a close friend Judy – Yehudit who was killed in a car crash. Only when our fourth and final child, David, is born two years after Jodi, do I insist on naming him for my brother David. With four small children at home, I may be ready to start dealing with my past.

David is born in 1967, an important year for the Jews of the world: the year of the Six Day War.

I am a busy, at-home Mom active in PTA and children's after-school activities. I have given up teaching, and Manny is making a good living, forever determined to make up for our honeymoon. We have moved to a larger home, and I am always volunteering to host kids' activities, parties, and guests there. I take the kids to movies and plays. New York has so much to offer, and I can indulge my own love for music while opening new horizons for them. I teach them to ice skate, and get on the ice with them. I don't consciously think back to the skating ponds of Piotrkow or learning to skate well in Sweden. I just know I love to skate and am good at it.

We live in a modern Orthodox household where women wear pants and t-shirts, don't cover all their hair, and don't think twice about buying tickets for the ballet when the ballerinas wear leotards. On the other hand, we have a strictly kosher home, following Jewish dietary laws with exactitude, and use timers to turn on lights on the Sabbath. We don't drive or use the phone on the Sabbath. We walk to the nearby Orthodox synagogue for services.

Manny and I relish our family vacations, piling the kids in the car and heading off to adventures. We take turns at the wheel as we show the children Washington, Hershey, Pennsylvania, National Parks, and Disneyland. We visit France, Spain, Switzerland, and Italy. We travel a lot, two adults with European parents who admire and love America. We roller-skate. We take dance lessons.

Manny is happy with such a busy household, particularly because I am independent enough to run it without having to disturb him in his business or his continued religious studies. He is devout and pious, but he's not self-righteous or preachy.

Every day, I find a love note from Manny somewhere in the house telling me how much he loves me. When I go to synagogue on Saturday, I find a love note on a yellow post-it tucked in my prayer book.

What impact does my Holocaust background have on my mothering skills? My daughter Naomi says that one time the kids were fussing about the food at a restaurant and were leaving most of it uneaten. I evidently lost control, telling them what I would have done for a slice of bread when I was their age. She remembers it because it was so unusual for me to have an outburst like that. "We all knew Mom was in the Holocaust, but it was something we didn't talk about," she says.

When Jodi wants to buy what we considered extravagant clothes, she has a contract – something similar to what I'd had with the Globes, to spend a fixed amount on her wardrobe. Ironically, she wants fancy clothing in Flatbush, but just the opposite when she goes to Israel where girls wear simpler clothing. I think most parents, attempt to teach their children to handle money and not connected to me being in the Holocaust.

Sarah Moskovitz's *Love Despite Hate* tells the story of the child survivors of concentration camps who were brought to Lingfield House, a children's home in England. They were from age three to teens, the age group I was in after the war. Because most of the child survivors were able to find the strength and courage to go on, she urged psychologists to rethink "the concept that early deprivation unalterably determines the course of life. Despite the severest deprivations in early childhood, these people are neither living a greedy, me-first style of life,

בס״ד אייר

My Precious Darling
On behalf of our entire family
I thank You for giving us
guidance and direction in life.
Your moral compass always
show the right way to go.
Your conduct is something to
be emulated. All about
You is perfection.
Your dedication to Hashem
and to mankind is legendary.
I pray for Your well being,
good health and a good life.
Hashem bless You.
forever,
Love
xx

בס״ד אייר

To The Most Magnificent
Person in the entire
Universe.
P.S. It definitely is a
Person of size. You are my
wife, and this makes me at
Peace with life. Besides
adoring You, I so much
respect and admire You. I
truly try to be worthy of You.
Everything You do is to perfection
Your smile light up my life,
It also lights up the room
Everything about You is
Perfection. I thank Hashem
+ You that You are my
wife
Love
xxx

Some of the notes Rena has found from Manny around their home.

בס״ד בריק חלקי

My Wonderful Darling Rena
Once again I begin by thanking
pen for helping me to meet You.
Then I thank You for being, by
far, the most wonderful person
in the entire Universe.
All of us, Eli, Sherry, Michel and I
thank You for a most wonderful
vacation that You planned. Everything
You plan and do is perfection.
No wonder we all adore You.
I so much look forward to every
moment with You. Especially
We look forward to our next
vacation in Eilat + Lavie.
Love foreva
xxx

בס״ד

Darling Rena,
I am so lucky to be your
husband
To spend life with the
nicest Person in the world,
nicest in so many many
ways.
Most of all when You
are near people,
You bring out the best
in people
Especially me.
So thank You
And of course
I love You more +
more
every moment of every day
all my
love
foreva
xx

nor are they seeking gain at the expense of others. None express the idea that the world owes them a living for all they have suffered. On the contrary, most of their lives are marked by an active compassion for others." I relate to this. I never feel I'm owed special consideration because of my past suffering.

I have often heard it told that survivors become hoarders and obsessed by food. At our home, I make sure there is always lots of food, a full freezer, well-stocked cupboards of staples. But are my cabinets any different from those of my American-born neighbors in Brooklyn? I doubt it.

Am I more fearful for my children? I don't think so. Maybe the opposite. I'm adventurous and encourage them to be.

Some say we survivors put greater emphasis on our children doing well in school than our American-born neighbors.

Do I push them harder to succeed than American-born parents? I have no way to measure this. The children are smart and good students and pretty much self-motivated. If they need help on homework, we help them like any other middle-class parents. I've always been confident that they'll all do fine in school, and they do.

It's important to Manny and me both that our children be educated, faithful and respectful Jews. They all seem to identify strongly and follow our manner of observance.

I love the role of being a mother with a car full of kids, a place of parties and gatherings and late-night homework sessions. I don't find instilling religious education a burden. Quite the opposite. I love to see the children growing up as knowledgeable and proud Jews.

An important part of our connection to Judaism is our love of Israel. Israeli Independence Day in 1967 is

May 15. The children come home with Israeli flags with the number 19 for Israel's 19th birthday. On the same day, Egyptian troops begin moving into the Sinai desert south of Israel and massing near the border. Three days later, Syrian troops line up in the Golan Heights in the North. Gamal Abdul Nasser, President of Egypt, orders the United Nations Emergency Force, which has been stationed in the Sinai since 1956 to leave. The troops pick up and go. Egypt crows that now it will exterminate Israel, followed by a similar announcement by Syrian Defense Minister Hafez Assad. On May 22, Egypt closes the Straits of Tiran to Israeli shipping and ships headed for Eilat.

Our President, Lyndon B. Johnson, tries to organize an international flotilla to test the blockage, but he fails. Jordan's King Hussein signs a defense agreement with Egypt on May 30. He also wants to get in on the nearly certain destruction of the Jewish state.

In June 1967, the State of Israel is in grave danger. Arab armies are preparing to attack from the North, South and East. The Western border is the Mediterranean Sea. "We will throw you into the sea," they threaten.

Jews throughout the world are distraught, and in our neighborhood in Brooklyn we keep our radios on, waiting for every news item. How will little Israel face these bullies? The specter of the mass killing of Jews looms large. For me, it's not theoretical. I'm sick with worry.

On June 4, Iraq joins, too. Over 250,000 troops with more than 2,000 tanks and 700 aircraft surround Israel with its two million, four hundred thousand Jews.

On June 5, the Israeli air force makes a preemptive attack on Egypt, wiping out most of their airplanes on the ground. Israelis fight back attacks on all fronts.

In emergency meetings in synagogues, we pledge money to help Israel. We pray. After six fraught days, it's over. Israel has defeated the Arab armies determined to destroy the young state.

There is relief and ecstasy among world Jewry and all peoples who are pleased to see tyranny defeated. We all want to go and celebrate in Israel. We start to make plans for a family trip.

In September 1967, I have just returned home from giving birth to our son David. Out of the blue a woman phones and wants to know if I'm Rena Quint who is related to Leah Globe and who knew the Goldbergs who owned a furniture factory.

I'm suspicious and cautious. By now I have a family to protect. Immediately I think that someone might be a kidnapper. But as it turns out, this woman's sister, Zipporah, is married to my cousin Isaac Rushinek, son of my Aunt Leah. The Rushineks have moved to the United States – not far away on Long Island. They asked her to phone me because she's been in the US longer and speaks better English.

She understands the surprise of this call and rushes ahead with an explanation. She says that Isaac wanted to stay in touch all those years ago but the Globes had been advised by psychologists of the time that I should have a new beginning, not hampered by sad memories of the past. They'd closed the door to renewing ties. He, of course, wasn't in a position back then to adopt me or take care of me. Of course, Israel was a poor country and they were struggling financially.

I don't know if this is true, and certainly wouldn't confront them with it. The Globes gave me a new life, confidence, love. But now I'm an adult and can be in touch with whomever I want.

Isaac, I learn, was having a hard time making a living as a building contractor in Israel and now wants to try the

United States. He wants to see his American cousin: me. I, too, am eager to see them.

I am about to meet up with my surviving Piotrkow cousins for the first time since the Holocaust. Twenty-five years have passed since liberation in Bergen-Belsen.

We invite them to our home. Isaac and I haven't seen each other since Sweden – 22 years have passed. When I see him, I don't recognize him. He's a nice looking man, with curly blond hair, a little like mine, I guess. He's slim and athletic.

I have such a rush of conflicting emotions. Here is someone who knows me from "back there," who knew my nuclear family, who shares at least some of my DNA.

But he's also from the world that I have distanced. He's a stranger. What might he reveal to me?

We speak in a mixture of English, Hebrew and Yiddish. He isn't outgoing, and it's easier to talk with Zipporah, his wife. I learn that his father survived the war, but my Aunt Leah didn't. Isaac married and had two sons Lior and Doron. After our initial meeting, I invite him and Zipporah and the children to spend the Passover holiday with us. They are wary at first, probably because we seem so religious to them. After all, Manny is a Rabbi and wears a yarmulke. They assume we'll be praying all day and that we might coerce them to pray. Nonetheless, they accept our invitation.

I correctly anticipate their surprise at how holidays are in our Orthodox household. Instead of entering a Jewish equivalent of a monastery, their kids immediately begin playing basketball with mine. We have a joyous holiday meal, with lots of discussion and lots of food. The house is full of games and toys and the next day, a long Monopoly tournament is launched.

After the holiday, one of their sons says he likes our

house. Can he please have one of those yarmulkes and get an undershirt with ritual fringes like our son? The cousins like it enough to come back the following year.

When Lior is Bar Mitzvah, we stay in a motel near their house in Long Island, and volunteer to bring the food from Brooklyn. On Saturday night there's a party at an Israeli nightclub. One of the guests is another long lost cousin: Irving Cymberknopf. He has arrived from Venezuela! He's the cousin, now living in Venezuela, whom the Globes had found and who said he didn't want to have me join him because he couldn't take care of me.

He is ten years older than me. His mother, Aunt Bina, was so close with my mother. He, too, worked in the Hortensia glass factory. We may have shared the bunker we dug together as the liquidation of the Jews in the ghetto approached. We hid together in the small ghetto and may have been arrested together with his mother and brought to the synagogue/prison in Piotrkow.

I don't remember him at all. We do not sit and talk about Piotrkow. The memories are too painful. His parents were murdered within a month of each other when he was 17. He is an only child.

Cousin Irving has built an adventurous life for himself, moving to Canada and then Venezuela, and then back to Canada, and finally to Israel. Maybe we do have adventurous genes. He has done well as a jeweler, has even hired Rushinek to build a villa in the upscale town of Savyon for him. He also succeeded in exhuming Aunt Bina's remains from Poland and moving them to Israel.

Irving has what he calls a "complex relationship with Jewishness." He is bitter about the murder of his family and the price Jews paid in the Holocaust. On the other hand, he feels a pull to Judaism. He likes meeting us enough so that on his next visit to New York, he stays with us for Yom Kippur, the most solemn day of the year. Even on this heavy day, we don't talk about that last terrifying Yom Kippur in Piotrkow.

Even though he has given up much of his childhood religious practice, he is moved and inspired by this solemn day which reminds him of happier days in his youth before the war. He stays on with us, helps us build a sukkah and stays for the entire eight-day holiday of Sukkot.

He also wants to pass on a strong attachment to Judaism to his children. Irving's daughter Beatrice, named for Aunt Bina, comes from Venezuela, to attend Stern College, the women's division of Yeshiva University, in New York. She and her friends become regular visitors to our home in Brooklyn. They often eat their Shabbat meals with us, and reciprocate by babysitting Saturday nights so that Manny and I can have an evening out.

When I relax into it, I feel wonderful reconnecting with blood relatives. They aren't, however, always an accurate source of information. My aunts are dead, but Irving Rushinek's father has survived World War II. He should be a great source of family knowledge, but he insists, for instance, that I had two sisters who were killed. I remember only brothers. He keeps asking how it is possible that I don't remember these cute little girls. This is very upsetting for me, until records show that there never were two little girls. (It turns out that his post-Holocaust memory isn't accurate at all.)

When I get together with these cousins, we don't talk much about our childhoods in Piotrkow. We shy away from these still-open wounds.

Then one day the phone rings. There's a woman with a heavy European accent on the other end asking for Fredzia. I am busy in the kitchen cooking and automatically answer that it's a wrong number.

And then I freeze. Did she say "Fredzia?"

Luckily, the woman calls again and insists I don't hang up. Her name is Lily Koslowsky. She has seen my photo in a Jewish newspaper because Manny and I have received an honor. She saw my mother's face in mine. She is a distant cousin of my mother's and was "as close to her as a sister" she says. This wasn't without context. Beatrice has visited her in the Bronx where she lives and has told her about "the cousin in Brooklyn." Everything seems to have come together. She, too, should be a valuable source of information about my mother. But she breaks down in tears every time she mentions my mother and can't answer even my simplest question. She is so miserable when she remembers her dear cousin and friend Sarah that I quickly change the subject.

Later I will meet Lily's son, Dr. Menny Koslowsky, head of the department of psychology at Bar-Ilan University near Tel Aviv. He confirms that Lily remained unable to discuss her Holocaust experience until her death. All he knows is that she spent two years in Auschwitz – she did have a number on her arm – but couldn't trace her path from Piotrkow to Auschwitz. When the Steven Spielberg film and video archives came twice to film her, she became so emotional she was unable to recount her experiences.

In 1969, Manny and I forgo buying new furniture, and instead fulfill our dream of organizing a family summer trip to Israel.

The weather in Israel in the summer is hot and dry. We plan a trip that's full of fun with swimming and hiking, but we also want to visit the newly accessible Jewish historic sites. We visit the Cave of the Biblical Patriarchs and Matriarchs in Hebron: Abraham, Isaac, Jacob, Sarah, Rebecca, Leah. My children go to Jewish schools and kindergartens, and know those names, which also resonate with the names of those in our family.

Outside of Bethlehem, we stop at a small stone building where matriarch Rachel is buried after dying in childbirth. According to Jewish tradition, she awaits the return of the Jewish people. The words from the prophet Jeremiah are posted on the wall, "A cry is heard in Ramah – deep anguish and bitter weeping. Rachel weeps for her children, refusing to be comforted – for her children are gone."

How grateful am I to be here with my husband and four children. I try not to feel the yearning for those who never got to live a life like mine. I cry out for them like matriarch Rachel.

In the 1960s, every fourth person in Israel is a Holocaust survivor. There are three main reasons so many survivors have come to Israel. First, it is a refuge, receiving survivors with open arms, if limited resources. Every Jew becomes an instant citizen, Second, most Holocaust survivors are Zionists. In cities like Piotrkow, the Zionist movements were strong. No one had to tell the Jews of Europe how important having a Jewish state was. Third, many survivors have family in Israel. Even a distant cousin is now a cherished family member.

Holocaust survivors in Israel were circumspect about their war experiences when they first arrived. They didn't share what they'd gone through and the courage that was required to start again. I understand them. Like me, they didn't want to talk about the difficult past.

There's another reason for reluctance about speaking about the Holocaust. For these new Israelis, there is an embarrassment about the supposed helplessness of the Jews in the Holocaust. The ethos of pioneering a new Jewish country fighting back against its enemies doesn't jibe with the image of starving prisoners in striped pajamas. Only after the capture of Adolf Eichmann by Israeli Mossad agents in May 1960, outside of Buenos Aires, Argentina and Eichmann's public trial in Israel a year later does the heroism of Holocaust survivors begin to take its place in public understanding.

Adolf Eichmann was an *Obersturmbannfuher* – a lieutenant colonel in the Nazi SS who was in charge of deportation to extermination camps. He is reported to have said, at the end of the War, that he would "leap laughing into the grave because the feeling that he had five million people on his conscience would be for him a source of extraordinary satisfaction."

The trial is a major event in Israel. We Jews have developed a long arm to bring to trial those who have murdered our family members, decades after the crime. But even more than the cry for justice – there could be no justice for my parents and brothers who were murdered for no reason other than their Jewishness – is the impact of listening to the soul-wrenching testimony of survivors. For the sake of convicting this monster, they overcome their reluctance to recall the past, and words come spilling out. The details of the hellish oppression are beyond imagination. The depravity of the Nazis, a culture that had grown up within what was considered the most cultured nation in the world, defies understanding. Survivor after survivor testifies as Eichmann sits stoically in his glass booth. He's not sorry. There is no remorse.

In Israel, a new appreciation for survivors emerges from hearing the testimony. In a country that has prided itself on the victories of its scrappy military and the energy of ingathering of exiles, the strength, ingenuity and resourcefulness of the men, women and children who emerged from the boiling cauldron in Europe startles those who have belittled or ignored them.

Now there is a realization that despite the most gruesome tests and trials, survivors retained their humanity, took up arms to defend fledgling Israel and committed to bringing up new families. Israelis are now secure enough to hear this and to begin recognizing the enormous contribution survivors have made to the State of Israel.

This appreciation would come together most vividly in 2003, when three F-15 pilots, originally invited to Poland to celebrate the Polish Air Force's 85th birthday, fly over Auschwitz carrying the names of all those recorded murdered in Auschwitz on that date 60 years earlier. There is fierce competition among Israel Defense Force pilots to take part in the fly-over. Why? Because so many of them had grandparents who are survivors. They all desperately want to show that we are not helpless anymore.

I know from Barbara Sofer, who is the Israel Director of Public Relations for Hadassah, that most of the brilliant doctors in Hadassah Hospital are the children of Holocaust survivors. Their message, after the Holocaust, was not to waste their lives on revenge, but to devote them to healing.

Still, when Manny and I come to Israel with our children, I don't present myself as a survivor. I arrive in Israel as an American Jewish tourist showing the country to her children, all of whom are enrolled in Jewish schools where Israel is a major source of love and pride. I don't think much about the once-upon-a-time plan for me by the representatives of the Jewish Agency in Sweden that I should move to Israel with the other orphan children. I do visit my friend Lucia, Sarah Ben Ari, at her home in Haifa. But the search for my past stays on the back burner, even after my family trip to Israel.

In the early 1970s, Jacob Globe is diagnosed with

cancer. I take him to his chemotherapy appointments. I care for him. And then, in 1972 my beloved adoptive father dies. By now I know about funerals. I arrange his. At a Jewish burial, the Rabbi or a woman appointed by the Rabbi tears the collar of the shirt or coat of close relatives as a sign of mourning. Leah's clothing is torn, and Jacob's sisters and brothers, too. But then the Rabbi hesitates. I'm not Jacob's real daughter, he says. I don't really have to tear my collar. The words "not real daughter" ring over and over in my ears.

Many of the mourners have no idea what is going on. They can't believe I'm not the biological daughter. What difference does this make? Jacob's sister and brother, not as religiously bound as we are, express their horror at my exclusion. Fortunately, a different authority, Rabbi Zalman Sharfman, steps forth and insists that I be included in the mourning circle.

When Leah, my mother, dies in Israel many years later, there is no question about me being an authentic mourner.[4]

For my children, Leah and Jacob are full grandparents. I didn't bring them up mourning their murdered biological grandparents. I may have been wrong in excluding my personal history in order to shield them. I wonder if I am disrespectful to my biological parents and my other mothers by not mentioning them, as I honor the death of my adoptive parent. I'm simply not ready yet.

David is five when Jacob Globe dies, and insists that Grandpa isn't really dead. Grandpa had promised to give him a dime, and "Grandpa always keeps his promise." He couldn't have left without giving him a dime.

---

4   When Nechama Leibowitz, a prominent educator, died without children, hundreds of her students tore their clothing to mourn her.

I think of all the hopes and promises that have been broken in my life as we walk around the block together, a tradition that marks the end of the mourning period. How will I break the news to David that those who have passed away can't keep promises? We're on a dead end street with a bridge walkway. There, on the bridge, is a single shiny dime. David picks it up. "I told you he didn't forget," says David. "He sent me a dime from heaven." He is comforted.

.

Chapter 17

THE SEARCH FOR MY MOTHERS

The first time I speak about the Holocaust is to my son David's eighth grade class.

By now, we are a well-established family. Manny is even chairperson of the Board of Education, and I'm active in Jewish clubs, the PTA, and community activities.

David has volunteered me as a speaker about the Holocaust. The teacher phones me. "David said the strangest thing in class today. He claimed that you were a Holocaust survivor. It's not true, is it?" Not only is the teacher surprised, but so are his friends and their parents.

I arrive at the school feeling nervous. How much should I say? Won't the children be frightened?

I tell my story haltingly. I am missing so many details. Leah has come to listen, too. This increases my discomfort. I don't want to hurt her feelings talking about my birth family. I don't want to reveal the difficulties I've had in the United States because that will hurt her feelings, too.

I am relieved when this talk is over. I am embarrassed about how little I know for sure. I won't do this again, I tell myself. But just in case I'm in a position to speak of it again, I'd better find out more. With this "excuse" I begin a low-key search for my roots.

Manny isn't pleased. He objects to this pursuit. Why dig up the hurtful past? I consider going to an organization for Holocaust survivors, but he discourages me. He is clearly worried that I will upset an ideal marriage. Why would I want to disturb the balance I have achieved by focusing on the anguish of the past? He wants to protect what we have created as a family.

That's not only his attitude towards the Holocaust, but on most issues. When the kids grow up and I consider going to a group in the community center for empty-nesters, he doesn't think this is a good idea, either. He comes from a generation without too much faith that psychological investigation increases happiness.

Although I'm influenced by what my husband thinks, it's not the final word. Our marriage, like most, involves negotiated decision-making.

I realize that Manny's objection is just an excuse. I'm the one who is ambivalent. If I want this badly enough, nothing will stand in my way and Manny will come around to supporting me as he always does. He senses my ambivalence and reflects it, hoping to help me find the easiest and least painful way to go ahead. He can't stand to see me hurt.

Eventually I come to terms with my own ambivalence. I have postponed looking backwards, facing the pain and loss and uncertainty. I don't like hemming and hawing when I'm speaking about my past.

I admit to myself finally that I want to know more about my family, to take pride in them, and to recognize their valor facing the horrible fate of the Jews around them. It's hard to imagine as a parent what it must have meant to be unable to protect your children from mass murder. And of course, I am haunted by the memory of letting go of my mother's hand.

Leah, always so strong and sensible, doesn't discourage me from this quest. She seems to understand, and even offers to help.

I don't dive in. I dip my toe in the water, so to speak. I approach the YIVO Institute for Jewish research in New York City and tell them the outlines of my story. I can see the skepticism in the research assistant's eyes. How is it possible for this well-dressed lady from Brooklyn with an educated American accent to have survived alone in Holocaust Poland? She speaks to me as if I'm just another New York City whacko or an imposter. She says, and not so nicely, that no child could have survived without a parent or sibling.

How can I possibly start to explain that I had a golden chain of mothers who pulled me from the jaws of death?

My experience at YIVO is discouraging. I'm off to an abysmal start. But I'm never a quitter. The researcher's patronizing attitude gets under my skin and strengthens my determination to show her that she's misjudged me.

I go back to YIVO. The same woman isn't on duty. Now I say I'm looking for "my friend's" history. Can they help me?

The librarians on duty are nicer. They give me an introduction to the challenges of Holocaust research. They explain that the first problem with looking for someone in Holocaust records is the unreliable alphabetization and spelling. Even if I find the Polish or German spellings of my friend's name, I can't be sure it's been recorded correctly.

Nor are listings straightforward. For instance, when the British took over Bergen-Belsen, they made good records of the survivors, but they admittedly were so overwhelmed by what they experienced and the rapid pace of death around them that they didn't write down all names.

I don't find "my friend" Fredzia Lichtenstein on my first try. I sit at the big desk and go over lists. A librarian helps me peruse them in the book *Sharit Hapleta* (What Remains). The lists turn out not to be perfectly alphabetized, and we find "my friend's name" out of place. I feel triumphant. You see, I exist. I don't say this, of course. I tell her that "my friend" will be thrilled.

Years later, at Yad Vashem in Jerusalem, a German volunteer will find "Fredzia Lichtenstein" on a list that says "unaccompanied children." Nine years old! That's me!

There's an additional barrier in gathering information, akin to the attitude I first encounter at YIVO. When I meet Holocaust survivors, particularly in Israel, they are more European than I am. For all intents and purposes, I'm an American. I speak English like an American. I speak Hebrew and Yiddish with an American accent, and I don't speak Polish or German or Russian. Even when I attend the ceremonies for survivors of Piotrkow, I'm somewhat of an outsider. The others meet and know each other. I always feel as if they look at me as an imposter – maybe a second generation (the child of a survivor) – but certainly not the little girl who spent her early childhood years in the Piotrkow ghetto. Their meeting and talking has reinforced their memories over the years, as they fill in blanks for each other. They always seem so certain about what happened, while my memory is a patchwork quilt.

I feel rejected by these other Holocaust survivors. Imagine what this means for someone like me who has had to work hard to form her identity.

I don't have a numerical tattoo on my arm. These were only issued in Auschwitz camp and not even always there.

I once helped a survivor who knew she was in Auschwitz, but couldn't prove it because she had no tattoo. It turned out that she was one of three cousins who were dispatched to an ammunition factory, but she fainted and was presumed dead while the others were being tattooed with numbers. When the others were dispatched to the ammunition factory, they managed to revive her. Hence, she had no tattoo.

I went with this woman to the archives at Yad Vashem and managed to find her name on the list of those deported from her town and also at the ammunition factory. The Auschwitz listing wasn't there, which corresponds with her story. I could understand her relief at having her memory and words corroborated. For her, this had the added benefit of being able to get restitution, which she needed as an elderly and impoverished survivor living in the United States. All she needed was someone to give her a little encouragement and help to find her records.

There has been a lot of discussion of the so-called "Second Generation," the children of Holocaust survivors. Back in 1979, Helen Epstein wrote a popular and emotional book called *Children of the Holocaust,* in which she talks to children whose parents are survivors. Writes Epstein:

"For years it lay in an iron box buried so deep inside me that I was never sure just what it was. I knew I carried slippery, combustible things more secret than sex and more dangerous than any shadow or ghost."

Epstein herself and those she interviewed were all the children of survivors, but she perfectly describes the combustible history I carried as a survivor.

In early 1981, I read a magazine called *The Voice,* published by survivors from Piotrkow. The editor and writer is a Piotrkow-born survivor named Ben Giladi. Ben has taken on the mission of recording the history of the Jewish community of Piotrkow and also keeping in touch with former residents around the world. The strong attachment to the original Jewish communities where most of our families met their death is a fascinating part of Holocaust history. On one hand, we feel little attachment to Piotrkow, but on the other, our identity is forever connected to our birthplace in Poland.

In the magazine that Ben publishes, I read the story of Yidele and Frieda Jaffa, two Piotrkow children who are still looking for their identity. I wonder if I can learn anything about my roots from these folks. With some hesitation, I phone Giladi, who lives in Kew Gardens, Queens, New York. Ben is friendly and welcoming. He is ten years my senior. He doesn't remember me, or sadly, anyone from my family. After the Holocaust he returned to Poland and graduated from university there. He lived in Israel, and then eventually moved to the United States. He'll be so happy to meet me.

In March 1981, Manny and I attend a Purim Party organized by Ben and his wife Guta Giladi with others from Piotrkow in the community center in Queens. Lily Koslowsky is there. She's the only person at the party I know. Once again, I don't find others who know my family or me. Ben tells us about the World Gathering of Jewish Holocaust Survivors in Jerusalem that is going to take place in the summer. This is good news for me. We are already heading for Israel for our daughter Menucha's wedding.

I am 46. I realize that with a daughter getting married I am at a new stage of my life. I feel more secure. It's time to become more active in my search. After all, what will I tell my grandchildren?

Our family gathers in Israel in July before the wedding. I register for the conference and daily excursions connected to it.

One of these trips is to the Etzion Bloc, a cluster of towns between Jerusalem and Hebron. What I remember most from the trip is a stirring Hebrew song that we learned on the way – *Mekimi m'afar dal*, God lifted me up from the dust. It resonates for me and becomes a sort of personal theme song. Other words of wisdom I absorb on the trip inspire me, too: "When you are cold and want to light a fire, first go out and cut the wood. It warms you twice, first the cutting and then the fire."

Six thousand survivors of the Holocaust and their children are gathering in Israel for the first World Gathering of Jewish Holocaust Survivors in Jerusalem. My hopes are high.

The meeting is in Jerusalem, in Binyenei Ha'Uma, the National Convention Hall. It's like a giant reunion with everyone seeking long lost relatives or friends from decades past. There are opportunities to put up signs seeking anyone who knows me. I go to the meeting hall with Leah, who has moved to Israel to be near Menucha, with whom she has always been so close.

Many survivors find other survivors who know them or their families. There are shouts of joy and tears. I feel leaden. I don't find anyone. No one knows me. No one remembers my family. Everyone seems to be meeting someone from their past except for me. It's awkward to go there with a mother and then explain that my biological mother was from Poland and she was murdered, perhaps at Treblinka.

People keep asking me when I came to the United States. 1946, I say. They ask Leah why she went back to Poland if she came to the US in 1906. Of course, she didn't, but they assume she was my mother in the Holocaust. They're puzzled. She doesn't want to explain. "Ask my daughter," she says.

The meeting is a huge disappointment for me. Imagine attending a class reunion when you don't know anyone there. Then imagine that you are looking for your own family and no one knows what you're talking about.

But I don't give up. Once again, my frustration stirs

me to do more research and establish my past. I write to the International Tracing Service in Bad Arolson in North Hesse, Germany.

The huge archive, opened as early as 1943, was set up within the British Red Cross, on the initiative of Allied Forces HQ, to begin the work of tracing people. North Hesse, Germany was chosen because of its central location between the four occupied zones and because it had large, undamaged buildings and good telegraph and telephone connections.

The officials at the archive send back a letter, recognizing me as a little girl who was in Piotrkow, Czestochowa and Bergen-Belsen! I am thrilled. At last, confirmation. You see, I want to shout to the world, everything I tell you is true. Everything I remember is true!

A few additional words about Holocaust research. At the beginning, there were only lists on paper that needed to be perused. It's easy to miss something, particularly when dealing with spelling mistakes and lists that aren't in order.

Later, computers became a wonderful aid, but they, too, are only as good as the programming. For instance, when I was looking for myself back in YIVO, I had to check one list at a time.

Today, computers programmed at Yad Vashem and other Holocaust websites have the ability to look for a name that "sounds like" an American spelling. It has taken decades to digitize Holocaust records and possible spelling corrections. But computers have limitations, too.

My last name, Lichtenstein, in its variations is a common name among many Jews in Europe. I can't find any record of my father until I take a short course in doing research. I suddenly realize that he might be listed under his secular/Polish name of Ignis, and not just Isaac.

And then I find him – there all the time – listed on the transport to Buchenwald. After that, the trail goes cold.

I still haven't found my mother or brothers on any list of the living or dead. Although I know logically that they cannot be alive, emotionally there is no closure.

I continue looking in every source I can. I'm always looking, and asking and hoping.

Chapter 18

MOTHER IN ISRAEL

Israel is always in our thoughts and hearts. Manny and I begin visiting every year. We both know we might have grown up there if circumstances had been different. We love watching Judaism come alive in the modern State of Israel. We never think of danger when we are there, just the pleasure of finally being in the Jewish homeland.

On every trip, we hunt for an apartment to buy in Jerusalem as a first step to a possible move. We look at dozens of apartments, but nothing feels right. One apartment is too dark, one too small, and still another on the wrong street.

And then Leah Globe, my energetic and practical mother who is busy with volunteer work and helping with her growing brood of great-grandchildren, finds us the perfect place nearby her home.

Sight unseen, Manny makes an offer over the phone for the large apartment on Graetz Street. The street carries the name of German-born Heinrich Graetz, who was one of the first historians to write a comprehensive history of the Jewish people. The apartment is in what is called the "German Colony."

For Manny, as a real estate attorney, arranging the purchase is easy. So, without seeing it, we buy a spacious four-bedroom apartment on the second floor in a beautiful building. We know the location is convenient, but don't realize that within a few years this will become one of the trendiest neighborhoods in Jerusalem.

Rena's mother, Leah Globe.

When we finally see the apartment, we love it. It is time to pack up our lives in New York.

Before we actually moved to Jerusalem, Rabbi David and Bobbie Hartman's daughter Devora and her two children move in. Devorah's husband IDF pilot Aharal'eh Katz is missing in action. Eventually, the young mother learns that her husband is dead. We are glad that we are able to provide a comfortable home for a family undergoing such a trauma.

We get ready to move. We sell our Brooklyn home and downsize our belongings. Manny will carry on his law practice from afar, and will engage in his favorite pastime of teaching Jewish law.

The apartment turns out to be a perfect fit. From the beginning, I feel compelled to invite others to stay with us or at least come for dinner. Hundreds of visitors have slept over in the guest room. Literally thousands have broken bread with us in the large dining-living room. I have an obsession with inviting guests. I like to share stories, and I like to expose them to the beauty of Judaism that they can experience at our table. I love eating a leisurely Shabbat meal with them in my own home. I wonder if my biological mother was like this, or if I picked up this hospitality trait from my mother, Leah.

In Jerusalem, I am teaching English at the Hebrew University, but still have time to spoil my grandchildren, and of course to explore my interests. I became a volunteer guide in Yad Vashem. It's a museum and research center. Teachers come from around the world for practical courses in Holocaust education. The name Yad Vashem comes from the book of Isaiah, 56:5. "And to them will I give in my house and within my memorial and walls a name (a 'yad vashem') ... that shall not be cut off."

There are numerous Holocaust museums in the world. Most of them provide an introduction to the Holocaust for those who know little about it, but Yad Vashem is the advanced course. Over a million visitors come each year, and it's a place of pilgrimage for survivors and our families. The names of the dead, or at least as many as have been recorded, are listed in the Hall of Names. A huge registry allows survivors to fill in chapters of their family history. It's also a repository of Holocaust memorabilia.

My first volunteer assignment is to guide visitors in the art museum which occupies one wing of Yad Vashem. This is the largest collection of "Holocaust art" in the world. Today there are more than 10,000 items in the collection. It includes the works of Jewish artists before and during the Holocaust, and scenes of the Holocaust. Many of the artists risked their lives to create these pictures. I learn about the artists and pictures and tell their stories to groups. Just being among the pictures and sculptures is both healing and inspiring. The art bridges the world of words to capture pain and passion, love and hope. Erudite Manny helps me prepare, doing research to fill in the background and adding his intellectual muscle to my endeavors. Only sometimes I have to remind him that the language is too legalistic.

I realize, with dread, that I need to go back to Europe to gather information. In 1987, Manny and I make plans with another couple, Jane and Marvin Klitsner, to visit Scandinavia. We fly from Tel Aviv to Copenhagen. Part of our plan is to visit Sweden to see the place where I was taken for rehabilitation. Funny, but we never state this as the reason for the trip. It's the elephant in the room when we get together to plan our vacation. I'm embarrassed to talk about it, even with close friends. Maybe they're embarrassed, too.

We rent a Volvo and get maps. There is an easy ferry ride across the Oresund Straits, and a short car ride from Malmo to the site of my rehabilitation.

We haven't set up any appointments. I am still in the toe-dipping stage of my exploration. Our friends are happy to go along with this interesting side trip, but I don't want to burden them with extensive exploration. We didn't, for instance, book hotels nearby the hospital where I was treated or visit the local municipality archives.

Once there, we rely on asking people we meet. The Swedes are friendly and ready to help. The young people we meet speak excellent English, but have no idea of the events of 1946. The older folks we meet don't understand English. At last we meet a police trooper in black boots on a motorcycle. He introduces us to the kiosk owner who points out what is still an "alien camp," a center for immigrants in Tinsgryd. We spot a hospital in Hassleholm, but we have come on a Sunday and there is no one to speak to in the office. The policeman shows us the lake surrounded with apple trees that I remembered so well.

As time goes by, I know that I need to go back again and do a more serious search for my roots. The Yad Vashem Holocaust Museum has occasional educational trips to Poland. In 1989, after registering, I find that I'm terrified, but Manny encourages me and promises to come, too. We are told that if we want to do any research to come prepared to pay for information. We bring dollars, coffee, chocolate and leather belts – consumer goods that are scarce in Soviet-era Poland.

I am scared when I land in Poland. The airport is ugly and small. Everywhere there are guards who look mean and threatening. I hold Manny's hand.

Our luggage gets lost. All of our kosher provisions

are gone. There is nothing kosher to buy except mealy apples that taste like potatoes. Fortunately, the luggage is found, but we are off to a rough start.

Among the first places we visit is Treblinka. The camp was totally razed. Somewhere there may be the ashes of my mother and brothers, scattered in this soil.

My husband, who is a *Kohen,* never goes to cemeteries because of the prohibition of *Kohanim* to come close to the dead. But on this day he stands by my side.

There are 17,000 stones put up by the Polish government, but there is no map, and I can't find the stone of Piotrkow. This makes me sad. Manny advises me to light my memorial candle anywhere I like. It's not as if anyone is buried under these stones. My hands tremble as I light the match.

Rena lit the memorial candle and placed a placard with the names of her birth parents and brothers in Treblinka.

We take a day off from the group itinerary and hire a guide named Maria to help me do research in Piotrkow. We get to the Town Hall to look for my birth certificate. The clerk asks me for my American passport. "You can have it, but you'll find that the name is different, where I was born is different, my mother's name is different. The date I was born is also wrong. Maybe it says blond hair, green eyes. That's about all you'll find."

The clerk is puzzled. Maria explains it all in Polish. The town keeps old records in large, black hand-written ledgers. Each year has its own ledgers. I am grateful that the clerk is willing to read all this old handwriting.

First she looks at records for 1936. No mention of Fredzia Lichtenstein. Nor in 1937. Then the clerk has another idea and looks back in 1935.

"Here it is," she says with satisfaction. In the hand-written ledger, my birthday is recorded: December 18, 1935. My heart is pounding. I am excited, and also feel profound relief.

Remember, this is the first time I've seen my birth certificate.

I start dancing with delight. "I exist, I exist. *Mekimi m'afar dal*. I have risen from the dust."

I make Manny look and read aloud. I continue dancing, telling my friends and husband that I was born. Now most persons don't have to affirm that they were born, but to me, this was confirmation of my memory and the story of my life. Because the birth certificate shows that I was born two months before Fannie, whose birth certificate I've been using, I am two months older. That makes me laugh.

The certificate confirms my Piotrkow origins and most important, the accuracy of my memory. It has my parents' names and our address, confirms that they came

Rena found her childhood home at 2 Plac Czarnieckiego in Piotrkow.

from Piotrkow, and says they were both 26.

I need to pay for the stamps to get a copy with an official stamp. You can imagine that I am ready to pay any amount. I'm glad we have all those dollars with us.

Just to get a sense of the gaps in the economic situation of Poland and western countries at the time, the total bill comes to 18 US cents.

Later, the same helpful clerk sends me a copy of my parents' marriage license and my brothers' birth certificates. The marriage license is the document in which my mother is listed as six years older than my father. I also learn the names of my grandparents and realize for the first time that I am named for my maternal grandmother Fredzia.

The location for the Lichtenstein's mezuzah was clearly visible when Rena revisited the apartment where she lived as a child before the Holocaust.

With Maria's help we find my house. I am short of breath as I look up at the balcony. I remember it. The Fredzia part of me comes alive.

How can I convince the current occupants to let me in? I am dressed up to make an appearance as a rich American who wouldn't be interested in coming to live in a Polish home. I have chocolates and coffee and leather belts.

My heart is beating fast and my hands are shaking as I knock on the door. I see that the location for my family's mezuzah on the doorpost, though it has been painted over, still exists. I run my palm along the stone banister. I know this place.

A white-haired Polish woman answers the door. The translator explains who I am. The woman says she remembers my father! She invites us to come inside.

I step into the living room. I think I remember it. The house is old and in ill-repair, but still beautiful. It's spacious and elegant with parquet floors and high ceilings. There's a ceramic stove for heating in the living room that I remember. My feet remember the stairs where I ran up and down. I remember standing on the balcony.

I ask the woman if she has anything left from my family. I tell her I am willing to pay whatever she asks. She shakes her head. She thinks there were "green dollars" hidden here once, but the previous tenants didn't know what they were and burned them.

I look around, wondering whether the breakfront and its contents belonged to us. Did my mother sit on these chairs? I don't want any of these, but I'd like to know about them, run my hands over the furniture. That's impossible, We stay less than an hour talking. What is there to say?

She says she worked with my father. She remembers him as such a nice man. She tells me the war was hard for the Polish people, too.

There is an embedded sense of familiarity and even comfort in being in this building. I am finally back home.

Here's something strange.

All these years I remember a kiosk where I ate my first ice cream. It's still there. No one is selling ice cream, but I can remember the texture of it on my tongue. I remember my mother buying me ice cream, but I can't picture her face. I breathe deeply, trying to inhale the past and awaken a memory.

Later, I will learn that my mother sold one of her shops to buy this house after I was born. We have the records to prove ownership, but it is not possible to claim this property. My mother bought the apartment in 1936. Germany took it over in 1939, the Soviets in 1945, and the

Polish government in 1961. After that, it was purchased on the private market.

In 1989, I record my own testimony in Yad Vashem. This is the first time I speak for the historical record. I do not enjoy the experience. The interviewer has a confrontational tone, like a police inspector. She keeps grilling me about what I remember and don't remember. Her job is to establish facts, but my memories from childhood are sketchy. I keep saying, "I don't remember exactly, but I know," which she doesn't like.

I have heard other Holocaust survivors describe their childhoods with absolute clarity and wondered how they knew exactly if their shoes were brown or black.

My daughter Menucha sometimes complains that I didn't share enough of my Holocaust history while she was growing up. I couldn't visit those memories back then. I was too invested in being a good wife and mother, and I didn't want my personal suffering to impinge upon my children. As a result, they haven't become involved in meetings of "Second Generation."

I find it easier to talk about this to my grandchildren now that my children are adults. The dialogues I have with my grandchildren are somehow healing, while I feel more defensive with my own children. When I was bringing them up, on one hand, I didn't want to burden them with the history of horror and death. On the other hand I wanted them to appreciate the proud traditions and heroism of their ancestors. It's hard to get this balance right and I never feel totally at ease with it. I take some comfort in knowing I'm not alone in this struggle.

In his book, *Against All Odds*, William Helmreich confirmed that for most survivors, discussing the Holocaust with their children was one of the most difficult issues they faced. The majority dealt with it, although it hurt, at some stage in their children's lives, but usually – like me – after many years or even decades had elapsed. Others are unable to broach the subject at all. In the early years after the war, the shock and drama of liberation, combined with the plight of the survivors, kept the story in the forefront of the news. But then, beginning in the mid-1950s, a "curtain of silence" descended, allowing people to put what had occurred out of their minds.

Our children weren't learning about the Holocaust in school when Menucha was young. General awareness of the Holocaust has increased over the years, also forcing us survivors to confront our pasts. By the time David, our youngest child, was in school, there was a beginning of a discussion on the Holocaust.

I change volunteer jobs at Yad Vashem and become a guide in the Valley of Communities, where each town and city has a stone monument. I expand my knowledge of Holocaust history.

In 1996, I am interviewed by author/historian Lyn Smith for London's Imperial War Museum. The testimony appears in her book, *Forgotten Voices of the Holocaust*. Her interview style is much warmer, and by now, I'm more articulate about my past, able to stitch together more pieces of the quilt.

By the early 2000s I become a frequently invited lecturer, telling my personal story and meeting with a wide array of groups interested in the Holocaust. Groups begin to request me as their guide. I gain a reputation as a guide and speaker, partly because of my American English. Sometimes it works against me.

Once the esteemed violinist, Isaac Stern, was in Israel to teach a master class in the Jerusalem Music Center in Yemin Moshe. Stern and the students, many from Asian countries, want to come to Yad Vashem. I am thrilled to be asked to guide them. I am a lover of music and a huge fan of Stern's.

So I do my homework and learn about his family's Ukrainian/Polish background. Stern came with his parents as a toddler to the United States from Kremenet in 1921. In the Holocaust, the Nazis murdered all but 14 of the 15,000 Jews who remained there. I begin to speak of it, but Stern does not want to hear anything I have to say.

Stern is known as a pleasant, personable superstar, but he can't bear what he assumes is a third-hand description of the Holocaust.

When I say I want to take him to the memorial for his hometown, he says he isn't interested. I ask my friend Renee to stay with him while I give the tour to the rest of the group.

I am insulted, but continue to guide the group of 28 master class students. Sometime during the tour I mention that I was a child in Bergen-Belsen.

Stern's face drains of color. He comes forward to apologize for his rudeness. He tells me that he figured "that some American woman who had studied about the Holocaust from a book had little of worth to tell him." He didn't realize that I am a survivor.

I accept the apology. He subsequently sends me a box of his concert tapes to say he is sorry. Maybe he did learn something from my tour, after all.

One of the common questions I get from my audiences is how I believe I got to be the one in my family to survive. Was I chosen, just lucky, stronger and smarter than others? My answer? "I don't know why."

It's easier for me to answer the question with stories. One of the stories I tell at Yad Vashem originated in the orphanage of Dr. Janusz Korczak in Warsaw.

An
Inspirational
Presence

Holocaust Survivors Volunteer at Yad Vashem

Rena is a frequent volunteer guide at the Yad Vashem Holocaust Museum in Jerusalem.

Korczak was a forward-minded educator and popular author who allowed the orphans freedom and self-government. His educational theories were so famous that the Germans would have allowed him to live, but instead he chose – like our Rabbi Lau – to go to the death camp Treblinka with his flock.

The orphanage wasn't religious in terms of strict Sabbath observance, but Jewish traditions were observed. There was a communal Seder on Passover, complete with "stealing" part of the ceremonial middle matzo, the afikomen, and hiding it until the Seder leader ransomed it back.

On Seder night in the orphanage, when it was time to steal the afikomen, two hundred eager children sat around the table hoping they'd get to "steal it." The lucky child

In 2006, Rena was formally recognized for her volunteer service and received the award from Jerusalem Mayor Uri Lupolianski. She has also received many prizes and awards from communal organizations like Hadassah, Emunah and Amit, as well as from the National Geographic.

מתנדבים מקבלי אות
ראש העיר
לשנת תשס"ו 2006

גב' רינה קווינט החלה את פעילותה ההתנדבותית לפני כ-20 שנה. כחברה בסניף ירושלים של ארגון "אמונה". רינה פעילה מאוד בתחום קליטת עליה וביתה פתוח לרווחה לכל עולה חדש ותייר, אותו היא רואה כעולה חדש בפוטנציה.

יחד עם עוד חברת אמונה, הקימה רינה את המרכז ללימודי השואה ע"ש יוסי ברוגר, במכללת אמונה. רינה מנהלת את המרכז, עוסקת בגיוס כספים לעזרת תלמידות הרוצות לנסוע לפולין.

פעמיים בשנה, בערב יום השואה וכליל הבדולח, רינה מארגנת לתושבי ירושלים כנס זיכרון גדול: לזכור ולא לשכוח את שעבר על העם היהודי בשואה.

חלק גדול מספריית השואה במרכז, מושתת על תרומותיה של רינה. ספרים, סרטים קלטות וציוד אחר.
בכל עת מוכנה רינה להדריך סיורים ב"יד ושם" ובמגדל דוד, ובדרך זו היא מצליחה להדביק את כולם באהבת ישראל וירושלים.

גב' רינה קווינט

who could take part in this ritual would find a filbert inside his matzo ball in the soup. One of the few survivors told about everyone searching for the filbert and how he was lucky enough to be the one to find it in his soup! "I prayed very hard and I got it."

Finding the nut saved his life. He ransomed it for a few zlotys. When the war started, the boy was able to pay for his transportation out in a carriage to Russia with those zlotys and was saved.

Was his being saved chance or destiny? This is a huge question in Jewish philosophy, which elicits strong opinions in both directions. Some argue that every leaf falling from a tree is the decree of God, while others leave room for chance.

How often have I asked myself why I survived when my brothers didn't? I have no clear answer, but feel that because I was able to survive, I must make my life meaningful and dominated by good deeds.

When I take a group of nine-year-olds, among them my granddaughter Shani (Naomi's daughter), to Yad Vashem, they are too young to visit the museum itself, so I give them a grand tour of the outdoor sculpture garden. I create a sort of scavenger hunt, with me asking the children to find symbols and emblems related to Judaism: a Jewish star, a Hanukkah menorah or a Torah scroll. I also include the sculpture of Dr. Korczak in the game.

There is a magnificent sculpture by Boris Saktsier of Dr. Korczak holding children. All the children have the same scared face, with their heads hanging low. Dr. Korczak has his arms around them. There's a cut in the hand to show his helplessness. I explain it to the children.

Afterwards, I take the children to a nearby playground, the Jerusalem Monster slide. But when they send me a thank you note – an oak tag with all of their comments, the part of the visit they liked most was seeing "the man with the broken hand."

Another time, I am babysitting for Odelliah and Moriah, two of my older granddaughters, while leading a tour group at Yad Vashem. We go to the art museum. I am ambivalent. Should I take them to the Children's Memorial, too?

Let me describe the Children's Memorial. You enter from what is usually the bright Jerusalem sunshine into an underground cavern hollowed in the hillside. A funnel of stone draws you into a dark space. There are photos of children and a voice, speaking in Hebrew, Yiddish and English, reads the name of a murdered child, his or her age, and their hometown. The darkness is offset by flickering lights, three memorial candles infinitely reflected throughout the hall.

Here we remember the million and a half children – a quarter of the Six Million murdered by the Nazis and their collaborators. The Children's Memorial was designed by world-famous Israeli architect Moshe Safdie and was donated by Abraham and Edita Spiegel, themselves survivors. Their son Uziel, the name of a Biblical angel, was murdered in Auschwitz at the age of two and a half.

I decide to take the children in. "I'm going to hold your hands," I tell them. We walk slowly. "Are you sad? Afraid?" I whisper.

"No," answers Odelliah, who is Menucha's daughter. "It's so beautiful. God promised the Israelites that we would be like the stars in the heaven, and here are all these children like stars."

I think of my brothers, her great uncles, as stars shining and I am comforted.

The Future Generation – Eli and Shani Silverman, Rena's grandchildren, carry a wreath at the "Dor Hemshech" commemoration program at Yad Vashem in Jerusalem.

How do I live with my lapses in memory that still trouble me even after the visit to a psychologist? I try to accept that these lapses are a common symptom for survivors. Take the story of Elsa Pollack, for example.

When I was still guiding in the art museum section of Yad Vashem, artist Elsa Pollack spoke about her powerful sculpture "Auschwitz," a tall chimney with six sections. When she and her parents were in Czechoslovakia, they were told to go to the *umschlagplatz*, a plaza used as a gathering place. At some point, they were ordered to leave their bundles behind, including her father's tallit and tefillin. As they boarded the train, her father was so distraught to be leaving his tallit and tefillin behind that he couldn't be comforted. Elsa, just a child, ran back and, among the thousands of packages, found his tallit and tefillin, and gave it to him on the train. Her parents were murdered in Auschwitz. Her father probably never used the tallit and tefillin again. She vowed at that time that she would never cry again. She'd used up all her tears.

But when this sculpture was unveiled in Yad Vashem and her friends and family were there, she broke down and wept. The people asked why she was crying then when she didn't cry when she was sick or lonely. She answered, "What merit did I have to survive when my pious parents died?"

One of her guests answered, "It says in the Bible, if you honor your parents you will live a long life. Maybe your saving your father's tallit and tefillin is the reason." I often repeated this story while guiding.

Years later, Pollack is once again at Yad Vashem. I have a chance to talk to her and tell her how important her story is to me.

I am leading a group near the sculpture and see Pollak. "Here is the great artist," I shout to my group. "You are so lucky! She can tell you the story herself." But Pollak defers to me, the guide, to tell her story.

When I finish, I am surprised and upset to see that she has turned white. "Where did you hear that story?" she asks. I remind her that she told it herself. "Impossible," she says. "I don't believe in God and would never tell such a story. But the story is true."

I often have young people come up to me after hearing my story to ask to speak to me personally. Many want to talk about their personal challenges. Some are adopted and want to discuss this with me.

High school students from Jewish schools in Israel and the Diaspora visit Poland to internalize the events and lessons of the Holocaust. I have frequently been invited to accompany the students, tell my story, and answer their heartfelt questions. The groups are usually part of a program called "The March of the Living." The march

Rena, at the site of the memorial stones in Treblinka.

itself is 1.8 miles from Auschwitz to Birkenau.

The groups include teachers and guides and medical staff. On one trip, we are traveling in seven buses on a Polish highway. There is a major accident in the opposite direction. We stop to help. Our Israeli doctors and nurses run to the scene. Some of our youngsters protest that we shouldn't help the Poles who have been so cruel to the Jews. We explain that our own obligation to act as moral human beings has to overcome any fear or anger we have. We are commanded in the Torah not to stand by idly while our fellow human being's blood is being spilled.

We visit Treblinka, where my mother, brothers, and aunts and uncles were likely murdered. On my previous trip, I was unable to find the stone for Piotrkow, among the 17,000 memorial stones. This still bothers me. I share this personal disappointment with the group of students and ask for their assistance to find the Piotrkow stone.

Suddenly a boy with dyed dreadlocks, headphones for music and earrings comes running up to me. "Rena," he says. "Rena! I found it! I prayed that God would help me find it and I did. I grew up in Argentina where no one in my community was religious. There were few Jews. I know that God answered my prayers and not only did I find your stone, but I understood for the first time that I am also a part of the Jewish people."

Not all of the visits to Poland are so moving. We run into anti-Semites, too. Skinheads and others taunt and threaten us. We have guards with us, of course. Our own teens want to do battle with the skinheads, but, of course, we don't allow this. On one trip, on Shabbat afternoon, I am taking a walk with a group of adults. Some Polish kids mock us: "Jid, Jid, Jid." I freeze. Security moves forward. Afterwards, one of the men with me says something interesting. "I never thought of myself as a Jew, just an

Rena, at the Piotrkow stone in Treblinka.

Israeli." He discovers his Jewishness in Poland!

No matter how many times I go to Poland, when I see these Jewish young adults carry the Israeli flags through the concentration camps it makes me choke up.

In October 2007, I face a particularly tough challenge. I am invited to Bergen-Belsen by the Foundation for Memorials in Lower Saxony. I do not want to go. I never want to see this place again. But then I convince myself. This is not just a graveyard. There's a new Memorial in Bergen-Belsen being created, along with a double-volume set of the names of former prisoners, dead and alive. I'm in that book.

In his introduction to the *Book of Remembrance*, Bernd Busemann, then Minister of Education and Cultural Affairs of Lower Saxony and chairperson of the Board of the Foundation for Memorials in Lower Saxony writes: "A name is closely bound to the personality and dignity of each and every person in each and every culture. The National Socialists sought to debase their prisoners in the concentration camps by reducing them to mere numbers. With the loss of their names, the prisoners were supposed to lose their personalities and eventually their will to live. This process of the destruction of millions of human lives ended in the burning or anonymous burial of the bodies in mass graves. In Bergen-Belsen, even the camp records office was burned down in order to wipe out the traces of the crimes and the names of the victims."

The Lower Saxony State government and German Federal Government have provided the financial means to compile the material and print the books.

Through their search of the records and personal testimonies, a master list was created. The total number of prisoners in the Bergen-Belsen concentration camp was estimated by the researchers to be around 120,000. Because the records were burned, the researchers drew their list from parallel and alternative records. Of the estimated 50,000 who died, fewer than 10,000 names have been recorded. The records from certain parts of the diverse camp were better than others. As you might expect, the records for the "Detention/Exchange Camp" in which Jewish prisoners intended for exchange and the families in the "Star Camp" are far better than for those of us who came at the end of the war, long columns of prisoners dumped in the camp to die. It's fragmentary at best. Not even after liberation were our names fully listed

The inscription on this memorial in Bergen-Belsen reads:

**ISRAEL AND THE WORLD SHALL REMEMBER
THIRTY THOUSAND JEWS
EXTERMINATED IN THE CONCENTRATION CAMP
OF BERGEN-BELSEN
AT THE HANDS OF THE MURDEROUS NAZIS**

EARTH CONCEAL NOT THE BLOOD SHED ON THEE!

**FIRST ANNIVERSARY OF LIBERATION
15TH APRIL 1946 (14TH NISSAN 5706)**

**CENTRAL JEWISH COMMITTEE
BRITISH ZONE**

in the rush.

To get to Bergen-Belsen from Israel, Manny and I fly to Hamburg, then Hanover and stay at the Crowne Plaza Hotel in Celle. I'm usually a good traveler, but I am very agitated on this visit. From the first minute, I don't want to remain in Germany.

Because of the nature of the group there is a lot of security. I find the German men and women in uniform intolerable. There seems to be endless inspections of our bags, orders to get in line, calls to take off our shoes.

Although I'm a sociable person, I can't find my place among the other survivors. I don't want to talk to anyone.

Instead, I became obsessed about Sabbath services. I was promised that there would be kosher food and religious services on the trip.

I am concerned that no Sabbath prayer services have been organized, and that Manny will not be able to pray in a quorum, where a minimum of ten men is needed to recite certain prayers, among them *Kaddish*, the prayer for the dead.

The idea that among all these Jews and all the Jewish souls buried here, there will not be an organized Jewish prayer service galls me. Instead, there is a tour of the area, which takes place on the Sabbath.

My inability to organize a prayer session awakens an old feeling of helplessness.

In general, I'm not a person who interferes with the lack of observance of others. I have family and friends who are Sabbath-observant and others who aren't. Here I feel hurt and offended by the lack of interest in Judaism in this place where so many Jews suffered and died. I can't shake my miserable mood.

On Sunday we visit the beautiful new museum. I am relieved, as always, to find myself in the computer. But this doesn't assuage the gloom I feel.

There's a mountain of dirt where the dead are buried. It reminds me of an archaeological hill, called a "*tel*" in Hebrew, where archaeologists dig up remnants of bygone civilizations. Bygone, indeed. Had the British liberated us a few days later, my bones would have been in that hill. That's an unnerving feeling. Whereas other chapters of my personal story are best-possible-guesses, I know I was in Bergen-Belsen. I remember being here: the fear, the hunger, the stench.

This place makes me sick with sadness. Bergen-Belsen is too much for me. I can't wait to leave. I shudder when I think of it.

I do not expect to ever go back to Poland or Germany again, but in 2010 I visit Piotrkow again with a group of survivors. Most of those who come are family groups or extended families who have known each other since childhood. My friends Esther and Greer come with me. Their roots aren't in Piotrkow, but in Czestochowa, an hour's ride away. They have become part of my extended family in Israel.

In the Piotrkow synagogue I attend a ceremony with Naphtali Lavi who is celebrating his second Bar Mitzvah. His father was our honored Rabbi. Naphtali has grown up to be an ambassador.

After the ceremony, we walk to the building where he went to preschool and school, today one of the most elegant pubs in town. A Klezmer concert had been arranged in the ambassador's honor by the local municipality.

Visiting the cemetery and the forest where so many of our family members were murdered is difficult, but a moral necessity. So many of those who were murdered have no living descendants. Through our presence their memories are honored.

Most of my fellow survivors are older than me and remember happy times in Piotrkow before the war. My own memories are overlaid with the ghetto, fear and death.

In April 2013, my grandson Boaz accompanies me on a speaking tour in South Africa. I'd been invited after Mary Kluk, the leader of the Board of Jewish Deputies in South Africa and Director of the Durban Holocaust Centre, heard me speak at Yad Vashem in Jerusalem. She asked me to speak to many groups in South Africa. Boaz carries my suitcases and makes sure we arrive on time at the airports. I feel uncomfortable that he has to hear my

In Durban, South Africa. (R-L) Mary Kluk, Rena Quint, Rev. Bongani S. Hlatshwayo, and Rena's grandson, Boaz, 2013.

From Wendy Kahn, National Director South African Jewish Board of Deputies

Dear Quint Family: Hi from South Africa. I'd like to start by thanking you all for sharing your wonderful wife, mother, and grandmother with us. It has meant so much to us to learn not only from Rena's powerful Shoah story but also the many life lessons that she has left us with.

Everybody with whom she has interacted has been inspired and changed through their interaction with her. Her story has left each one of us enriched.

The journalist from one of our leading women's magazines said this of her interview, "In the 25 years that I have worked at Fair Lady magazine, I have never done such a meaningful interview".

Rena conducted a vast range of radio and print interviews, each of them leaving the journalist 'speechless' with her words of wisdom.

Yesterday she stood up in front of well over 1000 people on the stage in front of a statue of 6 Shofarot and she told her story without a piece of paper in front of her.

Before I sign off, I'd like to also thank you for sending Boaz to accompany Rena. Boaz in his own right was quite a hit here - particularly since he is studying in Gush, where many South Africans including my husband studied. He is a real special person and it was so wonderful spending time with him. His attentiveness and devotion to his grandmother was truly inspirational and we are hoping that it is not the last time he visits our shores.

Regards, Wendy Kahn
April 8, 2013

story over and over at each of the venues. Boaz doesn't seem to mind.

We are invited to a women's prison in Durban, South Africa. Rev. Bongani S. Hlatshwayo, the warden, heard me speak on the radio. I was nervous before the interview, warned that there might be many anti-Israel callers who would harass me. Fortunately, the interviewer became so engrossed in my story that he didn't leave time for callers, or maybe he wanted to protect me.

After the show, the warden gets in touch with me. He says he wants to motivate his women prisoners. None of them has gone through the horrors I have, and they can see that I have survived and have turned out well. He thinks it will encourage them.

I am uncomfortable when I walk in and the heavy prison doors lock behind me. The prisoners are singing hymns. I ask myself what I am doing there. But as I begin to speak and feel the rapt attention of the prisoners – many of whom are unaware that the Holocaust has taken place – my heart warms to them.

"No matter how down and out you were, no matter what you have gone through, you, too can be a positive person," the warden says to them. "Just look at this survivor. She went through worse than you did and she is okay."

I continue to seek clues to the gaps in my personal history. Jacek Bednark continues to search archives in Piotrkow and elsewhere. I am still reading books and listening to testimonies at Yad Vashem. I'm always looking for additional sources of information.

In 2015, I learn about a woman named Helena who was in Sweden with me. I get her telephone number from Lucia and contact her to meet.

Driving from Jerusalem to Ramat Aviv, Barbara Sofer and I talk about everything except the upcoming meeting. I'm a little nervous, yet very excited. Otherwise, why would it take me three phone calls to get the correct address for the GPS?

Helena, only a year older than me, lives in an assisted living home in a posh section of Tel Aviv. The building is beautiful white stone, with a swimming pool, pilates studio, and art classes.

I don't know what to expect. Is Helena frail? A slim brown-haired woman in a pink-checked blouse and dark pants greets us and hugs me hello. I don't recognize her. I'm sure she doesn't recognize me either. But we both remember each other as children.

The living room is attractive with a European elegance. A lemon tree is blooming on her balcony.

Helena was born in a small town, and came to Piotrkow as a toddler when her parents went to work in an uncle's flour mill. Unlike mine, her family lived outside the Jewish area. They spoke Polish at home.

Helena was in Bergen-Belsen, too. She remembers me from Sweden, from 1945. We are in 2015. I do the math, 70 years ago. Helena has been living in Israel all this time.

Helena tells me that she remembers Anna Philipstahl and Sigmund. She remembers me leaving Sweden with them.

I listen to her life-story, its own narrative of horror and sorrow. It resonates for me, too. When she lost her mother, her father's new woman-friend shielded her. This replacement mother, about whom Helena is ambivalent until today, must have felt Helena's anger and resentment. Still, she provided for her and protected her long after they had parted from Helena's father.

Female relatives – aunties – who worked in the

kitchen in Bergen-Belsen took risks to provide her with additional food.

Her story confirms what I had long maintained – an untold story of the Holocaust – the need to mother and be mothered was stronger than the fear of death.

Despite our similar background, Helena and I don't have much in common. She hates talking about the Holocaust. She is a nurse. She never married. So much of my life is centered on my family. On the other hand, she has kept in contact with many more Holocaust survivors than I have. They have made up her social circle. She is so certain of every detail of her past. I wonder if I had spent more time with other survivors would my narrative be different, with others filling in missing pieces of my history?

When I leave Helena, we say we will stay in touch, but I wonder if we will. Is the memory of Sweden enough to renew a friendship?

The meeting makes me think about a theory of the Holocaust that girls and women had a better chance of survival. At first I waved away this idea as absurd. But maybe there's something to it. Women mixed more with Polish women and spoke the language better with a less identifiable accent. Girls often went to public schools. They had no outward symbols of being Jewish, but the men were circumcised. Sometimes I wondered if my parents made a greater effort to save me because they knew my brothers, who were circumcised, had no chance of passing as non-Jews and surviving.

The natural ability of women to connect and form relationships was another advantage.

In 2017, there are fewer than 170,000 of us Holocaust survivors living in Israel. Two thirds of us are women.

Rena and Manny host a group from China in their home.

Most of us are over 80. My hope of filling in the remaining blanks of my history is dim.

I feel compelled to tell my story. I continue to meet thousands of people who want to hear it. Most of these lectures are at Yad Vashem, but I am also invited to almost every public venue in Israel. I host many groups at my own home, groups of Germans and Chinese have come to tea, ambassadors and college students, Rabbis and priests fill our living room.

Where does this compulsion to speak come from?

I'm reminded of the Talmudic story of Rabbi Honi Hama'agal, literally Honi the Circle Maker, who was a miracle working Rabbi of the first century. One day he was traveling along a roadside and observed a person planting a carob tree – known even then to take 70 years to bear fruit. Honi asked him if he was certain he'd live for another 70 years. "I found carob trees in the world. As those who came before me planted them for me, I'm planting for my children." The Talmudic story goes on.

Rena, at Yad Vashem, continues to relate her Holocaust experience.

Honi falls asleep and wakes up 70 years later. He sees a man gathering carobs. "Are you the man who planted the tree?" he asks. The man shakes his head: "I am his grandson."

I am the lucky woman who already has grandsons and granddaughters and great-grandsons and great-granddaughters to tell my own story to.

At Yad Vashem we tell our stories and plant trees, literally and figuratively. It's no coincidence that the trees we plant are also carobs. Avenues of carob trees line the museum.

We have another Talmudic story about sage Rabbi Shimon bar Yochai and his son who hid in a cave to escape the Roman conquerors. They were sustained by the carobs from a tree that grew at the mouth of the cave.

One of my greatest pleasures is visiting these carob trees, together with the "Righteous Among the Nations," those holy men and women who risked their lives to save

Jews. Sometimes I meet their grandchildren, too.

Those who didn't survive charged those of us who did with telling the world what happened. When I speak of the Holocaust, I'm doing my part to keep it from being forgotten.

I loved the trip to South Africa with my grandson. We met wonderful audiences of Jews and non-Jews. I have an offer to visit Australia and New Zealand to tell my story. Will I travel to those far lands to reach the hearts of men and women there? I will speak for as long as I have a voice and can tell my story cogently. I pray that God will give me the strength to continue.

Rena and Emanuel Quint.

For the last 59 years, I have been married to one wonderful man: Emanuel Quint. As soon as I met him, I felt the love of God reflected in him. I consider myself the luckiest woman alive to have such a fine and loving husband and large, wonderful family. Together with Manny and me, we have a family – a tribe really – of 55 persons counting children, their spouses, grandchildren, their spouses and great-grandchildren. Add to this, many good friends whom we cherish.

I know much about the complexity of motherhood. I am a mother of four, a grandmother of 22 and a great-grandmother of 22.

Despite my horrendous childhood, I think of my life as joyful. I have had a wonderful life. I am grateful to all my mothers. I owe my life and my accomplishments and my ability to wake up with a song in my heart to these selfless women. Maybe they were not entirely selfless.

By loving and caring for someone else, we also preserve ourselves. Every mother knows this.

I honor all of the mothers who saved me and loved me and all of the mothers, biological and non-biological, who are dedicated to passing on the good to those who come after us. I honor all my mothers who provided the love and nurturing for a new generation. I honor you all on Mother's Day and every day.

Rena and Manny's son and daughters.

*Rena with her family and friends dancing
at her surprise 70th birthday party.*

Rena and Manny with their family on the occasion of the Bar Mitzvah of the their grandson, Yossie.

Rena and Manny with their children and grandchildren at Ariah and Chamutal's wedding.

Rena and Manny's grandchildren and great-grandchildren.

Chapter 19

MANY MOTHERS

Here in Israel, Mother's Day is celebrated on the anniversary of the death of a valiant woman named Henrietta Szold. She was born in 1860 in Baltimore and moved to Israel when she was in her 50s. She never married and never had children.

When the Nazis took power in Germany and began spreading their tentacles throughout Europe, young Jews were suddenly left without jobs or schools. A Rabbi's wife in Berlin named Recha Freier suggested that they begin moving to pre-State Israel, even without their parents.

At first, the idea seemed outrageous. Who would take care of them? Miss Szold, as most called her, was recruited to organize this. She traveled to Europe and saw the desperate situation.

Young people began to arrive. Henrietta Szold met their ships. Few of the youngsters would ever see their parents again. They called her "*Ima,*" Hebrew for mother. They all had personal relationships with her. If anyone was unkind to them, they wrote home to their Mother and this petite American-born lady arrived to put matters in order.

Israel chose the anniversary of her death as the right day for Mother's Day, today renamed Family Day. Parenting, it was decided, was far more than a biological function. I have been blessed with so many mothers. None of us, with or without biological children, is exempt from helping to shelter and mentor the next generation. That's what I'm trying to do. The next generation and the next and next.

> *"The need to mother*
> *– and be mothered –*
> *is stronger than the fear of death."*
>
> Rena Quint

SIX QUESTIONS FREQUENTLY ASKED OF RENA QUINT

1. How can you be so normal? They say that the formative years are the most important and yours couldn't have been worse.

   Answer: I don't have an answer except to say maybe my biological mother gave me a lot of love in utero before I was born and then for the first three and a half years of my life. After that, I guess I was lucky until the age of ten to have different mothers who were supportive. Then I got really wonderful parents at the age of ten who gave me all the love and caring, and I have a wonderful husband and children who returned my life and nurtured my soul.

2. Do you believe in God?

   Answer: Yes, I very much believe in God. I am a religious woman and my husband and children all maintain fully observant lives. We couldn't be good religious people if we didn't believe in God. I don't understand how God could have allowed six million of His chosen people to be destroyed, and I also don't understand how the Germans, who are also God's people formed in the image of God, acted the way they did. I believe with all my heart that I could not have survived unless God was watching over me.

3. Why did you come to live in Israel?

   Answer: We always felt we belonged in a Jewish state. We brought our children up in a Zionist home and when our children got older, they all wanted to come to Israel.

First our oldest daughter got married and moved here and then our third daughter came to study at the university here. Our son went to yeshiva and our second daughter, who got married in the states, said she and her husband would come after graduation, so we just followed.

4. Could the Holocaust happen again?

Answer: I pray and hope that it doesn't. But when you realize what is happening in Syria and with groups like ISIS, you see that a Holocaust is happening to those people right now. How is it possible that civilized people could put a man in a cage, douse him in gasoline, and have his family and the whole world watch him burn and die in agony? Isn't that a holocaust?

5. How does it feel to be adopted?

Answer: I never really think about it. From the age of ten I had two wonderful parents, aunts, uncles and cousins and, even though they weren't biological, I had a family. My children had grandparents, and my children had each other and an extended family. I wish I had known my parents, but I guess God gave me a second chance.

6. What is the message you want us to take home?

Answer: Hitler wanted to annihilate all the Jews. He succeeded in killing six million of our brethren, a million and a half children, but you are here. I hope that all of you who are Jewish will marry a Jewish spouse. It doesn't matter if they are orthodox, conservative, or reform. The Jewish people are dwindling and if we assimilate and intermarry, Hitler will have won a posthumous victory. We can't afford to let him win.

TIMELINE

January 30, 1933: Adolf Hitler is appointed Chancellor of Germany.

March 5, 1933: Reichstag (Parliament) elections. Hitler gets 44 percent of the vote, forms a coalition government.

March 22, 1933: Dachau, the first concentration camp, is set up near Munich. First prisoners are mostly Communists, Social-Democrats and homosexuals, or those accused of such.

September 15, 1935: Nuremberg Laws. Reich strips Jews of civil rights in Germany.

December 18, 1935: Fredzia Lichtenstein is born in Piotrkow, Trybunalski, Poland. (This date became known in 1989 when Rena was able to retrieve a copy of her birth certificate.) She lives in Plac Zydowski (now Czarnieckiego 2). The Germans will rename this square Judenplatz. She has two older brothers and her parents are delighted with the little girl.

February 15, 1936: This is the birth date that Rena uses on all of her official documents until today. In 1946, she entered the United States as Fannie Philipstahl, and this was Fannie's birth date.

August 1, 1936: Olympic Games held in Berlin and succeed in fooling the world that everything is okay in Germany.

October 25, 1936: Mussolini signs the "Axis" alliance with Hitler.

March 13, 1938: The Nazi Reich annexes Austria. This is called the Anschluss.

July 6, 1938: American President Franklin D. Roosevelt proposes an international conference in Evian, Switzerland. Twenty-nine countries come, but no one agrees to open gates wide for refugees.

August 17, 1938: Jews in Germany are required to add middle names of Israel and Sarah to their identity cards. Jewish baby names are restricted so that German names aren't used.

September 29, 1938: England and France accept Germany's annexation of the Sudetenland, a province of Czechoslovakia at the Munich conference.

November 9, 1938: Pogrom called Kristallnacht because the glass in Jewish stores and synagogues was shattered. One hundred Jews were murdered, 30,000 arrested.

September 1, 1939: The Germans invade Poland. Four days later Piotrkow is occupied by the Germans. Fredzia will soon be four. Anti-Jewish *Aktions* begin. All of Poland is occupied within a month.

October 8, 1939: Jews outside the Jewish neighborhood are ordered to move there.

October 12, 1939: The *general gouvernment* is established as the Nazi's means of ruling Poland. A Jewish Community Council of 12 members is set up in Piotrkow to carry out orders of the Germans within the community. Germans decide to isolate Jews by establishing a ghetto. Jews outside of the ghetto reportedly don't listen to orders to leave their homes and are forced out by the Germans.

October 31, 1939: Deadline for moving into the ghetto.

November 1, 1939: The first Nazi ghetto is created in the Jewish neighborhood of Piotrkow. Restrictions are put in place. White skull signs will mark borders.

July 1940: A ghetto census is taken. Refugees from other areas crowd into the ghetto.

Winter 1940-41: Typhus epidemic on Hanukkah, new commander Buss takes over ghetto.

Spring 1941: The Germans create a payoff system which allows Jews certain rights. For instance, matzo is allowed to be baked for Passover. Fredzia, 5, celebrates Passover with her family.

June 22, 1941: Germany attacks the USSR. The rural Jewish communities around Piotrkow continue to supply the ghetto with food.

July 1941: *Judenrat* chairperson Zalman Tenenbaum and other members of the ghetto administrative staff and members of the Bund are arrested.

September 1941: Several of arrested Jewish officials are deported from Piotrkow and apparently murdered following the discovery of their underground activities. A second *Judenrat* is appointed. Dr. Shimon Warschawski is the new chair.

April 1942: The ghetto is sealed, its borders narrowed, and the overcrowding intensifies. Two young men from Chelmo relate the ghastly news of Jewish massacres in other places. The news isn't generally believed. Fredzia should have begun school, but there is no formal school education.

Spring-Summer 1942: Germans send forged greeting cards to the ghetto from Jews who had been deported from various cities and were now supposedly held in forced labor camps in the East.

July 23, 1942: The first recorded killings in Treblinka. Also, the Jewish fast day of Tisha B'Av (the 9th of Av). Jews continue to be caught hiding in cellars under the city market; they are murdered on the spot or sent to the ghetto in Tomaszow Mazowiecki, which is being liquidated. Several hundred Jews caught in the small ghetto without work permits are concentrated in Piotrkow Trybunalski's synagogue where they remain for several weeks. They are shot to death over several days in Rakow forest.

August 1942: Piotrkow Jews hear of the deportation of the Jews of Radom and Kiełcze.

Fall 1942: Annihilation of the Jews is expected. By the Jewish New Year, September 11, Rosh Hashanah, residents realize what awaits.

September 21, 1942: Yom Kippur. Crying is heard from homes. Rabbi Moshe Chaim Lau delivers his farewell address before Yizkor, the memorial prayer for the dead.

September 22, 1942: In Piotrkow, Jews hear of Nazi *Aktion* in nearby industrial city of Czestochowa where many have relatives.

October 1942: Jews from Srock, Tuszyn, Wolborz, Przyglow, Sulejow, Rozprza and Kamiensk are transferred to the Piotrkow Ghetto. They are allowed to bring large quantities of material possessions.

October 12, 1942: Ukrainian units arrive in the city. The factory directors of Hortensia, Kara and Bugai order their workers including Fredzia's father and uncle to take up residence at their work places.

October 14-22, 1942: *Aktion* begins in Piotrkow. SS and Ukrainian militia, organized by *SS-Hauptsturmführer* Willy Blum, surround and seal the ghetto at 2 a.m. A thousand elderly people are shot; 6,000 at a time are deported in 52 cattle cars, in each of four transports: a total of 22,000 Jews. The last transport, including Rabbi Lau and dignitaries, isn't full; 2,000 Jewish workers in the glass factory can see the trains leave. The trains are sent to Treblinka where the Jews are gassed upon arrival. In addition to the legal workers, between 1,000 and 2,000 illegals remain in hiding after the *Aktions.*

November 2, 1942: Group of captured "illegals" are held in the synagogue, then sent to Tomaszow Mazowiecki, from where they were deported to Treblinka together with the Jews of Tomaszow.

November 19, 1942: One hundred Jews, mostly elderly, are taken first to the synagogue, and then shot in the Rakow forest.

November 25, 1942: Effort made to find hiding Jews by telling them they can now register for work. This is a bluff, but many come out and are held in the synagogue. Reports of babies' heads bashed. Eight children are burned by Ukrainian guards. Several prisoners succeed in negotiating their way out.

December 19, 1942: There are 42 men taken from the synagogue to the Rakow forest and ordered to dig burial pits. Most are shot, but some escape. A total of 520 Jews, in groups of 50, are murdered in the Rakow forest.

Winter 1942-43: Gradually, over one thousand Jews come out of hiding places and infiltrate the forced labor camp which has been established in the small ghetto. Numbers increase to between 3,600 and 4,000. They work in the factories and workshops, as well as in collecting and sorting the belongings of deported Jews. The small ghetto has a curfew at night, and any Jew who is found outside of the block is shot.

Beginning 1943: From the small ghetto, 500 Jews are sent to the munitions factory in Skarzysko-Kamienna.

March 21, 1943: Purim. Ten Jews are selected for so-called exchange with Palestinian Germans. Instead they are massacred.

April 21, 1943: Pesach *Aktion*, workers instructed to stay in Hortensia.

July 1943: The small ghetto is liquidated; 500 Jews are murdered. Factory workers remain in barracks near the factory. Germans hang a sign at the Piotrkow Trybunalski train station: "Piotrkow Trybunalski is Judenrein (free of Jews)." Fredzia is seven.

November 25, 1944: Hortensia and other work camps are liquidated. SS takes the Jewish men to work in the armaments factory in Czestochowa and the Buchenwald concentration camp in Germany. Most of the Jewish women were sent to the Ravensbruck concentration camp in Germany. Others reportedly are sent to Bergen-Belsen, Mauthausen, and Auschwitz.

January 15-16, 1945: Because of the success of the Soviet offensive, the SS evacuates camps in Poland close to the front. Around 5,000 prisoners are sent to the concentration camps Buchenwald, Gross-Rosen and

Ravensbruck where most of them perish. Jewish resistance fighters of ZOB (Zydowska Organizacja Bojowa) fight unsuccessfully against the Germans until June 1943.

January 16, 1945: Piotrkow is liberated by the Red Army.

January 20, 1945: Ignis Lichtenstein, Fredzia's father, arrives in Buchenwald from Czestochowa. He is never heard from again.

April 15, 1945: British troops liberate Bergen-Belsen. They find Fredzia Lichtenstein alive among the piles of dead bodies.

May 9, 1945: VE Day, the German Army surrenders.

July 5-26, 1945: Fredzia leaves Bergen-Belsen via the Lubeck, Germany port and on the Kastleholm ship. She is sent to Aliens Camp in Bjarred, Sweden (near Malmo) for medical care and possible adoption.

August 6, 1945: The United States drops an atomic bomb on Hiroshima, Japan.

August 10, 1945: In Sweden, Fredzia is hospitalized in Hassleholm for diphtheria and typhus. August 15, 1945: Japan surrenders.

September 2, 1945: Formal Japanese surrender in Tokyo. World War II ends. Out of the estimated 28,000 Jews who had been imprisoned in the Piotrkow ghetto, 1,600-1,700 have survived, either in the camps or in hiding. Prior to World War II, 3.3 million Jews lived in Poland; 380,000 survived.

September 28, 1945: Fredzia is sent to a recuperation camp in Tinsgryd, Sweden.

October 1945: There are 370 Jews are living in Piotrkow.

March 26, 1946: Fredzia arrives in the USA on the Drottningholm ship sailing from Gothenburg, Sweden. According to the records, she's now a girl from Germany, and her name is Fannie Philipstahl. Her name will soon be changed again to Frances Philipstahl.

September 18, 1946: Anna Philipstahl (born August 18, 1903 in Ochtendung, Germany) dies in New York in Park East Hospital. She's 43. Her husband Julius had died in 1944. Fredzia/Frances is once again an orphan. Fredzia (now using the name Frances) spends a weekend with Leah and Jacob Globe, Brooklyn, NY.

December 2, 1946: Fredzia goes to live with the Globes in Brooklyn.

December 5, 1946: The Philipstahl's official guardian is Anna's cousin, Louis Goldberg, North 4th Street, Lindenhurst, Long Island.

June 24, 1947: Fredzia's name is officially changed to Rena, which means "joy."

October 28, 1947: The Globes advertise through the American Joint Distribution Committee for surviving relatives of Fredzia. Uncle Rushinek, by marriage, is found in Israel. Cousin Irving Cymberknopf is living in Canada, later to move to Venezuela. No distant cousins are interested in adopting Rena. November 10, 1947, Jacob and Leah Globe become Rena's official guardians.

May 20, 1949: Case closed of unaccompanied children.

October 24, 1949: Rena is adopted by Leah and Jacob Globe.

December 30, 1952: Rena Globe becomes a US citizen. (She knows who George Washington was, also the Dodgers.)

Summer 1958: Rena, 23, visits Israel for the first time with the Young Mizrachi movement.

March 15, 1959: Rena, 24, marries Emanuel Quint.

1980: Rena goes to YIVO library of Jewish Research, HIAS and Agudat Yisrael and (Vaad Hatzalah) and the Joint, looking for records about herself.

1981: Rena attends the gathering for the 36th Anniversary of the Liberation of all camps. For the first time, she seeks information about her past. She is invited to speak in a high school about the Holocaust.

July 1984: Rena makes Aliya with her husband and four children.

1985: Rena becomes a guide in the art museum section of the Yad Vashem Holocaust Museum.

1989: Rena finds her birth certificate in Piotrkow.

1989: Rena gives testimony in Yad Vashem. Rena becomes a guide in the Valley of Communities in Yad Vashem.

1996: Rena is interviewed by Lyn Smith for London's Imperial War Museum.

October 2007: Rena visits the site of Bergen-Belsen.

October 2013: Speaking tour in South Africa.

December 18, 2015: Rena celebrates her 80th birthday.

AFTERWORD
Barbara Sofer

I am sitting with Rena Quint in her living room. On the glass serving cart near the kitchen, four blue, round candleholders are standing together. This week marked the tenth of Tevet, the memorial day for those whose graves are unmarked. She has lit candles for her parents, for Yossi and David, but hasn't yet thrown away the empty containers.

The rest of her large living room has been cleared in anticipation of a family celebration this week. Why go to a hall when Grandma Rena's house is available? Seventy relatives are expected for a ceremony called *Pidyan Haben*, the redeeming of the firstborn son. No challenge for the indefatigable Rena.

Last year, Rena's grandson Yinon, one of Menucha's dozen children and a soldier in the Israeli army, married his girlfriend Naomi, a college student. They had a son, Ben Zion.

The *Pidyan Haben* ceremony takes place on the thirty-first day of the infant's life, and it's customarily followed by an elaborate meal and many toasts and speeches. The requirements for the ceremony are that this must be a mother's first born healthy baby boy. A *Kohen* – a member of the priestly tribe of Jews – must be present. Rena's husband Manny, the great-grandfather and a Kohen will be present and officiate in the ceremony. Manny has done this enough so that he has his own ritually-approved silver coins, as mandated by Jewish law, used in the ceremony.

The Torah says that the firstborn Israelite boys in

Egypt were redeemed when the firstborn boys of the Egyptians died in the tenth plague. That meant that the firstborn Jewish boys were forever consecrated to God's service. The ceremony emphasizes that children are a gift from the Creator and must be dedicated to the continuation of our people.

The baby will be brought into the room on a silver tray and the women – Rena included – will fill the tray with their own jewelry to show that the baby is worth more than all the gold and silver in the world. The parents will recite blessings and go through motions of "returning" the coins to Grandpa Manny. It's an old ritual, this Redemption ceremony, and a good excuse for a party.

Redemption. The word makes me think of Marc Chagall's stained glass window of the Biblical Joseph. He emerged from imprisonment in a dungeon to become the CEO of the greatest empire of the ancient world, saving all of the empire from starvation. On the top of the window, Chagall depicts hands, with a bloody finger, his symbol of the Holocaust. The hands hold a *shofar*, the ram's horn blown on Rosh Hashanah and Yom Kippur. Chagall said the world was silent during the Holocaust and the shofar stood for the absent wake-up call. It's also a symbol of the time of Redemption, when war is no more.

The Nazis created the concentration camp as a new weapon for the oppression of millions. Through manipulation of body and mind, they were able to oppress and murder without restraint. From the early ghettos to the Death Marches where men and women and children were murdered for stumbling as they walked through snow, they sought total control over human beings in their power.

But they never had total control. Rena is proof of that.

Rena and I talk about the seating and menu for the party. The great-grandchildren will picnic on a blanket on the floor while the adults fill their plates with chicken, salads and couscous at four long tables. "I have plenty of tablecloths," says Rena.

I can't help it. I think of her mother's dowry.

Does she see the connection between the memorial candles and the ceremony? Her parents must have had the same ceremony when her older brother was born.

"No," says Rena, who insists on honest answers instead of those we might assume she'd make. "I think of myself as two persons – the one who lights the memorial candles and the one who is ebullient at the gathering of her growing family." Then she adds, "I do hope Hitler is looking up from the grave and writhing as he sees another Jewish child come into the world."

I have heard her speak dozens of times. Her voice is never stilted or halting. She can always find the right words.

An hour later, one of Rena's grandsons calls me. His name is Ori – Hebrew for My light. He's been visiting Grandma and she mentions the book.

He wants to tell me about a Passover picnic the family had in a park in Netanya, a seaside city. All of the offspring – Rena's children, grandchildren and great-grandchildren were dressed in green t-shirts as they gathered in the park. "We are our own March for the Living," says Ori. "A passerby asked what we were doing, and we said we were all descendants of a Holocaust survivor. He said, 'All of you from one survivor? What a miracle.'"

Barbara Sofer

RENA QUINT

Rena Quint grew up in Brooklyn, never telling her classmates that she had spent her first years in a Nazi ghetto, in forced labor, in concentration camps, or that she'd lost every member of her family. Today she is the premier English speaker at Israel's Holocaust Museum Yad Vashem, every year addressing thousands of men, women, and children from around the world. She survived as a child alone in Nazi-occupied Poland because of a series of women who mothered her until they, too, died. She emerged from the Holocaust with her belief in God and love intact. She has received numerous awards, and is often interviewed by the media in Israel, the US, England, Germany, and South Africa. She and her husband, Emanuel Quint, a lawyer and Jewish scholar, have four children, tens of grandchildren and great-grandchildren. Rena is the archetypical example of the power of feeling you are a survivor, and not a victim.

Education:
- BA with a major in Education, Brooklyn College
- MA in Remedial Reading, Brooklyn College

Teaching experience:
- Adelphi University
- Hebrew University
- New York City public school system

Organization activities: (all as a volunteer)
- Vice-chairperson, World Emunah
- President of Jossi Berger Holocaust Center, Jerusalem
- Board member of Association of Americans and Canadians in Israel, Jerusalem
- Sisterhood President of Young Israel of Flatbush
- President of many local benevolent and charitable organizations in the United States

Communal activities: (all as a volunteer)
- Guide at Migdal David, Museum of the History of Jerusalem
- Guide and lecturer at Yad Vashem
- Visiting lecturer for schools, colleges and tourist groups about the Holocaust

Speaker to many audiences, including the following, in person, on radio, and television, giving testimony in Israel, the United States, and South Africa.
- AACI
- Achva Summer Camps
- Aish HaTorah
- Amit
- Bakaa Collage
- Beth Jacob of Washington
- Beth Midrash LaTorah

- Beth Sholom of Texas
- Bnai Akivah
- Bridges For Peace
- British Missions
- Camp Ramah
- Canadian Missions
- Christian Embassy
- Christians from the Bible Belt
- Emunah
- Emunah in Los Angeles
- Emunah in New York
- Emunah in New Jersey
- Gulf War Support Groups
- Hadassah
- Hebrew Union College
- Hebrew University
- Horeb
- Israel Center Jerusalem
- Israelite
- Machone Gold
- March of the Living
- Mayanot for Men
- Mayanot for Women
- Michlalah
- Midreshet Lindenbaum
- Midreshet Moriah
- Morasha in Israel
- Nifty
- Rainer Camp
- Second Generation Groups
- Shoshanot Yerushalayim
- Students in Bet Shemesh
- Sulam

- Survivors Course in Yad Vashem
- Survivors of Lodz
- Survivors of Theresienstadt
- UJA Fellowships
- UJA Leadership groups
- UJA Missions
- World Union of Jewish Students
- Yad Vashem groups, students, teachers, survivors,tourists, dignitaries
- Yeshivah of Flatbush
- Young Israel
- Young Presidents groups

BARBARA SOFER

B arbara Sofer is a prize-winning journalist, author and inspirational speaker who also serves as the Israel Director of Public Relations for Hadassah, the largest Jewish organization in the world, with over 300,000 dues paying members.

In Israel, the United States and elsewhere, Barbara speaks to Jewish and Christian audiences about Israel, Judaism, women's issues, and spirituality. A graduate of the University of Pennsylvania with an MA from the Hebrew University of Jerusalem, her byline has appeared in the New York Times, Woman's Day, Reader's Digest, Parents, the Boston Globe as well as many other publications. She has written seven books and contributed to others. She writes a popular weekend column for the Jerusalem Post that deals with the challenges and miracles of everyday life in Israel, where she moved from the United States 40 years ago.

As the Israel Director of Public Relations for Hadassah, she has witnessed and documented the daily effort to create an island of peace and sanity within Jerusalem's biggest medical center. Because of the prominence of Hadassah Hospital in the news, she has worked with top-tier media, including "Sixty Minutes" and "Nightline" in formulating programs that show Israel in a positive light. She contributed to the Emmy winning CNBC program "Jerusalem ER".

Sofer appeared on Good Morning America's new Seven Wonders of the World series as an expert on the spiritual uniqueness of Jerusalem and likes to think of herself as a "magida," an itinerant teller of the stories of Israel, past and present. She has served as a scholar-in-residence and visiting lecturer in a variety of venues, including synagogues, churches, regional conferences of Hadassah, national conventions, communities, and at schools.

Her prizes include many Rockower awards for Jewish journalism, the Sidney Taylor Award for the best Jewish children's book, and the 2008 Eliav-Sartawi Award for creating understanding through Middle Eastern journalism. Sofer is married to scientist/writer Gerald Schroeder. They have five children and a changing number of grandchildren.

BIBLIOGRAPHY

Apfel, R.J., Simon B., *Minefields in their hearts, The mental health of children in war and communal violence,* Yale University Press, New Haven, CT, 1996.

Bachar, Eytan, Canetti, Laura, Berry, Elliot M., "Lack of Long-Lasting Consequences of Starvation on Eating Pathology in Jewish Holocaust Survivors of Nazi Concentration Camps", *Journal of Abnormal Psychology,* 2005.

Bardgett, Suzanne and Cesarani, David, *Belsen 1945, New Historical Perspectives,* Valentine Mitchell Pub., 2006.

Barel, Efrat, *Surviving the Holocaust: A Meta-Analysis of the Long-Term Sequelae of a Genocide,* University of Haifa and the Max Stern Academic College of Emek Yezreel; Marinus H. Van IJzendoorn, Leiden University; Abraham Sagi-Schwartz, University of Haifa; Marian J. Bakermans-Kranenburg, Leiden University; *Psychological Bulletin,* Vol. 136, No. 5.

Baumel, J.T., *Unfulfilled promise: Rescue and resettlement of Jewish refugee children in the United States 1934-1945,* Juneau, AK, Denali Press, 1990.

Blatman, Daniel, *The Death Marches, the Final phase of Nazi Genocide,* Cambridge, MA, Belknap Press of Harvard University, 201, also footnote p. 423, quoting Doris L. Bergen, *Death Throes and Killing Frenzies: A Response to Hans Momsen's 'The Dissolution of the Third Reich: Crisis Management and Collapse, 1943-5',* Bulletin of the German Historical Institute, 21, 2000.

BBC coverage of liberation of Bergen-Belsen, http:// isurvived.org/Frameset4References-3/-Bergen-Belsen_LIBERATION.html

Camil, D. and Carel R.S., "Emotional distress and satisfaction in life among Holocaust survivors – a community study of survivors and controls", *Psychological Medicine,* Volume 16 / Issue 01 / February 1986, pp 141-149, Cambridge University Press, 1986, DOI, *http://dx.doi.org/10.1017/S0033291700002580,* 09 July 2009.

Chrisophe, Francine, *From a World Apart, a Little Girl in the Concentration Camp,* Lincoln, NE, University of Nebraska Press, 2000.

Cohen, Sharon Kangisser, *Testimony and Time,* Jerusalem, Yad Vashem, 2014.

Cymberknopf, Irving, *Memories of My Life,* self-published.

Dasberg, H., "Child survivors of the Holocaust reach middle-age: Psychotherapy of late grief reactions", *Journal of Social Work and Policy in Israel,* 5(6), 71-83, 1992.

Dasberg, H., "Adult child survivor syndrome on deprived childhoods of aging Holocaust survivors", *Israel Journal of Psychiatry and Related Sciences,* 38, 13-26, 2001.

Davidson, Shamai, *Human Reciprocity Among the Jewish Prisoners in the Nazi Concentration Camps, The Nazi Concentration Camps,* Yad Vashem, Jerusalem, 1984, Gutman, Israel, ed., Yad Vashem, Conference, 4th.

Davidson, S. and Charny, I., *Holding on to humanity: The message of Holocaust survivors - The Shamai Davidson papers,* New York: New York University Press, 1992.

DeWind, E., "The confrontation with death." *International Journal of Psychoanalysis,* 49, 302-305, 1968.

Des Pres, Terrence, *The Survivor; An Anatomy of life in the Death Camps,* New York, Oxford University Press, 1976.

Didion, Joan, *The Year of Magical Thinking,* Vintage, New York, 2007.

Dinnerstein, L., *America and the survivors of the Holocaust,* New York, Columbia University Press, 1982.

Durlacher, G.L.De zoektocht [The search], in translation, Amsterdam: Meulenhoff, 1991.

Eisenberg, A., *The Lost Generation: Children in the Holocaust,* NY, Pilgrim Press, 1982.

Eitan, Rachel, *http://www.jewishvirtuallibrary.org/jsource/ Holocaust/UK/belsensurvivor0545.html* (from Bergen-Belsen trial testimony).

Eitinger, Leo, *Concentration Camp Survivors in Norway and Israel,* London, Allen and Unwin, 1964.

Epstein, Helen, *Children of the Holocaust,* New York, Bantam, 1979.

Feldman, Dina, Samuelson William, *New Bulletin 1,* 1982, p. 31 http//www.u. org/en/holocaustremembrance/ docs/ Poem Contributed.

Finkel, Sidney, *Sevek and the Holocaust, the Boy who Refused to Die,* self-published, USA, 1976.

The Foundation for the Benefit of Holocaust Victims in Israel 2014 Annual Report, April 2014, http:k-shoa.org

Gedenkbuch, Book of Remembrance, Prisoners in the Bergen-Belsen Concentration Camp, Foundation for Memorials in Lower Saxony, Bergen-Belsen Memorial, April 2005.

Gilbert, Martin, *Atlas of the Holocaust*, William Morrow & Co. New York, 326, 1993.

Gilbert, Martin, *The Holocaust – The Jewish Tragedy*, William Collins Sons & Co. Ltd, London, 1986.

Gilbert, Martin, *Holocaust Journey – Travelling in Search of the Past*, Weidenfeld & Nicolson, London, 1997.

Gilbert, Martin, *The Boys – Triumph over Adversity*, Weidenfeld & Nicolson, London, 1996.

Gilbert, Martin, *The Day the War Ended*, HarperCollins, San Francisco, 1995.

Gill, Anton, *The Journey Back from Hell – Conversations with Concentration Camp Survivors*, Grafton Books, London, 1989.

Goldhagen, Daniel Jonah, *Hitler's Willing Executioners: Ordinary Germans and the Holocaust,* Knopf, New York, 1996.

Grant-Marshall, Sue, "I survived Bergen-Belsen," *Fairlady*, Johannesburg, June 2013, 63-66.

Gutmacher, Yisrael, Mendelsohn, Ezra, *The Jews of Poland Between Two World Wars*, Waltham, Brandeis University Press.

Gutman, Israel, ed. *Encyclopedia of the Holocaust,* Macmillan Publishing Company, New York, 1990.

Hantman, Shira and Solomon, Zahava, "Recurrent trauma: Holocaust survivors cope with aging and cancer", *Social Psychiatry and Psychiatric Epidemiology*, Issue 5, May 2007.

Harel, Z., Kahana, B. and Kahana, E., "Psychological well-being among Holocaust survivors and immigrants in Israel", *Journal of Traumatic Stress Studies*, I (4) 413-428, 1988.

Harel, Z., Kahana, B. and Kahana E., *Predictors of psychological well-being among survivors of the Holocaust*, Springer, 1988.

Helmreich, William B., *Against All Odds*, Simon and Schuster, New York, 1992.

Herzberg, Abel J., *Between Two Streams, A Diary from Bergen-Belsen*, translated by Jack Santcross, I.B. Tauris, London/New York, 1997, in association with European Jewish Publication Society.

Hilberg, Raul, *The Destruction of the European Jews*, abridged 1986, Holmes & Meier Publishers Inc, Teaneck, New Jersey, 1986.

Hilberg, Raul, ed., *Documents of Destruction*, Quadrangle Books, New York, 1971.

Hitchcock, Alfred, Documentary of Bergen-Belsen, 1945.

Holocaust and Rebirth, Bergen-Belsen Memorial Press, New York-Tel Aviv, 1965.

Integration of Immigrants in Sweden 1945-1975, *Finnish Yearbook of Population Research* XLV, 2010, 103-122.

Jaffe, R., "Dissociative phenomena in former concentration camp inmates." *The International Journal of Psychoanalysis*, 49(2), 310-312, 1968.

Jiong, Li, Vestergaard, Morgens, Cnattingius, Sven, Gissler, Mika, Hammer Bech, Bodil, Obel Carsten, Olsen, Jem, "Mortality after Parental Death in

Childhood: A Nationwide Cohort Study from Three Nordic Countries", *PLOS*, 2014.

Keilson, Hans, *Sequential Traumatisation in Children. A clinical and statistical follow-up study on the fate of the Jewish war orphans in the Netherlands*, The Magnes Press, The Hebrew University, Jerusalem, 1992.

Kestenberg, J.S., & Brenner, I., *The Last Witness: The Child survivor of the Holocaust*, Washington, DC: American Psychiatric, 1996.

Keys, Ancel Benjamin, "Human starvation and its consequences", American Dietetic Society, New York, 1946.

Klein, Hillel, Zellermayer, Julius and Shanan, Joel, "Former Concentration Camp Inmates on a Psychiatric Ward", *Archives of General Psychiatry*, 8, 1963.

Krell, R., "Child survivors of the Holocaust – strategies of adaptation", *Canadian Journal of Psychiatry*, 38, 384-389, 1993.

Krell, R. and Sherman, Martin, *Medical and Psychological Effects on Holocaust Survivors*, Transaction Publishers, Rutgers University, New Jersey, 1997.

Krystal, H., & Danieli, Y., "Holocaust survivor studies in the context of PTSD", *PTSD Research Quarterly*, 5(4), 1-5, 1994.

Kuch, K., & Cox, B. J., "Symptoms of PTSD in 124 survivors of the Holocaust." *American Journal of Psychiatry*, 149, 337-340, 1992.

Lasker-Wallfisch, Anita, *Inherit the Truth*, St. Martin's Press, NY, 2000.

Laub, D., & Auerhahn, N.C., "Knowing and not knowing massive psychic trauma: Forms of traumatic memory." *American Journal of Psychoanalysis*, 74, 287-302, 1993.

Laub, D., & Auerhahn, N.C., "Failed empathy – A central theme in the survivor's Holocaust experience."*Psychoanalytic Psychology*, 6(4), 377-400, 1989.

Levy-Hass, Hanna, *Diary of Bergen-Belsen, 1944-45*, Haymarket Books, Chicago, 2009.

Lubliner, Michael, *Chapters of Remembrance, the memoirs of Michael Lubliner, Vol. I, 1905 – 45* (PDF) translated by Coby Lubliner.

Luchterhand, Elmer "Prisoner Behavior and Social System in the Nazi Camp," *International Journal of Psychiatry* , Vol. 13, 1967, 245-264.

Marks, J., *The hidden children: The secret survivors of the Holocaust*, Toronto: Bantam Books, 1995.

Matussek, Paul, *Internment in concentration camps and its consequences*, New York, Springer, 1975.

Mazor, A., Ganpel, Y., Enright, R. D., & Ornstein, R., "Holocaust survivors: Coping with post-traumatic memories in childhood and 40 years later", *Journal of Traumatic Stress*, 3(1), 11-14, 1990, (January).

Modai, I., "Forgetting childhood: A defense mechanism against psychosis in a Holocaust survivor", in T. L. Brink (Ed.), *Holocaust survivors' mental health*, New York, Haworth Press, 1994 .

Moskovitz, Sarah, *Love Despite Hate*, Schocken Books, New York, 1983.

Moskovitz, S., & Krell, R., "Child survivors of the Holocaust: Psychological adaptations to survival", *Israel Journal of Psychiatry and Related Services*, 27(2), 81-91, 1990.

Preis, Lea, *Yad Vashem Studies (42:1 2014)*, Preis, quoting from the wartime account of Yaakov.

Krell, Mark, *Medical and Psychological Effects on Holocaust Survivors*, Mark Sherman, introduction by Elie Wiesel, 1997.

Krzepicki, "Jews from the World to Come: The First Testimonies of Escapees from Chelmo and Treblinka in the Warsaw Ghetto 1942-3".

Milgram, Abraham and Rozett, Robert, editors, *The Holocaust Frequently Asked Questions*, Jerusalem, Yad Vashem, 2005.

Philips, Raymond, editor, *Excerpts from The Trial of Josef Kramer and 44 others: The Belsen Trial*, William Hodge and Company, London, 1949.

Press, Krell, R. "Child survivors of the Holocaust: 40 years later", *Journal of the American Academy of Child Psychiatry*, 24, 378-380, 1985.

Rahe, Thomas, "Children in the Bergen-Belsen concentration camp", Bergen-Belsen Memorial, unpublished manuscript, January 2011.

Reichental, Tomi, with Pierce, Nicola, *I Was a Boy in Belsen*, Tomi Paperback, Obrien Press, Dublin, Ireland, 2011.

The Relief of Belsen, April 1945, Eye Witness Accounts, Imperial War Museum, 1991.

Robinson, Jacob, *Holocaust and Rebirth, Bergen-Belsen 1945-1965*, Bergen-Belsen Memorial Press, New York-Tel Aviv, Introduction by Josef Rosensaft.

Roger, George, photographer, Bergen-Belsen, *At the Gates of Hell, The Liberation of Bergen-Belsen*, Time, 1945, (photos online).

Rosensaft, Joseph, Collection of Bergen-Belsen, Yad Vashem archives, Jerusalem.

Shanon, Joel and Shahar, Orna, "Surviving the Survivors: Late personality development of Jewish Holocaust survivors", *International Journal of Mental Health*, 1989.

Sharfstein, Chana, *It was Evening, It was Morning, Scandinavia in the Aftermath of World War II*, Devora Publishing Company, Jerusalem, 2012.

Smith, Lyn, *Forgotten Voices of the Holocaust*, London, Ebury Press, 2006.

Sterling, Eric, Editor, *Life In The Ghettos During The Holocaust*, Syracuse University Press, Syracuse, NY, 2005.

Suedfeld, Peter, Krell, Robert, Wiebe, Robyn E, Steel, Gary Daniel, "Coping strategies in the narratives of holocaust survivors" *Anxiety, Stress & Coping: An International Journal*, Volume 10, Issue 2, 1997.

Trunk, Isaiah, *Judenrat – The Jewish Councils in Eastern Europe under Nazi Occupation*, University of Nebraska Press, Lincoln, 1996.

Tucker, Todd, *The Great Starvation Experiment: Ancel Keys and the Men Who Starved for Science*, First University of Minnesota Press, Minneapolis, 2008.

Wagenaar, W.A., & Groeneweg, J., "The memory of concentration camp survivors", *Applied Cognitive Psychology*, 4, 77-8, 1990.

Van der Hal-van Raalte EA1, van IJzendoorn MH, Bakermans-Kranenburg M.J., "Sense of coherence moderates late effects of early childhood Holocaust exposure", *Journal of Clinical Psychology*, 2008 Dec, 64.

Van der Hal-van Raalte, van IJzendoorn Marinus H., Bakermans-Kranenburg, Marian, "Sense of Coherence Moderates Late Effects of Early Childhood Holocaust Exposure", *Journal of Clinical Psychology*, Vol. 64(12), 1352-1367 (2008) & 2008 Wiley Periodicals, Inc. Published online in Wiley InterScience (www. interscience.wiley.com). DOI: 10.1002/jclp.20528

Van IJzendoorn MH, Bakermans-Kranenburg MJ, Sagi-Schwartz A, "Are children of Holocaust survivors less well-adapted? A meta-analytic investigation of secondary traumatization," *Journal of Trauma Stress*, 2003 Oct, 16.

Verolime, Hetty, *The Children's House of Belsen*, Politicos, London, 2005.

Walker, Patrick Gordon, *BBC Broadcast, Belsen Concentration Camp: Facts and Thoughts*, Belsen 1945, page 137.

Weiss, Aharon, *Categories of Camps-Their Character and Role in the Execution of the Final Solution of the Jewish Question. The Nazi Concentration Camps: Structure and Aims; the Image of the Prisoner; the Jews in the Camps*: Proceedings of the Fourth Yad Vashem International Historical Conference, Jerusalem January 1980. Ed. Yisrael Gutman and Avital Saf, Jerusalem: Yad Vashem, 1984. 115-132. Print.

Wilson, J., Harel, Z., & Kahana, B., *Human adaptation to extreme stress: From the Holocaust to Vietnam*, New York: Plenum Press, 1988.

Yehuda, Rachel, Kahana, Boaz, Schmeidler, James, Southwick, Steven M, Wilson, Skye, Giller, Earl L., "Impact of cumulative lifetime trauma and recent stress on current post-traumatic stress disorder symptoms in holocaust survivors," *American Journal of Psychiatry* 1995/12/1.

Yehuda, R., Elkin, A., Binder-Brynes, K., Kahana, B., Southwick, S. M., Schmeidler, J., & Giller, E.R., Jr."Dissociation in aging Holocaust survivors." *American Journal of Psychiatry*, 153 (7), 935-940, 1996 (July).

Yehuda, R., Schmeidler, J., Siever, L. J., Binder-Brynes, K., & Elkin, A., "Individual differences in post-traumatic stress disorder symptom profiles in Holocaust survivors in concentration camps or in hiding", *Journal of Traumatic Stress*, 10, 453-465, 1997.

Young, Kelly, *The Psychological Effects of Starvation in the Holocaust: The Dehumanization and Deterioration of its Victims, 2013*, National Collegiate Honors Council, Student Interdisciplinary Research.

Zullo, Allan and Bovsun, Mara, *Survivors, True Stories of Children in the Holocaust*, Scholastic, New York, 2005.

Websites

US Holocaust Memorial Museum: www.ushmm.org

Yad Vashem: www.yadvashem.org

http://en.wikipedia.org/wiki/Irma_Grese

www.deathcamps.org

www.yadvashem.org/yv/en/exhibitions/valley/
piotrkow/deportations.asp

www.recoveredmemory.org

http://psychology.huji.ac.il/.upload/articles/165.pdf

BBC Testimony Harold L3 Druillenenc:

www.bergenbelsen.co.uk/pages/Trial/Trial/
TrialProsecutionCase/Trial_010_Druillenec.html

Third Annual Report: New York Association for New
Americans, Inc, Leo Baeck Institute, NYC

http://psychology.huji.ac.il/.upload/articles/165.pdf

The Foundation for the Benefit of Holocaust Victims in
Israel 2014 Annual Report, April 2014, http:k-shoa.
org

www.u.org/en/holocaustremembrance/docs/

Yad Vashem Studies (42:1 2014) Dr. Lea Preis,
quoting from the wartime account of Yaakov
Krzepicki, "Jews from the World to Come: The
First Testimonies of Escapees from Chelmo and
Treblinka in the Warsaw Ghetto 1942-3"

www.jewishvirtuallibrary.org/jsource/Holocaust/UK/
belsensurvivor0545.html (from Bergen-Belsen trial
testimony)

Nizkor Project: www.nizkor.org

www.ushmm.org/wlc/en

Piotrkow - www.yadvashem.org/yv/en/exhibitions/
valley/piotrkow/ghetto.asp

https://en.wikipedia.org/wiki/
Piotrk%C3%B3w_Trybunalski_Ghetto

Bergen-Belsen - http://bergen-belsen.stiftung-ng.de/
de/home.html

APPENDIX

IMPRESSIONS

Once a year, on Yom HaShoah – the Memorial Day for victims of the Holocaust – as the sirens wail, I stand in my mother's place. Once a year, instead of being the daughter of the vivacious blonde power force who is constantly moving and doing, I become a little girl, alone in the world, hungry, sick and surrounded by horrors unimaginable even after we have seen the pictures.

With the siren wailing, I become her. I feel the emptiness, the knowledge that as bad as things are they can always get worse, the simple unfairness of how life was taken from so many, the sheer evil that becomes a background for one's life. I feel the cold and the hunger and the loneliness and the inability to understand how one can live like this.

When the siren stops, in the remaining few seconds of silence before the world starts moving again, cars honking, people talking, I reflect on the wonder of how my mother, the woman who gave birth to me, who brought me up, arose from that darkest place of all, to lead such a full life, such an active life.

I grew up in a house with my two older sisters and younger brother. The house was always full of friends, ours and my parents, full of food, noise, activities. My parents were active participants in our schools and synagogue, my mother head of the Ladies Auxiliary and my father Chairman of the Board of Education. Love notes from my father to my mother were taped throughout the house. Hospitality was a core value, the door was always open and everyone was welcome.

Till today the dissonance, the incongruence, of a

person whose formative years were passed basically in Hell, in circumstances we cannot fully fathom, that can make a house like that, boggles the mind. I am amazed each day by the sheer strength of will, desire and determination to go from that childhood – if one can call it that – and become the woman that we grew up knowing.

I think of myself as a child, probably complaining that I didn't like this food or another, that the teacher was mean to me. I imagine myself in such circumstances telling that child to be grateful for what she had. Not my mother. She never looked back, never compared our easy and bountiful lifestyle with her past. She gave us the gift of enjoying life as we were born into it, and for that too I am grateful.

Till today, my mother is a force of nature. Nothing stands in her way – illness, pain, logistics – she just keeps going and achieves whatever is needed in that moment.

She, with my father, have raised a small dynasty of their own, hard to keep track at any given moment how many great-grandchildren are on the way. I know she sees this wonderful, large family as her answer to the Holocaust, as her proof that even through the worst, beautiful things can grow. I know she is right.

...Jodi Patt, Rena Quint's daughter

Have you had a bad day? Bad week? Maybe a lot longer? That's normal but know that things will get better. My mother taught this to me; it's not at all surprising when you know the story of her life.

My mother escaped from the grip of death as a child in the Holocaust, and now lives a beautiful life in gorgeous Jerusalem – the ultimate home for the Jewish people. Yet she has never forgotten how to persevere. Just recently my mom, the great-grandmother, slept on the hard floors of the hospital for days in order to keep my father company, who was a patient there, and pushed a heavy wheelchair up hills and more and more.

The Torah states that one who lends money with interest is penalized heavily in life, as it is illegal. But why does the Torah single out this prohibition as life altering? The Sages say that you have to believe that God controls all, and He can ensure that you will earn your money within the confines of the law.

So too, God has challenged my mother, and in her case the big picture has gone so well.

We can never figure out the tragedy of the Holocaust. Even scholars who can explain away the big picture of God's ways can *never* explain the horrors of the Holocaust, but through my mother we can see there is a big picture.

Hopefully, the reader will see it as quickly as my mother was able to, though some might have to wait for the next world. My niece once remarked how all the mothers up in Heaven collectively look out for my mother and together thank each other. What a beautiful and true statement.

... David Quint, Rena Quint's son

Dear Buff, The story of your life has been a part of me for as long as I can remember. I have heard your story on many occasions and in many places, and I'm grateful for all those opportunities.

When I was only six years old, I spoke at our shul ceremony for Yom HaShoah. I stood with a paper saying "Zachor" on one side, and my short speech on the other. I said that when my grandmother was my age, she was doing slave labor in a glass factory.

When I was age ten, you took me and my summer camp friends to Yad Vashem. My friends and their parents still remember that powerful experience.

The next year, you invited me to your shul in Jerusalem for the Yom HaShoah program. I spoke before the audience, and I was honored to light a candle before your keynote speech.

When I went on the school trip to Poland, I thought of you all the time, especially when seeing a sign to Piotrkow.

Fast forward to my years in Hesder Yeshiva. One of the most important trips in my life was accompanying you to South Africa. You spoke about your experiences to Jewish groups, and you were interviewed on the radio. And of course, your speech in the prison was unforgettable.

Last year, you came to my Yeshiva in Gush Etzion to speak to the students who were about to travel to Poland. You inspired many people. Even though it was a difficult time, everyone appreciated all that you said.

...Boaz Silverman, Rena Quint's grandson

Dear Buff, my special Savta, When we look around and see the magnificent family that surrounds you, we are all amazed.

As a child, you lost everything you had. Your parents, your brothers, your belongings – you were left with nothing.

With our very eyes, we can see the hand of Hashem that took you from there and rebuilt your life. You started off by living the pasuk, "...through the valley of hell", though quickly advanced to the pasuk, "Hashem is my shepherd, I will not go on missing..." The continuation reminds us of your blessed Friday night Shabbat table, surrounded by family and friends.

Buff, in Poland you were the one and only survivor from your family. Look around, you are now crowded in your lovely home in Yerushalayim with sixty family members. Your parents named you Fredja, which means Joy. How correct they were for naming you so, as you grin with joy here. Your parents and brothers must be grinning with joy in Olam Haba, both proud and amazed.

Buff, you are a living example of the Jewish nation. One who seems to have had no chance of survival, yet grew stronger to a wonderful life filled with success, joy and happiness.

I am so proud to be your grandson, and we will carry on everything you taught in many more years to come.

... Eli Silverman, Rena Quint's grandson

When you read my mother's book, you will understand that she didn't have a childhood. Because of this, my mother made sure that her children, and later her grandchildren, had a delightful childhood.

The children in Bergen-Belsen were only able to dream about playing and dancing and traveling. My mom made sure that we kids actually played and danced and traveled.

Parties were a big part of our family life. Birthday parties and family Chanuka get-togethers were a natural occurrence each year.

My mom took us ice skating. I remember many Sundays at the rink with my mom and sisters, and we always brought a friend or two, or more, to add to the fun.

We traveled as a family to Israel shortly after the Six-Day war. In subsequent summers we returned to Israel, stopping at locales such as Switzerland, Paris and Holland. Highlights of our trips were the ice sculptures at the Jungfrau where I wore my mom's cashmere sweater, finding my "lost" baby brother, saying *Shema Yisrael* at the Alkmaar Cheese Market, and hopping on an overnight train for an impromptu visit to Paris. This all in stark contrast to the confinement of Bergen-Belsen.

We were always the house that entertained, always the address ready for a party, always having Shabbat guests. My mother was always the first to volunteer to host an event at her home, always the first to be the class mother.

Kindness and being nice to everyone, as well as a love of fun were always part of her message to us. This didn't stop when we grew up either.

Mom, the new generation, your grandchildren, benefited from your tireless efforts to find joy in the world.

My children enjoyed traveling with you and Daddy to London, Paris and Washington. I still enjoy hearing stories from my kids about "Pizza Rini", and kosher ice cream in Washington, and Tehillim at Legoland.

Thanks Mom for always being there for all of us.

... Naomi Silverman, Rena Quint's daughter

It was the summer of 1982 when I met my mother-in-law. Naomi had invited me to her house for a barbecue. I didn't know her well, and had never been to her house.

As I got close, I saw a good looking middle-aged couple standing at the barbecue grill. I approached them and asked if I was at the right place.

Naomi's father, Rabbi Quint, answered me with a question: "Are you Jewish?" When I replied, "Yes" – he said, "then you are in the right place." How right he was.

I went on to fall in love with Naomi and both of her parents.

What I came to learn was that this attribute of *Hachnasat Orchim*, of welcoming guests, was not just for the barbecue, but actually an entire way of life for the Quints.

Over the years, I grew to love Rena and my admiration for her kindness, hospitality, and desire to provide love for her family, which knows no bounds.

... Bob Silverman, Rena Quint's son-in-law

ARTICLES

"Quintessential Yiddishkeit"
By Greer Fay Cashman
Published in the Jerusalem Post (November 1994)

ANYONE WHO asks Emanuel or Rena Quint what
they do will get varied replies depending on the time of
day. Emanuel Quint might he teaching, lecturing, working
at his computer on a new chapter of yet another book,
going to a board meeting – or believe it or not, vacuuming
the carpets.

Rena Quint might be preparing a meal for some
30 people, guiding at Yad Vashem, the Tower of David
Museum or the Supreme Court, rushing off to care for
a sick person, planning an event for one of the several
organizations in which she is active, answering one of the
scores of telephone calls she receives each day, or making
up the bed for yet another house guest.

The Quints, though they talk freely about each other,
are more reticent when talking about themselves. They
may say something about their mutual enjoyment of the
arts, the dinners they attend for any number of good
causes; the pleasure they get from traveling through Israel
or abroad – but they're unlikely to pinpoint exactly what
they do.

Those who know them, wax long and loud about their
qualities. But in a nutshell, the Quints are in the business
of doing mitzvot. They cheerfully open their home and
their hearts to anyone with a problem, and do everything
they can to solve it.

This can involve finding answers to halachic or legal

questions; providing a roof and a bed for someone who is temporarily without accommodation; allowing the use of their home for weddings, sheva brachot, britot, fund raising functions or shiva services for the newly bereaved; feeding the hungry or creating a warm, friendly environment for people of all ages who want to participate in an informal Jewish studies program.

Brooklyn-born Emanuel Quint attended Law School and Yeshiva concurrently. In 1955 he passed the Bar examination and was ordained as a rabbi. A partner in the highly successful law firm of Quint, Marx and Chill, he specialized in real estate and commercial litigation. In his spare time he worked in a voluntary capacity for numerous Zionist and educational organizations and institutions, invariably finding himself on the board – often as president or vice president. He was an officer in many synagogues and yeshivot as well as in several branches of Young Israel. He gave classes at Yeshiva University and together with Professor Neil Hecht wrote two books on Jewish Law.

At age 54, he retired from practicing law. "I figured that all I could do was make more money," he says. Two of the four Quint offspring were already living in Israel, and a third had set the date for her own aliya. Their son and daughter-in-law are also contemplating aliya.

Ten years ago, the Quints came to Israel, barely knowing a soul. Now their circle of friends is so large, that they've had to compile their own personal telephone directory, which every few weeks is updated and expanded.

Rena Quint, born in Piotrkow, Poland, was approximately three years old at the outbreak of World War Two. Transported to several labor camps, she wound up in Bergen Belsen, which was liberated by British forces. She was subsequently sent to Sweden where she was taken in by another Holocaust survivor whose own daughter had died. The woman brought her to the US in 1946, and passed away soon after. The 9 year-old girl was then taken in by the Globe family, who with love and devotion turned her from a wild, angry child into a caring and sweet tempered woman. Twelve years later, she met Emanuel Quint, and after a whirlwind three weeks courtship, they married.

A teacher by profession with a Masters degree in remedial reading, Rena Quint taught elementary school and English as a foreign language to Russian students at Adelphi University. After making aliya, she also taught at Hebrew University for one summer.

The Quints always had open house in America, and they have continued the tradition in Israel. "Our place is always open to someone who doesn't have a place to stay," says Emanuel Quint, who on settling in Israel quickly immersed himself in a wide range of volunteer activities. Together with Rabbi Adin Steinzaltz, he founded the Institution of Jewish Law of which he is the dean. On Thursday nights he conducts Talmud classes in his home, with some 60 people congregating each week. He is on the boards of the Jerusalem College of Technology, the Israel Center, Keren Or, the Rabbinical Council of America and Young Israel – and yet always has time for other people.

"We really are very busy from morning to night – and we like being busy," says Rena Quint, who is vice chairman of World Emunah and president of the Yossi Berger Holocaust Center.

The Association of Americans and Canadians in Israel and the Voluntary Tourist Organization are always sending visitors to the Quint home; and the Quints themselves will often approach strangers at the Hovevei Zion synagogue where they usually pray and invite them to dinner.

The Quints say that one of the smartest moves they ever made was coming to Israel. "Not many people get a chance to start again like this, except with a second marriage," says Emanuel Quint. "So let's pretend it's a second marriage, except that it's with the same partners."

"We have absolutely no regrets about coming to Israel," declares Rena Quint with a smile to match the statement. "We've met more people from the US, England and other countries than we ever could in the US."

What she fails to add is that the majority of these meetings have taken place in her own home.

"Surprise"
By Greer Fay Cashman
Published in the Jerusalem Post (February 2006)

MOST PEOPLE have only one birthday, the one according to the Gregorian calendar. Some people, who also take note of lunar calendar dates, celebrate their lunar calendar birthdays as well, which sometimes coincide with their regular birthdays, and can also be as much as a month apart.

Child Holocaust survivor Rena Quint doesn't observe her lunar birthday, but nonetheless has two birthdays, one in December and the other in February. The reason: Until some 25 years ago, she didn't know the date of her real birthday. Quint was brought to America on false papers. They belonged to a child who had perished in the Holocaust, and the little girl's mother, whose relatives in America sponsored her migration to the country, felt sorry for another little girl who had lost both her parents and her two brothers.

Soon after their arrival in America, the woman – who had been very frail after her ordeal in the camps – died. Her relatives did not want to keep the little orphan girl and passed her on to a childless couple who gave her a warm, loving home and a new lifestyle. Because she had no papers other than those of the dead child, her new family always celebrated her birthday in February, the date of birth listed on the documents. Quint was already the mother of four grown children when she decided to go to her native Poland with her husband, Rabbi Emanuel Quint, to try to find details of her biological parents and her real date of birth.

She discovered that she was actually two months older than she had always presumed. Because her family had always celebrated her birthday in February, she didn't make a big fuss about the December date, but when her friends learned her story, many of them chose to celebrate both December and February with her. Last December, she turned 70, and nobody made a big deal of it because around the same time, two of her grandsons, one from Israel and the other from America, were celebrating their Bar Mitzvahs.

However, unbeknownst to her, a huge 70th birthday party was in the offing. Amazingly, despite the large number of invitees, all of whom were relatives or close friends, the party remained a surprise until the last moment.

One of Quint's granddaughters told her that she was making a surprise party for another relative and that she wanted her grandmother to come festively attired to add to the party atmosphere. It was only when Quint and her husband arrived at Kibbutz Ramat Rahel on the outskirts of Jerusalem, where everyone was already gathered, that the penny dropped. An elated Quint went around kissing and hugging everyone, and sat with tears in her eyes as her husband read to her a love poem that eloquently expressed how much she is the center of his universe. Quint's excitement kept mounting as she watched a video prepared by one of her grandsons that showed the highlights of her life – primarily her own wedding, the weddings of each of her children and the weddings last year of her two eldest granddaughters, each of whom will this year make her a great-grandmother.

Her first great-grandchild is due to be born some time between Purim and Pessah, and the second around Shavuot.

Quint told her guests that until she was 10 years old, she had never celebrated her birthday, let alone had a birthday party. When she came to live in Jerusalem around two decades ago, she knew hardly anyone. In synagogue, only one person came over to introduce himself — and he, like she, was a new immigrant. She recalled telling her husband that it was just as well that they weren't having any family simha in the immediate future, because unlike the situation in Flatbush, where they had lived before among hundreds of friends, in Jerusalem, they had hardly anyone to invite. This is no longer the situation.

Community conscious almost to an extreme, both husband and wife joined numerous organizations in which they were intensely active and continue to be, in addition to which they opened up their home to scores of organizational events, hosting as many as 70 people at a time. Their amazing hospitality is legend not only in Jerusalem but also in the US. It is not unusual for some Emunah leader in America to call Rena Quint and ask whether she can put up visiting guests in her home, or whether she can make her home available for a welcome reception for an Emunah family mission.

Quint is also a volunteer guide at Yad Vashem, and a firm favorite with visiting groups from the US, who make a point of asking for her to guide them.

She also guides at the David Citadel Museum; volunteers at Yad Sarah and other welfare organizations; regularly attends lessons and lectures on Jewish texts; and is the first to instantly come to the aid of any of her friends who fall ill, lose their keys or have their pockets picked. In addition, she has never forgotten what it means to be alone, and she hosts birthday luncheons and dinners for friends and even chance acquaintances who have few or no relatives in Israel.

The little orphan girl, who came to America homeless, friendless and almost inarticulate for lack of education, today has 21 grandchildren, 18 of whom live in Israel. Two of the three who live in America came with their father to be with her on this special day in her life. That was probably the best surprise and the best gift of all. Her three daughters, Menucha, Naomi and Jodi, live in Israel and she sees them all the time. Her son, David, who lives in New York, has work pressures which make it difficult for him to get away. He was in Israel in December-January for the two Bar Mitzvahs, and she was sure that she would not see him again for months.

At the party, Quint apologized to anyone who had been left off the invitation list, "but I had nothing to do with it."

Still there's always a chance to rectify such omissions. The Quints will be celebrating their 47th wedding anniversary in mid-March.

MESSER-LICHTENSTEIN PRENUPTIAL AGREEMENT

Translation
Repertorium NO.242.

On 25 of February 1930 before me, Teodor Gorzynski, a notary at the land registry section of the city court of city Piotrkow, in my office in city Piotrkow at the Trybunalski Square no.7 appeared, unknown to me but fit for legal activity: 1) Icek Lichtenstein, son of Jankel, a tailor and 2) Sura Messer, daughter of Icek, unmarried, a trades(wo)man, legal inhabitants of the city of Piotrkow and (having?) legal residence, whose identity was authenticated by (persons?) who possessed the required by law attributes, Tobiasz Fisz and Edmund (?)yszkowski, both resident in the city of Pruszkow and entered into the following agreement:

1. Icek Lichtenstein and Sura Messer declared that, intending to bind themselves in a marriage tie, they arrange their financial relations during their marriage in the following way.

2. The property which each of the future spouses presently possesses and will possess at the moment of contracting the marriage, as well as everything which each of them will obtain during the marriage by inheritance or donation, will constitute the exclusive property of the party; thus concerning this property they establish separation of property. On the other hand, everything that the future spouses will gain during the marriage by work, saving or through chance, will be the joint property of the spouses.

3. Sura Messer declared that her property presently consists of the sum of six thousand zloty in cash and the dowry and furniture valued at 2500 zloty, namely:

1: closet with two mirrors, light oak,
2: two large beds of light oak with mattresses,
3: light oak table,
4: six Viennese chairs, light
5: ottoman upholstered in plush,
6: wall clock by "Beckier",
7: large mirror with a table, light,
8: two sewing machines for gents tailoring,
9: tailoring table, oak,
10: pine dresser, white painted,
11: kitchen table, white painted,
12: golden lady's wristwatch,
13: three plush bedcovers,
14: bed, personal and table-clothes, three sets each.

4. Icek Lichtenstein declared that he presently does not disclose his property, at the same time he mentions that his future wife Sura Messer has contributed to his home the above mentioned objects and furniture as well as the sum of six thousand zloty in cash until writing up the deed and (?) such (?).

5. According to article 208 of Civil Codex, the present notary has advised the parts that, under the rigor of annulment, this prenuptial agreement has to be disclosed in the civil act of marriage. An extract of this deed will be sent to the district court in Piotrkow as a registry court. (?) cash was charged and registered in the repertorium under the number 242, stamps and intercises 9 zloty, (?) 10% extraordinary surcharge 1 zloty 30 grosz and on behalf of the notary together

with preparation of the principal extract forty zloty (articles 4 and 10 (?)). The principal extract should be handed to Sura Messer.

This deed was read to (?) and its contents and its consequences have been understood by them and as being in accordance with their will, was accepted and undersigned.

SIGNATURES